The Strategy Game

Craig R. Hickman

McGraw-Hill, Inc.

New York   San Francisco   Washington, D.C.   Auckland   Bogotá
Caracas   Lisbon   London   Madrid   Mexico City   Milan
Montreal   New Delhi   San Juan   Singapore
Sydney   Tokyo   Toronto

Library of Congress Cataloging-in-Publication Data

Hickman, Craig R.
    The strategy game / Craig R. Hickman.
        p.   cm.
    Includes index.
    ISBN 0-07-028724-4 (hc)   ISBN 0-07-028725-2 (pbk)
    1. Strategic planning.   2. Corporate turnarounds—Management.
I. Title.
HD30.28.H5114   1993
658.4'012—dc20   93-9581
                                                      CIP

First McGraw-Hill paperback edition, 1994

1 2 3 4 5 6 7 8 9 0 DOC/DOC 9 9 8 7 6 5 4 3 (HC)
1 2 3 4 5 6 7 8 9 0 DOC/DOC 9 0 9 8 7 6 5 4 (PBK)

ISBN 0-07-028724-4 (HC)
ISBN 0-07-028725-2 (PBK)

The sponsoring editor for this book was Karen Hansen, the editing supervisor was Frances Koblin, and the production supervisor was Suzanne W. Babeuf. It was set in Palatino by McGraw-Hill's Professional Book Group composition unit.

Printed and bound by R. R. Donnelley & Sons Company.

If you would like to receive information on any of the following: a Software Version of *The Strategy Game*; a Trainer's Guide for *The Strategy Game*; or *The Strategy Game* Workshop, please write to: *The Strategy Game*, P.O. Box 50148, Provo, Utah 84605 - 0148.

Contents

Preface

I've written this book with two overriding purposes in mind: (1) to *educate* employees at every organizational level to become better strategic thinkers, decision makers, and implementers, a need recognized by a growing number of senior executives in the United States as a vital ingredient to building a new level of business competitiveness for the twenty-first century, and (2) to *entertain* business and nonbusiness readers alike by plunging them into the exciting world of strategic business dilemmas and perilous decision making, an approach based on Henry David Thoreau's once astonishing assertion made over 150 years ago, that people learn faster and better when they enjoy the process.

Through the unique combination of two proven methodologies, the *business case study*, originating from the distinguished halls of the Harvard Business School, and the *choose your own adventure format*, used by some science fiction and fantasy writers, *The Strategy Game* offers a really different kind of business book that both educates and entertains. I hope that you will find your strategic thinking improving as you read and play the game and that the game will broaden and deepen your awareness of today's diversified and interrelated strategic demands, allowing you to internalize your learning so you can apply it in the real world. In the game ahead you will personally and sometimes painfully experience the consequences of your own strategic choices as you work your way through the leading-edge principles and practices of strategic management. Most of all, however, I hope you have fun as you play out the suspense-filled decisions you'll be making.

I would like to offer some cautionary words before you begin *The*

Strategy Game. Although you are asked to make strategic decisions in situations that are intended to simulate real life, you may occasionally be presented with choices you consider extreme, inflexible, or contrived. Remember, it is only a game. I suggest that you consider any such circumstances constraints not unlike many similar circumstances imposed upon most CEOs in business today. You may occasionally feel there is a lack of sufficient information. As this occurs all too often in real life, use what you do know to stretch your thinking and make the best decision.

Finally, feedback from reviewers with diverse backgrounds who have played *The Strategy Game* indicates that you'll learn many things about yourself and about your strengths, weaknesses, biases, hopes, and fears. Winning is fleeting. How you play the game is lasting.

Craig R. Hickman

Acknowledgments

I wish to thank the many people who helped me with this book. First, to my literary agent and collaborator, Michael Snell, who for the past decade has patiently shaped and edited my work. He continues to be a most valued guide through the many mazes of the writing game. Adept word processing of the manuscript in the able hands of Mary Kowalczyk, who handled all aspects of the initial draft, and Mindy Gordon, who worked through the many revisions, made the writing much less of a chore.

A diverse panel of reviewers made up of medical professionals, business leaders, friends, and family members played and critiqued *The Strategy Game* as it unfolded, recording their experiences and helping me iron out many of the flaws. For any defects that remain, I must accept full blame. The panel included Paul Anderson, a medical technologist in the Hematology Department at Utah Valley Regional Medical Center, who generously interrupted his busy schedule to walk me through all the many aspects of blood analysis and diagnosis and then reviewed the manuscript for technical accuracy; Doug Nielson, M.D., a skilled neurosurgeon; Joe Cannon, Chairman and CEO of Geneva Steel; Stan Varner, builder and owner of Goldstone Place; Eric Marchant, former president of Management Perspectives Group and a management consultant; Mark Calkins, former vice president of marketing research for Novell; Marcello Hunter, a graduate student at the London Business School and a former technical writer for WordPerfect Corporation; my wife Pam, a gifted dramatist; my son Jared, a budding poet and novelist; my father Winston, a retired engineer and executive from EG&G; my brother Larry, a former financial executive with Union Pacific; my brother Mark, a computer programmer with EDS; and my sister-in-law Kim, whose enthusiastic review was greatly appreciated.

In addition to the panel of reviewers, several others offered technical, financial, and general input to the process of developing *The Strategy Game*. Paul Dunford, physician specialist for Coulter Corporation, the leading manufacturer of blood analyzers in the world, provided essential insights into the Coulter organization and the medical instrument industry. Roger Connors and Tom Smith, both management consultants to several medical device and diagnostics companies, gave me a broad and deep understanding of the strategic struggles and triumphs of organizations in the industry. Dave Winder, a managing partner at KPMG Peat Marwick, and his associates Jim Evans and Marty Van Wagoner, helped me develop the financial information on MedTech. As a management consultant over the last several years, I have worked with health-care administrators, physicians, nurses, and other medical staff at Intermountain Health Care in Salt Lake City, Cedars-Sinai Medical Center in Los Angeles, Samaritan Health Services in Phoenix, Century Health Care in Tulsa, Foundation Health Corporation in Sacramento, and Beverly Enterprises in Los Angeles. Countless people in these organizations gave me important background knowledge and insight into the health-care, medical equipment, and biotechnology fields.

Also, I am indebted to the Harvard Business School, which immersed me in business case studies for two years from 1974 to 1976, and to a host of fantasy and science fiction writers, whose "choose your own adventure" novels entertained my son Jared and, through him, me.

This book is dedicated to Jared Winston Hickman,whose voracious reading in his early years introduced me to the world of "choose your own adventure" books, which combined with my own earlier indoctrination into the world of business case studies, to spawn the idea for *The Strategy Game*.

Finally, I want to thank those unmentioned others who have contributed in countless ways to my writing and to this book. To them I am most grateful.

Introduction: The Adventure Begins

You are about to embark on an adventure. Your mission: to revitalize a troubled $150 million company. Your reward, if you succeed, will be a lot of personal satisfaction, a bright future as a top executive, and substantial financial remuneration. If you fail, you could lose everything you've achieved in your career.

The situation is a simple one: You've just become the CEO of MedTech, a medical instruments division of the $7 billion pharmaceutical giant, Benton Pharmaceuticals. You deserve this opportunity because you've chalked up an impressive record at another Benton division, where you worked for eight years as marketing vice president, then chief operating officer.

The challenge, however, is daunting. Benton acquired the 14-year-old MedTech six years ago on the assumption that its impressive history of innovation in the field of blood analysis, collection, and monitoring would fit perfectly into Benton's fast-growth philosophy. Since then, however, MedTech has performed sluggishly, averaging 4 to 6 percent annual sales and profit increases that fall well below Benton's 15 percent growth expectations. When your predecessor, John Ramsey, couldn't reverse the trend, Benton executives forced him into early retirement and tapped you to replace him.

You have in hand a report on MedTech (see the following pages). This report tells you how Benton Pharmaceuticals is organized and where MedTech fits in the organizational structure. It includes a summary of MedTech's financial position. The report also gives you some basic information about MedTech's facilities and officers.

Like most of today's CEOs, you will probably never possess all the

MedTech, Inc.

MedTech, Inc., is a wholly owned medical instruments subsidiary of Benton Pharmaceuticals and part of its Medical Products and Systems Group. Benton Pharmaceuticals consists of 62 divisions and subsidiaries organized into five groups: Pharmaceuticals Group (31 percent of revenues, 40 percent of profits); Medical Products and Systems Group (27 percent of revenues, 22 percent of profits); Diagnostic Products Group (21 percent of revenues, 20 percent of profits); Alternative Site Products and Services Group (17 percent of revenues, 15 percent of profits); and Industrial Products Group (4 percent of revenues, 3 percent of profits). For the most recent year ending September 30, Benton Pharmaceuticals reported revenues of $7.1 billion and operating profits (earnings before interest, taxes, and extraordinary items) of $2.1 billion. MedTech, Inc., was acquired by Benton six years ago for $200 million in cash. That year MedTech had grown from $72 million in revenues to $101 million, with operating profits climbing from $21 million to $30 million.

This year MedTech's worldwide revenues increased 5.2 percent to $147 million; U.S. sales were $118 million with international sales of $29 million. Sales have remained relatively flat due to increased competitiveness and lower pricing in the blood analysis, collection, and monitoring market. MedTech's worldwide market share has decreased slightly from 7 to 6.8 percent.

Operating profit decreased 4.6 percent to $32 million this year, primarily as a result of higher administrative expenses, increased cost of sales, and a restructuring completed in July. The restructuring was part of a major strategic analysis conducted for the entire Medical Products and Systems Group and included a reduction of administrative staff at MedTech. Cost of sales has been increasing in recent years, but the negative trend was arrested during the latter part of this fiscal year. Marketing expenses and R&D investment remained constant as a percent of sales, increasing 4.9 and 5.3 percent, respectively.

MedTech's capital expenditures, including additions to the pool of blood analysis, collection, and monitoring instruments leased to customers, were $10.2 million this year, compared to $13.8 million in the previous year. Most of the expenditures this year were directed toward improving manufacturing processes.

The following table provides a summary of selected financial data for the past five years.

Selected Financial Information
(Dollars in Millions)

| | Year ended September 30 | | | | |
	This year	Year 4	Year 3	Year 2	Year 1
Operations					
Net sales	$147.3	$140.0	$133.8	$128.5	$121.5
Cost of sales	52.7	48.3	46.0	43.4	41.4
R&D	15.2	14.6	13.5	12.7	12.4
Marketing	31.5	30.1	28.4	28.0	26.9
G&A*	15.8	13.4	12.7	11.8	10.9
Operating profit	32.1	33.6	33.2	32.6	29.9
Financial position					
Current assets	81.3	77.7	69.5	63.8	67.1
Current liabilities	45.4	40.1	38.8	34.8	37.6
Working capital	35.9	37.6	30.7	29.0	29.5
Other assets	24.5	25.8	27.0	26.2	28.8
Property and equipment	79.8	69.3	62.9	57.4	61.0
Total assets	185.6	172.8	159.4	147.4	156.9
Other data					
Capital expenditures	10.2	13.8	14.4	13.2	12.9
Depreciation and amortization	9.1	8.4	7.8	7.1	7.4
Return on sales	21.8%	24.0%	24.8%	25.8%	24.6%
Return on assets	17.3%	19.4%	20.8%	22.1%	19.1%
Number of employees	1052	1139	1122	1106	1088

*General and administrative expenses

MedTech has four manufacturing facilities, twenty-eight sales offices, and two research and development laboratories located in fourteen states in the United States and in Canada, England, Italy, Japan, and Australia.

Officers of MedTech include:

(*Your Name Here*), President and Chief Executive Officer
Richard Riley, Vice President of Research and Development
Edward Yates, Vice President of Production
Kenneth Y. Matsumori, Vice President of Management Information Systems
Amos A. Gill, Vice President of Finance

(Continued)

Katherine Saunders DaVaeno, Vice President of Marketing
Susan Carter, Vice President of Human Resources
Robert T. Shay, Vice President of Sales
Victor F. Gomez, Vice President of Technical Service
Mitchell P. Cavanaugh, President, Medical Products and Systems Group
Robert L. Koontz, Chairman and CEO, Benton Pharmaceuticals

information you would like before making tough strategic decisions; however, this report gives you the basic facts, and you will learn more about the situation and the people as you settle into the task of charting a successful future for the company. At the outset, you will encounter an either/or option, which will propel you down one of two avenues, each of which continues to branch off into a multitude of paths as you continue to make critical decisions about MedTech's future.

Some paths come to rather abrupt endings as a series of decisions fails to get results. Others lead gradually to varying degrees of success. Regardless of what you encounter as you move through the book, you can always go back to earlier critical junctures and try your hand again. Moreover, no matter how successful or unsuccessful a particular outcome, you will always gain some valuable insights into why a set of decisions turned out the way it did.

Before you begin playing the game, I want to offer some words of *caution* and explanation: While *The Strategy Game* represents real-life strategic decision-making situations, it is still only a game, and, as such, may occasionally present you with choices you consider extreme, unyielding, unsubstantiated, or otherwise contrived. If this happens to you while you're playing the game, I suggest that you view any unseemly choices or convoluted circumstances as mere constraints imposed upon you from the outside, not unlike the many constraints imposed upon today's CEOs, who often find themselves with no choice except to respond to circumstances. Further, whenever you feel a lack of sufficient information, which also occurs all too often in real life, make your best assumptions based on what you do know, stretching the breadth and depth of your strategic thinking, and making the best available choice.

Finally, on the basis of feedback from a diverse panel of reviewers who have played *The Strategy Game* and analyzed their experiences, I think you'll learn many new things about yourself and your biases, strengths, weaknesses, unique insights, blind spots, hopes, and fears. Winning is fleeting. How you play the game is lasting.

That's all you need to know before you begin. Have fun. And good luck!

1
The Current Situation

Your track record as vice president of marketing and then chief operating officer at another division of the $7 billion Benton Pharmaceuticals landed you the job as CEO of its MedTech subsidiary, a maker of medical instruments. After three months at the helm, and the closing of the current fiscal year, you have zeroed in on the single most important issue that will determine both your future and the fate of the company: achieving the parent company's growth goals with an organization beset by far more serious problems than you imagined when you accepted the job.

MedTech was built upon a line of blood analysis, collection, and monitoring products introduced 14 years ago and marketed to a wide range of health-care organizations. The company's blood analyzers range in price from about $10,000 to $200,000. The $40,000 to $70,000 midpriced line accounts for 42 percent of MedTech's revenues; the other blood analyzers, reagents, and peripheral products, such as blood bags, intravenous catheters, and blood pressure gauges, account for the balance. After initially purchasing a blood analyzer, the typical MedTech customer will spend from $500 to $10,000 annually on MedTech products.

Over the last 14 years the division has grown to its present $147 million sales level, with operating profits (earnings before interest, taxes, and extraordinary items) of $32 million. However, its last substantial sales increase came four years ago when the company introduced the Bloodgard closure, a device that protects health-care personnel from contact with a patient's blood. Bloodgard augments all MedTech product lines. Since then, however, MedTech has not introduced a major new product and has suffered stagnate sales and profit growth below 6 percent per year, well under Benton Pharmaceuticals' standard of 15 percent. In addition, MedTech's operating profits as a percent of net sales and total assets have remained below Benton's goals of 25 percent ROS (return on sales) and 30 percent ROA (return on assets).

Your predecessor, John Ramsey, who at the tender age of 57 had worn himself out in recent years, was forced to retire four months ago because he could not turn things around. Ever since then rumors have been flying that if MedTech does not show real progress in the next year, Benton will sell it, though your own discussions with senior executives at Benton neither prove nor disprove such rumors. With morale in the division much lower than you initially thought, you've learned that several key people are looking for jobs both inside and outside Benton.

Strategically, you've been reviewing alternatives for the past three months. A major strategy study was recently conducted by McKinsey & Company for Benton's Medical Products and Systems Group. The consulting firm recommended two possible directions for MedTech based on the following summary of MedTech's strengths and weaknesses:

MedTech Strengths and Opportunities for Growth

- Strong corporate history and tradition in technology development and product innovation
- Substantial reputation among customers for producing reliable, leading-edge blood analysis, collection, and monitoring instruments
- Widespread employee commitment for "working to save lives"
- Competent and capable senior management team
- Numerous attractive avenues for future new-product development
- Above-average to good quality of existing products
- Solid potential for improvements in cost and quality of existing products
- Opportunity to take advantage of an industrywide trend toward enhancing marketing and sales activities as another way (besides new-product development) to achieve growth
- Capability to exploit various domestic and global expansion opportunities through intensified marketing and sales efforts
- Abundant acquisition and joint-venture prospects
- High projected annual industry growth rates (over 25 percent) for medical instrument and equipment companies over the next decade

MedTech Weaknesses and Needs for Improvement

- Declining market share and weakening competitive position as evidenced by four years of low sales growth in a high-growth blood analysis, collection, and monitoring market

- Slow responsiveness to a fast-changing and increasingly competitive market

- Inadequate market segmentation analysis and target segment selection

- Requirement for increased investment in R&D to develop new products

- Need to reduce time getting new products to market

- Underdeveloped customer service orientation

- Incomplete and confusing definition of core competence (key organizational skills and capabilities)

- Lack of effective coordination, integration, and synergy among company functions, departments, and locations

- Diminishing vitality of sales force

- Declining morale throughout the organization

- Increasing government regulation and potential for major industry changes

- Continuing industrywide pressure to lower prices

- Growing strength of competitors, particularly BBX Systems, in new-product development, product quality, marketing, and sales

After several discussions with the McKinsey project leader and the in-house team that worked on the study with the McKinsey consultants, you've decided that the two strategic options outlined by the study do, in fact, represent the most viable choices. Although there are a host of strategic issues confronting MedTech that must each be addressed in turn, you believe first and foremost you must weigh the two McKinsey recommendations for stimulating the required sales and profit growth: focus on R&D for new products or improve marketing and sales of existing products. Each course requires such a major investment that, while improvement in both areas makes sense, the company cannot finance both alternatives simultaneously.

Competitors in the medical products industry currently win the sort of competitive advantage that sustains growth and development by outperforming rivals in one of these critical areas. Each route can, if properly supported, ensure success, regardless of the particular market within the industry. All successful companies in the industry perform both functions well; however, in the most outstanding companies one function dominates in decision making. Although MedTech once enjoyed both powerful R&D and strong marketing and sales, it currently can claim neither as a guiding strength. This situation, according to the McKinsey study, must change.

Your own analysis of MedTech's situation suggests that either strategic alternative could turn the tide. If you decide to invest heavily in R&D, you feel that a number of promising areas could yield viable innovations. With a steady stream of new products, the division could eventually develop the necessary marketing and sales expertise, through either its own sales force, alliances with independent marketing and sales organizations, or joint ventures with other Benton divisions or outside companies.

On the other hand, if you decide to beef up your marketing and sales efforts, you believe you can outperform R&D-oriented competitors, who often lack the marketing and sales prowess to exploit their innovations fully. With stronger marketing and sales capability, the division could attract new products from a variety of sources through licensing arrangements, alliances, joint ventures, or acquisitions, thus keeping its marketing and sales machine loaded with products.

As you approach this crucial, future-shaping decision, you find your senior team divided on the issue. Your marketing, human resources, finance, and sales vice presidents naturally favor the marketing and sales choice, while your R&D, production, management information, and technical service vice presidents understandably prefer to focus on R&D and new-product development. After several sleepless nights, you realize you can wait no longer to make a decision.

If you decide to focus on R&D for new-product development, turn to Chapter 2.

If you decide to strengthen marketing and sales, turn to Chapter 3.

2
Building an R&D Focus

Your senior management team greets your decision to focus on R&D and new-product development with a good deal of enthusiasm. Even those who had favored the marketing and sales option, relieved to see any action that could remove the uncertainty surrounding MedTech's future, applaud your decisiveness. However, at the next management meeting tempers flare as the team debates whether to emphasize the development of new, breakthrough products or improvements and refinements of existing products. While the group seems prepared to unite behind the R&D focus, they express far stronger opinions than you anticipated about exactly how to implement that focus. The argument grows so intense that you delay making any further decisions about implementation.

In the next few weeks you become increasingly concerned about the emotional stability of the vice president of R&D, Richard Riley, who adamantly favors development of new, breakthrough products. He has become so committed to that position that he erupts with hostility and condescension whenever anyone raises the other alternative. His behavior, little short of temper tantrums, has gridlocked discussions among your management team. Oddly, his major opponent is the vice president of production, Ed Yates, who believes MedTech would be much better off emphasizing the improvement and refinement of existing products. Yates has even gone so far as to question the ability of the R&D department to come up with viable, genuinely innovative products within a reasonable time frame. This view touches off Riley's powderkeg, of course, causing yet another management meeting to deteriorate into a shouting match.

To diffuse the emotion ignited by this issue, you form a task force to examine the question of whether MedTech should emphasize development of breakthrough products or improvement of existing products. You ask the vice president of management information, Ken Matsumori, who has remained neutral during the debates, to direct the task force in a thorough, yet urgent, analysis of the issue.

While the task force examines this pressing question during the next six weeks, you hold several one-on-one sessions with Richard Riley to help him control the kind of extreme behavior that has been wreaking havoc in so many management meetings. To your dismay, Richard does not respond positively and refuses so stubbornly to soften his stance that you doubt more than ever his ability to manage MedTech's R&D function effectively. This really worries you; however, you do value Riley's commitment and vision. You wonder whether his emotional stance and refusal to compromise represent strengths or weaknesses, given MedTech's new strategic direction.

Finally, Ken Matsumori and his task force present their findings to the management team during a full-day retreat at a nearby resort hotel. Their conclusions stress two fundamental considerations: (1) the development of breakthrough products may offer the greatest long-term return, but such a course would require a strength the company has not demonstrated during the last few years, and acquiring that strength would require substantial beefing up of the R&D department; (2) improving existing products may offer greater short-term return, but such a course would also require a strength the company has not displayed in recent years, and building that strength would demand much better communication, coordination, and commitment among all departments. While the report clearly enunciates the options, it leaves you pretty much where you started, with the two sides of the debate no closer to resolution.

In light of this dilemma, you realize that you will once again have to make a strategic decision based on the information at hand. Time is running out. You know that the division's R&D group can, and will, emphasize both development of new products and improvement of existing products. But you also recognize that it would be a strategic mistake not to establish one of these thrusts as the division's top priority. Your own experience and your study of strategic decision making in other corporations has taught you that the worst management blunder anyone can make is to try to "do everything at once" or "be all things to all people."

As you approach this decision you conclude that long-term opportunities favor the strategy of breakthrough-product development, whereas short-term gains favor the strategy of existing-product improvement. Now you must decide.

If you opt to emphasize the development of new breakthrough products, turn to Chapter 4.

If you choose to stress improvement of existing products, turn to Chapter 5.

3
Focusing on Marketing and Sales

Stunned by your decision to focus on marketing and sales, Richard Riley, vice president of R&D, storms out of the management meeting in which you announce your decision. The rest of the senior team reacts with much less emotion, although a rousing discussion ensues for the next three hours. To your delight, the persuasive arguments of Kate DaVaeno, vice president of marketing, and Amos Gill, vice president of finance, finally settle emotions and convince even those vice presidents committed to an R&D focus that the marketing and sales emphasis can provide a key to success over the next 10 years. Kate and Amos cite several examples of the power of marketing in both the pharmaceutical and medical products industries. One example, American Home Products, comes up again and again as proof that even a company with a terrible R&D track record, but stellar marketing and sales abilities, can outperform its competition. Kate DaVaeno hands out copies of *Fortune* magazine's article on the pharmaceutical industry in which American Home Products garnered high praise for its marketing and sales prowess, resulting in a 46 percent return on equity, second only to Merck. Amos Gill chimes in with all the financial analysis he can muster to demonstrate that a marketing and sales focus would solve MedTech's growth and development problems faster and cheaper than R&D. "Once our marketing and sales operation are top-notch, then we can worry about bolstering our R&D effort," Amos reasons. By the end of the day, the MedTech senior management team, with the notable exception of Richard Riley, unites behind a five-year marketing and sales emphasis.

Two days later, after a long and stormy confrontation with Richard Riley, you accept his resignation. You decide to leave the position of vice president of R&D vacant until one of the three directors who reported to Riley is ready to take over. Then, at 4:35 p.m., just as you are getting ready to leave the office early after a string of 12-hour days, Bob Shay, vice president of sales, walks into your office and closes the door behind him. By the look on his face, you know he's upset.

"I've been in meetings the past two days with Kate DaVaeno," he begins. "We're trying to come up with a broad sketch of the marketing and sales strategy, but we're having real difficulty ironing out our philosophical differences. To be honest, I think we're stuck." As Bob finishes his last sentence, your secretary buzzes to tell you that Kate wants to meet with you as soon as possible.

You sigh. "Tell her to come up as soon as she can." So much for calling it an early day.

Shay responds with surprising enthusiasm. "Good! Maybe we can resolve this thing right now!"

While you're waiting for Kate, whose office is two floors below your own, you ask Bob to describe the philosophical differences as he sees them.

After a moment's thought, he says, "Kate believes our marketing and sales strategy should be based on a detailed market-segmentation process that allows for what she calls `micromarketing' or `database marketing.' She wants to reconfigure our product line and customize services based on the needs of multiple market segments, and she's not thinking in terms of just four or five segments, she's thinking thirty or more. In my view, our salespeople already do a good job of identifying and meeting different customer needs, so we don't need to analyze a bunch of different segments to death. We really should be worrying about new and better customer service. If we could increase our sales force by 25 percent, beef up our customer service information department, and add the technical and training services our customers want, I bet we can increase our market share by 30 percent."

At this point Kate comes in, just as Shay is summing up his position, "Our philosophical differences really boil down to service versus segmentation. Kate doesn't see the need to improve service; she just wants to figure out the peculiar needs of a hundred different customer segments."

Kate immediately launches into her own impassioned speech. "That's right! We don't need more services, we just need to provide our customers with exactly what they want, and that requires modifying product offerings and features, product-line extensions, and technical services to meet the very different needs of our customers—medical centers, community hospitals, outpatient surgery centers, large clinics, small clinics, doctors' offices, emergency centers, rural health-care units, nursing homes, test labs, research centers, etc., etc. The list goes on and on. And, in all honesty, we don't do a good job meeting all these different needs. Bob wants to play the game the same old way: increase the sales force, improve service, and smile a lot. It just won't work anymore."

As Bob and Kate argue back and forth for the next several minutes, you begin to wonder what Vic Gomez, vice president of technical service, thinks about all this. When you ask about that, Shay and DaVaeno concur, "He's ambivalent. He can see pros and cons on both sides."

After another hour of discussion, you say good night to Kate and Bob. During your half-hour commute home you think about the possibility of doing what they both suggest. Unfortunately, your division does not at the moment possess the financial resources to do both well. Besides, even if you tried to do some of both, one of the two approaches should take precedence, or you'd invite the same sort of squabbling you just listened to for two hours. Surely, such contention could do nothing but cause confusion and inefficiency. Your options suddenly seem obvious: segmentation analysis must determine how, when, and where to modify products or increase service; or overall customer service must improve across all segments.

As you pull into the driveway of your home at 7 p.m., you feel once again that a CEO's job boils down to playing "tiebreaker." You're tired, but confident that you can make the right decision in the next day or two.

If you decide to favor extensive customer segmentation and micromarketing as the basis of MedTech's marketing and sales strategy, turn to Chapter 6.

If you elect to improve customer service across all segments through additions to the sales force and an enhanced customer service function, turn to Chapter 7.

4
Emphasizing
Breakthrough
Products

Richard Riley is delighted with your decision to emphasize break-through products and comes to your office to express his enthusiasm.

"I know this decision hasn't been an easy one for you," he says with no trace of his old hostility, "but given this topsy-turvy industry, it's really the only thing we can do."

You steel yourself for the confrontation you have been planning for some time. "I appreciate your support, but, frankly, I'm concerned about our ability to pull it off."

A frown crosses Riley's face. "What do you mean?"

"I mean that we've got to strengthen our whole R&D effort from the ground up."

"Of course we do, and I'm ready."

"Yes, but do we have the right people to pull it off?"

A moment of tense silence ensues. As Riley looks away, he asks, "What are you really trying to say?"

"Sit down, Richard. You and I need to have a frank talk about the future."

For the next two hours you share with Richard your concerns about building the strength of the R&D function and your misgivings about his own management and leadership capabilities. Twice during the session, once physically, you have to restrain him from angrily storming out of your office. While you continue to express your respect for his technical brilliance and innovative passion, you strongly question his ability to orchestrate the upgrading and building of his department.

By the end of your meeting Riley has calmed down and steadfastly insists that he can and will do whatever it takes to push MedTech's

R&D efforts to the forefront of the industry. As he leaves your office he says, "I've been waiting for this chance my entire career, to create the sort of breakthrough products that can advance medical care and save lives. I can make this happen. I know I can. I won't let you down!"

Alone in your office you ponder all that has occurred in the last several weeks. Given Riley's continuing volatility, you have decided not to tell him, for now, about the preliminary explorations you've held with a small medical products R&D company, FutureMed, that has racked up an impressive record of new-product introductions during the last five years. Just two days ago you seriously discussed with them several affiliation options, ranging from acquisition of the company to exclusive licensing of its new products. Benton senior executives have given you the green light to structure some kind of partnership with the company, but in light of all the recent disagreements among your own management team and your concern about the abilities of certain executives, such as Riley, you have decided to inform only your vice president of finance about the FutureMed possibilities.

Faced with yet another tough, strategically important decision, you decide to leave the office early on Thursday afternoon for a long weekend getaway, where you can think through the problem. Later that weekend, while lying on a beach in the Caribbean, you toy with two alternatives: build the R&D function from the inside out, relying on Riley and other key people to accomplish the upgrade, or acquire the necessary R&D capability from the outside through a company like FutureMed. Building from the inside out could greatly strengthen the morale and the overall culture at MedTech, but it would take a lot of time to do it that way. Acquiring new R&D capability from the outside, either through FutureMed or some other highly innovative company, would provide a quicker solution. But it could devastate Riley and many of his R&D people as well as send a signal of "no confidence" to the rest of the MedTech organization, possibly creating widespread unrest.

As you watch the sun sink into the Gulf of Mexico, you know you must find an answer by Monday morning.

If you opt to acquire new R&D capability from the outside through acquisition of companies such as FutureMed, turn to Chapter 8.

If you decide to build the R&D function from the inside out, relying on the key people already working at MedTech, turn to Chapter 9.

5
Stressing Improvement of Existing Products

At an early morning meeting with all your vice presidents, you announce your tentative decision to focus on improving existing products, but because you have decided not to move forward without a strong consensus from the group, you present your position as a topic for consideration rather than as a final decision. The discussion begins with a thorough review of Ken Matsumori's findings, with each member of the team freely asking questions and clarifying the task force's conclusions.

"I'm not sure we're not right back where we started," observes one vice president. Most of the others agree, though Matsumori's clarification of the two fundamental considerations have made the choices clear-cut: breakthrough products bring more risk and higher potential return; improvements to existing products entail lower risk and more predictable return. Most importantly, the task force's report has defused much of the emotion that has surrounded the issue, giving the management team a much more objective forum in which to express their views. By midmorning, everyone feels ready to vote. Having set the ground rules that you want a clear consensus, you ask Ken Matsumori to summarize the day's discussion before each one casts his or her vote.

"It's a tough call," says Ken, "but I do think today's discussion has helped refine our insights. First, I think we agree that pursuing an R&D focus with emphasis on existing-product improvement will allow us to achieve the profit and sales growth we need quicker, so we can survive in the Benton environment. It's just good business sense to pursue a strategy that can get us out of our slump faster and easier. Yes, it's true that breakthrough products promise even greater profit and sales growth down the line; but that goal will take longer to achieve, and we may not have the time, given Benton's short-term expectations. Pursuing the track of existing-product improvement will allow MedTech to establish a viable performance base, quickly, with less risk. I don't see what we have to lose by unanimously supporting a strategy for existing-product improvement. We can worry about developing a breakthrough-product strategy once we get Benton off our backs."

As you call for the vote, you sense that everyone has come on board, with the possible exception of R&D head Richard Riley. However, after calmly reaffirming his usual position, Riley surprises you by casting the first vote in support of your decision. Everyone else follows suit, giving you the consensus you wanted. On your way home that evening you praise yourself for having gotten the full support of your team behind what you consider the best strategic decision, given MedTech's current circumstances.

During the next several weeks Ed Yates, vice president of production, works closely with Richard Riley to develop the first round of product-improvement projects. To your delight, the two departments are working together smoothly, and you praise both Yates and Riley for that fact. In a careful feasibility study, outlining probable costs and benefits, they eventually identify six strong candidates for product improvement. Since both Yates and Riley know that the company cannot pursue all six projects simultaneously, they have separated the projects into two groups: three of the projects focus on decreasing the production costs of existing blood analysis, collection, and monitoring products, while the other three aim at increasing the quality of existing products.

Now you face another vital choice between cost reduction and quality improvements. Again, it's not an easy call, because the feasibility studies make both avenues look equally attractive. The cost improvements would enhance MedTech's price competitiveness with the more cost-conscious clinics, doctors offices, and smaller health-care facilities, while the quality improvements would enhance MedTech's perceived uniqueness across all market segments. It all boils down to a low-cost strategy versus a high-quality strategy. As always, your limited resources dictate that you select one or the other.

Ken Matsumori reminds you that if MedTech were a "total quality management" company, it could achieve cost reductions and quality improvements simultaneously, but for now that seems impossible. You agree and say, "Maybe we'll have the opportunity to create such an organization at MedTech in time, but now we have to choose."

Committed to the consensus approach with your management team, you decide to present your tentative decision at the next group meeting and then give your vice presidents the power to endorse it or call for more discussion and analysis. Between now and then, you must make up your own mind.

If you want to recommend the quality-improvement projects, turn to Chapter 10.

If you would rather champion the cost-reduction projects, turn to Chapter 11.

6
Pursuing Customer Segmentation

You have given Kate DaVaeno and her department the go-ahead to move forward quickly with their ambitious customer segmentation program, and you have suggested that they enlist the help of an outside marketing consulting firm. Oddly, Bob Shay goes along with your decision with no objection. Had he just been positioning for power, or didn't he really believe his own arguments? You make a mental note to take a closer look at Bob Shay and the entire sales organization in the near future.

With your approval, Kate engages the firm of Yankelovich Clancy Shulman to assist in an in-depth segmentation of customers and a subsequent reconfiguration of product and service offerings to meet segment needs. After reading *The Marketing Revolution* by Clancy and Shulman, Kate decided that Yankelovich Clancy Shulman would provide MedTech with the right combination of marketing intelligence gathering, segmentation, and strategy development skills.

Two months later, with the first phase of their study (the segmentation analysis) completed, Kate and John Carbiggs, a principal from Yankelovich Clancy Shulman, present a preliminary report to the senior management team. In it they suggest that MedTech could successfully pursue an industrywide (i.e., all-customer segments) strategy of customized variations in product packaging and pricing, marketing approaches and channels, and service offerings to appeal to different segments. For example, MedTech products could be easily modified to meet the needs of different customer segments, with the number of blood analysis, collection, and monitoring options expanding or retracting depending on the segment. Specialized sales detailing teams (teams of salespeople that match product/service offerings with customer needs) could be assigned to different segments, with technical service reorganized into three groups that would tailor their levels of customer service to the various segments. Differentiation from competitors industrywide would come about through distinctly different marketing and sales campaigns and product and service configurations to each segment, a tactic Kate and John Carbiggs call "micromarketing."

However, the segmentation analysis has also identified a rapidly growing group of underserved market segments: small health-care units, clinics, and doctors' offices. Since industry trends show these small-size providers performing a steadily increasing number of blood analysis, collection, and monitoring activities, better serving these customer segments and their subsegments could represent a substantial opportunity. However, doing so would require sharp focus and tremendous resources, because mere minor modifications in packaging, pricing, marketing approaches, or services would not be enough to create dominance in these underserved segments. To be sure, MedTech could apply micromarketing to capitalize on the underserved niches in the short term, but both DaVaeno and Carbiggs believe it would only be a matter of time before a competitor exploits this opportunity with a full-fledged focus and an all-out commitment of resources, eclipsing those paying less attention to the niches. You realize that it would be almost impossible to direct MedTech's micromarketing efforts at all customer segments and at the same time give the underserved niches of small health-care providers extraordinary attention.

Before DaVaeno and Yankelovich Clancy Shulman move on to the second phase of their study, analyzing ways of reconfiguring product and service offerings parallel to company strengths and customized for different segments, you must decide whether to apply micromarketing industrywide or target the underserved niches of small health-care providers.

After more than three hours of discussion of the segmentation report, you suggest putting the question to a vote, but Amos Gill, vice president of finance, interrupts. "Can I say something before we jump on one of these bandwagons?" Gill, a quiet man in his early fifties, seldom asserts himself this way, so you invite him to speak his piece. You've never known him to open his mouth unless he has something really worth hearing to say.

Gill takes the floor. "We've all been through the Michael Porter competitive advantage stuff dozens of times, and everyone of us knows we can't be all things to all people, but making a choice between these two

alternative strategies would be a big mistake." After a somewhat the-
atrical pause, Amos continues, "We *must* do both. Otherwise we
negate the value obtained by going through this whole segmentation
analysis. Granted, maybe we can't do both simultaneously, with the
same organization, but I believe we must find some way, some how, to
apply micromarketing in each of these areas."

After a long silence, individual vice presidents, one after another,
express agreement with Gill. The ensuing discussion identifies two
approaches to enacting both strategies: sequencing or separating.
Sequencing would mean pursuing the industrywide strategy first and
the underserved niche strategy second, or vice versa. Separating
would involve creating two sister divisions within MedTech, each
pursuing one of the strategies.

At this point, you end the meeting without taking a vote. You need
some time to think about the discussion, and you realize, once again,
you're going to have to make this decision.

---

*If you opt for sequencing the two strategies, turn to Chapter
12.*

*If you decide on separating the two strategies, turn to
Chapter 13.*

7
Improving
Customer Service

While you value Kate DaVaeno's suggestions for sophisticated market segmentation and micromarketing, you prefer Bob Shay's more straightforward approach. Improving customer service will, you think, give MedTech the quickest sales increase and set the stage for a more comprehensive service-based strategy in the future. However, if you don't increase MedTech's sales by at least 10 percent this year, there probably won't be a next year to worry about.

Your senior management team accepts the decision, agreeing that it probably does represent the best short-term option. At the very least, it will buy MedTech the necessary time to take other steps in the future. When Kate DaVaeno questions you about the possibility of more in-depth customer segmentation and the reconfiguration of product and service offerings along the lines of both company strengths and segment needs in the coming months, you promise her that possibility, but only if she lends her total support to short-term customer service improvements.

During the next several months you work closely with sales vice president Bob Shay and technical service vice president Vic Gomez to maximize customer satisfaction at the least possible expense. First you add twenty new salespeople, who will increase contact with customers by 25 percent, then you hire and train four new customer service clerks to handle customer information requests, complaints, and reorders. You also develop a plan for beefing up technical service and launch a new leasing program for smaller healthcare customers aimed at encouraging them to perform more blood analysis and testing.

From the outset, the customer service improvements seem to be working beautifully. Sales rise 8 percent in the first nine months of the year, and you are hearing strong praise from Benton. As morale throughout the company rises, so does customer satisfaction. Then, disaster strikes. In July, a nimble competitor, BBX Systems, introduces a new product line for blood analysis, collection, and monitoring with significant advantages over MedTech's own lines. Within three months sales of MedTech's midpriced line drop by a full third, more than wiping out the 8 percent sales increase. In fact, by year's end your division finishes with an 8 percent decrease in total sales and a 12 percent decline in profits.

Morale at MedTech sinks to an all-time low as rumors of an impending sale of the company and a wholesale sweep of its senior management run rampant throughout MedTech and Benton's other divisions. Luckily, the sale falls through because of the buyer's uncertainty about MedTech's future, and Benton CEO Bob Koontz assures you that the board will extend your opportunity to turn things around, but only for one more year.

In the following weeks you conclude that while your strategic deci-

Selected Financial Information
(Dollars in Millions)

	Year ended September 30	
	This year	Last year
Operations		
Net sales	$135.2	$147.3
Cost of sales	48.0	52.7
R&D	12.8	15.2
Marketing	32.2	31.5
G&A	14.0	15.8
Operating profit	28.2	32.1
Financial position		
Current assets	78.5	81.3
Current liabilities	46.1	45.4
Working capital	32.4	35.9
Other assets	24.1	24.5
Property and equipment	85.2	79.8
Total assets	187.8	185.6
Other data		
Capital expenditures	5.6	10.2
Depreciation and amortization	9.2	9.1
Return on sales	20.9%	21.8%
Return on assets	15.0%	17.3%
Number of employees	1076	1052

sion to improve customer service would have worked well in a "continuous change" market, it failed when the market became one of "radical change." You chide yourself for not anticipating the kind of competitive attack launched by BBX. In hindsight, you acknowledge that service improvement, which began as a low-risk strategy that relied on refinements and improvements, became a high-risk strategy when it could not accommodate substantial changes caused by an aggressive competitor. Really, you should have known better. And why hadn't the Benton executives given you more guidance? Around and around you go, until you realize that you can only point the finger at yourself. The bottom line? Your strategy failed. You designed it to buy time, but you ran out of time. As a result, MedTech's performance failed to meet expectations, as shown in the accompanying table.

After contemplating these numbers and wondering whether you've been too hard on yourself, you realize that you must either hold firm to building a long-term service-based strategy or return to a more traditional product-based one. Your group vice president, Mitch Cavanaugh, argues for getting back to basics and forgetting about faddish customer service or marketing segmentation strategies. "Just worry about product costs and quality and you'll be fine," he tells you. Returning to a product-based strategy would obviously please Benton executives, but holding firm to building a service-based strategy could certainly offer more potential for real reform and advancement, particularly given the industry's increasing attention on the manufacturing-services interface. Sticking with a service-based approach entails a lot of risk because Benton's top brass view it with such skepticism. A back-to-basics product-based approach might minimize risk, but it would not turn MedTech into the kind of company you want it to be.

Deep down, you really do believe in the words of James Brian Quinn and his colleagues at Dartmouth, as stated in a recent *Harvard Business Review* article, "Beyond Products: Services-Based Strategy." According to Quinn, "The role of services in providing value is ever more important. Not long ago, most of a product's value added came from the production processes that converted raw material into useful forms (steel into auto bodies, for example, or grain into edible cereals). Now, however, value added is increasingly likely to come from technological improvements, styling features, product image, and other attributes that only services can create." You even send a copy of Quinn's latest book, *Intelligent Enterprise* to Mitch Cavanaugh. You attach a memo and quote a sentence from the book: "In a world where products are moving more toward commoditization and where services and intellect are increasingly the bases of differentiation, leading manufacturers are moving ever more toward service-based strategies."

Now, what will you do?

> *If you choose to go back to a product-based strategy, turn to Chapter 14.*
>
> *If you want to hold firm to building a service-based strategy, turn to Chapter 15.*

8
Acquiring FutureMed

After several weeks of painstaking research and analysis, you present your case for acquiring FutureMed to senior executives at Benton, who love the idea. They find especially attractive two of the small company's most recent product innovations: the FutureScan cardiopulmonary system and the FutureStar cell sorter. As you explain in some technical detail, these instruments represent major advancements in the pumping, oxygenating, and monitoring of a patient's blood when routed outside the body during open-heart surgery and in the prognostication of illnesses such as leukemia and other forms of cancer. Since both products have passed preliminary FDA reviews, there should be no difficulty gaining premarket approval and moving into production within the next several months. As a footnote to your presentation, you review FutureMed's current research projects, which include a promising blood culturing system that could revolutionize the industry in a few years.

At this point in the discussion, one of the Benton executives, Charles Doan, president of the Diagnostic Products Group, raises a question you anticipated but hoped wouldn't come up. "Explain to me," he begins, "why FutureMed should be acquired by MedTech rather than by a division in the Diagnostic Products Group?" Before you can answer, he raises his voice, making it clear he's not just posing a question, he's staking out a position. "It seems to me that FutureMed's strength lies in medical diagnostic devices, not blood analysis instruments."

After waiting a few seconds for the walls to stop vibrating, you calmly explain that FutureMed's basic R&D competence lies in the field of blood analysis, collection, and monitoring equipment, not in general medical diagnosis. You admit that the FutureStar cell sorter could be classified as a more general diagnostic product, but that it is also a blood analysis system, an area in which FutureMed maintains a 100 percent focus. Having already described FutureMed's blood-culturing project in detail, you reveal details about some of the company's other product development projects: A state-of-the-art injection and flow system that integrates both pharmacy and bedside management systems with bar-code programmability to ensure more accurate and cost-effective drug delivery into the blood system; a revolutionary system for the real-time measurement of cardiac function and blood flow in critically ill patients; and a host of related new products such as blood reservoirs, filters, and custom tubing packs. You conclude your remarks by insisting that FutureMed's R&D competence fits better with MedTech than with any other company in the Benton organization, and that a completion of the acquisition would greatly enhance MedTech's strategic position in the market. Charles Doan, apparently satisfied with your argument, changes the subject to a discussion of where to go for lunch.

In the end Benton approves your proposal to acquire FutureMed for $30 million, and you work hard on finalizing the deal over the next few months. Amos Gill, vice president of finance, and Winston Wallberg, legal counsel from corporate headquarters, prove invaluable in putting the deal together. At one point the whole thing comes close to unraveling because you can't come to terms with FutureMed's founders and owners on the details of the deal. The three FutureMed founders have different agendas that become evident only as negotiations intensify; tempers flare and you see your weeks and months of work going up in smoke. One of the founders, Jack Suhler, wants to remain on board after the acquisition and is willing to take a portion of his FutureMed equity in Benton Pharmaceuticals' stock, but the other two founders want to cash out and retire. By working nonstop over a critical weekend, Gill and Wallberg structure a buy out that meets everyone's needs through a combination of cash, stock, and seller's debt arrangements. Each of the FutureMed founders feels well-treated, and the deal is consummated.

Finally, six months after having decided to make research and development MedTech's major strategic focus, you have completed the FutureMed acquisition and must now find a way to integrate the new company into your own. The only casualty of the transaction is the resignation of Richard Riley, vice president of R&D, who saw it as an affront to his capabilities and an indication of your disrespect. In retrospect, you conclude that Riley's resignation is best for all concerned. He can get on with his career elsewhere, and you won't have to worry about his consciously or unconsciously sabotaging the integration of the two companies.

Until you can properly formulate a plan for that integration, you allow FutureMed to operate autonomously. You assign a team under the direction of Jack Suhler, one of the FutureMed founders, to plan the integration. To your chagrin, however, the team has reached an impasse: Should FutureMed and MedTech's R&D function be combined into a separate, autonomous R&D division of MedTech, or should FutureMed be brought into MedTech as an integral part of the company? While you can appreciate the pros and cons of each approach, you must decide on one or the other. The stand-alone R&D division would have the advantages of autonomy, concentration, and focus, as well as an R&D management approach directed solely at developing breakthrough products. The disadvantage of the stand-alone option would be the potential isolation and detachment of the division, which might cause it to lose touch with the marketplace. On the other hand, the advantages of integrating FutureMed with the whole MedTech organization would be the stimulation a fiery little innovator would bring to the party and the reorganization of all MedTech and FutureMed operations, including marketing and production, which always have trouble working smoothly with R&D. The disadvantages to this option would be the possible loss of FutureMed's spirit as it gets bogged down by the process of melding into the rest of the company. Again, you're stuck on the horns of a dilemma.

After thinking about and studying the situation for a week, you keep coming back to a sentence in *Third Generation R&D: Managing the Link to Corporate Strategy*, a book by Philip Roussel, Kamal Saad, and Tamara Erickson, consultants at Arthur D. Little: "The first and in many ways the most difficult obstacle to overcome is the gap between the worlds of R&D and the company's general management, two worlds with often disparate cultures and different outlooks." Finally, you arrange to meet with Jack Suhler's planning team first thing in the morning to let them know your position.

If you prefer to combine FutureMed and MedTech's R&D function to create a separate, autonomous division, turn to Chapter 16.

If you would rather fully integrate FutureMed into MedTech, turn to Chapter 17.

9
Upgrading In-House R&D Capabilities

Despite your serious reservations about Richard Riley as a manager and leader, and in light of the fact that building the R&D function from the inside would have to begin at the top, you conclude that Riley deserves the opportunity to apply his flair for developing breakthrough products. After all, as Riley himself has argued, MedTech has never really made R&D its primary focus, so how can you accurately assess him or anyone else in R&D on their recent performance? Giving Riley the go-ahead to create a new, powerful R&D culture would send a clear message throughout the organization that you are willing to give the people at MedTech every chance to prove themselves. This message could greatly strengthen the motivation of all MedTech people to succeed.

Over the next several months you work hard to develop and inspire the R&D management team. To secure state-of-the-art training, Riley, his three department heads, and eight team leaders attend advanced R&D management seminars at Stanford University at a total cost of over $300,000. Within months the training begins paying off as a series of new-product ideas move into development.

You and Riley also retain an R&D consulting firm to help MedTech set its new-product development priorities and establish a process for guiding product ideas through each stage of development and into production. As you predicted, the morale among R&D personnel shoots skyward, affecting the entire organization in a heartening way. Even senior executives at Benton comment on the vitality and enthusiasm of everyone at MedTech.

You had successfully convinced Benton executives that an in-house upgrading of R&D would take time but that the long-term benefits would be worth the wait. While you had projected sales would remain level for 18 to 24 months, you forecast increases of 20 to 25 percent over the next several years. Profits would decrease slightly during the buildup period but then would also rise at a 20 to 25 percent growth rate. While anxious and somewhat skeptical, the Benton executives had agreed to give you the time, provided you maintained sales at the current level.

After almost 12 months as CEO of MedTech and with the R&D upgrade process moving along beautifully, rival BBX Systems introduces their new blood analysis product line, causing MedTech sales to plummet by almost 50 percent. This blow devastates everyone at MedTech because the division still sits many months away from introducing any of its own new products. You can do little to blunt BBX Systems' competitive initiative. Not only does BBX's new blood analysis system outperform every other system on the market, its excellent component products (i.e., reagents, tubes, bags, filters, containers, and monitoring devices) can function with competitors' systems, even your own.

Though you immediately shift emphasis to shoring up marketing and sales, BBX's new line of products simply outperforms MedTech's. At the end of your first fiscal year, MedTech posts sales of $122 million, a 17 percent decline, and profits of $20 million, a 38 percent decline. The

Selected Financial Information
(Dollars in Millions)

| | Year ended September 30 | |
	This year	Last year
Operations		
Net sales	$122.2	$147.3
Cost of sales	45.3	52.7
R&D	19.7	15.2
Marketing	23.0	31.5
G&A	14.1	15.8
Operating Profit	20.1	32.1
Financial position		
Current assets	68.8	81.3
Current liabilities	56.3	45.4
Working capital	12.5	35.9
Other assets	23.2	24.5
Property and equipment	91.2	79.8
Total assets	183.2	185.6
Other data		
Capital expenditures	11.3	10.2
Depreciation and amortization	9.9	9.1
Return on sales	16.4%	21.8%
Return on assets	11.0%	17.3%
Number of employees	1054	1052

table on the previous page provides a summary of selected financial information. Unfortunately, the outlook for the coming year looks even bleaker, because your anticipated new products will not come on-line until the end of next year.

In January of the next year, Benton informs you that an Italian Pharmaceutical company, Beltrami, Ltd., has agreed to purchase MedTech for $140 million. You are asked to remain in your current position for the first six months of the transition, after which Beltrami will replace you with their own executive. Benton executives don't offer you much hope of another position within the Benton organization after the transition period. In fact, your immediate boss at Benton suggests that you start looking for a job immediately.

During the next few months, while doing what you can to smooth the transition from Benton to Beltrami ownership and searching for a new job, you take time to think about what went wrong. For a long time you chalk it all up to timing. If BBX just hadn't introduced their new line when it did, MedTech's fortunes would have fared much better. You remain convinced that your strategy was a good one and that it would have succeeded if you had only had time to implement it. Benton, you believe, was just too focused on short-term results to allow the strategy to work. After all, Beltrami was impressed enough with your efforts to build up the in-house capabilities of the R&D function that they eagerly pursued the company.

Later, after you move to a new job as vice president of operations for another medical supply company, your understanding of what happened evolves, and you come to recognize that your strategy to upgrade MedTech's in-house R&D capabilities rested on too many overly idealistic assumptions. With the benefit of clearer hindsight, you realize that such a strategy would only have worked in an ideal world free from the forces of short-term pressures, cutthroat competition and massive change. You vow you'll never make the same misjudgments again.

What would you do differently if you could move back the clock?

If you want to go back to your last strategic decision point, return to Chapter 4.

If you want to review an earlier decision, return to Chapter 2 or Chapter 1.

If you're still feeling the sting of defeat and believe you could have made your last strategic choice work in real life, you may be right. After all, this is just a game. However, if you return to your last strategic decision (the first option above) and select the other alternative, you will learn why the author considers it a better choice.

10
Making
Better-Quality
Products

When you present your recommendation that the division focus on quality improvements of existing products, production vice president Ed Yates suggests that the company collect additional competitor intelligence. After some discussion, everyone agrees that a little more probing would be smart, so you postpone the decision for two weeks, asking Ed Yates and marketing vice president Kate DaVaeno to find out what they can about your competitors' product plans. After the meeting you pull Ed aside to explore his concerns further. He admits to some misgivings about the quality-improvement projects, saying, "I'd feel much better about the cost-reduction route, but I can go the other way as long as we're confident that our competitors won't beat us at the quality game." You thank Ed for his candor and return to your office.

As you mull over the situation, you begin to question your consensus style of management. You still firmly believe that the market will welcome quality improvements, but you've now halted progress in that direction for two weeks. All your current customer surveys clearly suggest the willingness of several customer groups to purchase new, higher-quality blood analysis, collection, and monitoring systems; your management team, including Ed Yates, had reviewed that data, so why the delay? Maybe Ed is pursuing some other, hidden agenda?

Two weeks later, you ask Ed Yates and Kate DaVaeno to report their findings to the management team. Yates begins, "I found out from Bevans (one of MedTech's suppliers) that BBX is going to introduce a new and improved line of blood analyzers later this year. My contact at Bevans says the BBX people are unusually tight-lipped about the new line, but they're acting very confident."

DaVaeno concurs. "My information corroborates Ed's. One of our largest customers in Los Angeles, Cedars-Sinai Medical Center, has seen a sneak preview of a prototype. They said it outperforms our midpriced line in every respect."

While this news greatly troubles your team, you personally remain confident that quality improvement holds the key to your future. Mustering as much enthusiasm as you can, you conclude, "Well, I guess we'll just have to make our improvements even better."

However, your words do nothing but spark a rousing discussion that takes on a more and more negative tone. You end it by imposing your decision on the group. The time for consensus had ended. The quality-improvement projects will begin immediately. To justify your heavy-handedness, you cite BBX's head start, saying, "Look, I'm sure BBX is not the only competitor working on new and better instruments. This is a very quality-conscious environment, and we must meet the challenge, not shrink from it. Regardless of the quality of BBX's new systems, we must take them on and beat them. I *know* we can do it." Spurred on by your confidence, the management team gets behind the idea and displays an unusual level of common purpose as they prepare for the introduction of quality improvements in the company's midpriced line of blood analysis, collection, and monitoring products. Yates and Riley unite their departments in an effort to streamline the process and speed everything up.

Six months later, BBX introduces their new line of blood analyzers to rave reviews from customers, but MedTech's revamped line of blood analyzers, which hits the market only a month later, almost neutralizes the BBX advantage. Over the next few months MedTech and BBX Systems each fight aggressively to maintain their positions in the marketplace, but, unfortunately, MedTech's sales increase only slightly to $148 million for the year, with profits declining 6 percent to $29 million. Financial and statistical information for this year and last year are shown in the accompanying table.

While you win a certain amount of praise for fending off BBX's attack, it isn't enough to keep Benton from putting MedTech on the auction block. In December, several weeks after the end of the fiscal year, almost 17 months after you took the helm as CEO, you receive official notice that MedTech will be divested in the coming year. Merry Christmas!

Selected Financial Information
(Dollars in Millions)

	Year ended September 30	
	This year	Last year
Operations		
Net sales	$148.0	$147.3
Cost of sales	52.8	52.7
R&D	18.0	15.2
Marketing	31.8	31.5
G&A	15.2	15.8
Operating profit	30.2	32.1
Financial position		
Current assets	88.5	81.3
Current liabilities	47.1	45.4
Working capital	41.4	35.9
Other assets	24.9	24.5
Property and equipment	86.2	79.8
Total assets	199.6	185.6
Other data		
Capital expenditures	8.4	10.2
Depreciation and amortization	8.9	9.1
Return on sales	20.4%	21.8%
Return on assets	15.1%	17.3%
Number of employees	1050	1052

You are asked to stay on until the divestiture, at which time you can either remain with MedTech, if the new owners want you, or you can work with corporate human resources to find a position elsewhere within the Benton organization. You are pleased when two group vice presidents inquire about your availability and your corporate human resources contact tells you she won't have any trouble finding you another CEO position at a Benton subsidiary or division within the year.

Over the Christmas holidays you decide that your reputation as an up-and-coming executive has remained intact because you did a good job of damage control in the BBX situation, but you still wonder whether a more aggressive strategic posture would have kept MedTech in the fold. You conclude that your decision making was wise and calculated, but it wasn't brilliant. You pursued a safe course, not a growth course. What would you have done differently if you had the chance to relive the last 17 months?

If you wish to go back to your last strategic decision, return to Chapter 5.

If you choose to go back to an earlier decision, return to Chapter 2 or Chapter 1.

If you're still feeling the sting of defeat and believe you could have made your last strategic choice work in real life, you may be right. After all, this is just a game. However, if you return to your last strategic decision (the first option above) and select the other alternative, you will learn why the author considers it a better choice.

11
Producing Lower-Cost Products

You hear no hint of disagreement or disgruntlement among your senior team when you propose implementing the cost-reduction projects. Their consensus turns to active enthusiasm as firm plans and assignments begin to take shape. Even the normally recalcitrant R&D head Richard Riley gets swept up by the projects aimed at developing cheaper, simpler blood analysis, collection, and monitoring product lines that will cut costs in half to such customers as clinics, doctors' offices, and small health-care facilities and labs.

Marketing and sales, led by Kate DaVaeno and Bob Shay, respectively, get excited about how lower-cost, simplified product lines can open up their attack on several underserved and growing market segments, all of which will support MedTech growth. It gladdens you to see the formerly squabbling group pulling together as a real team.

When you ask finance vice president Amos Gill to review the project budgets to make sure they will adequately support everyone's objectives, he assures you that they are adequate to get the job done. Management information systems vice president Ken Matsumori will track the development of the lower-cost, simplified products, monitoring all costs and operating expenses by product line, and human resources vice president Susan Carter will review personnel needs with each of the vice presidents, and technical service vice president Vic Gomez will streamline all technical services to customers.

As the management team rallies around the program, you marvel at the tangible excitement and commitment in the air. Finally, MedTech is making real progress. You know more strategic decisions will crop up in the future, but for the moment you feel quite confident with the decisions that have brought the company this far.

Eight months later, MedTech introduces a midpriced "economy line" of blood analysis, collection, and monitoring products with immediate and widespread success among the targeted market segments. A couple of months earlier, competitor BBX Systems had introduced a new and improved midpriced blood analyzer that initially cut into MedTech sales by 10 percent, but the lost sales are easily regained as the new midpriced line racks up an amazing $40 million in sales by the end of the fiscal year. The curtain comes down on your first fiscal year as CEO with sales at $176 million, a 20 percent increase, and profits at $46 million, a whopping 42 percent increase. The table below compares performance for this year and last year.

Modern Health Care magazine devotes half its December issue to MedTech's cost-cutting approach to product improvement and puts your picture on the front cover. At its annual conference of corporate and division officers, Benton Pharmaceuticals honors you as the divi-

Selected Financial Information
(Dollars in Millions)

	Year ended September 30	
	This year	Last year
Operations		
Net sales	$175.8	$147.3
Cost of sales	59.2	52.7
R&D	18.1	15.2
Marketing	37.1	31.5
G&A	15.7	15.8
Operating profit	45.7	32.1
Financial position		
Current assets	93.6	81.3
Current liabilities	53.7	45.4
Working capital	39.9	35.9
Other assets	27.3	24.5
Property and equipment	84.9	79.8
Total assets	205.8	185.6
Other data		
Capital expenditures	8.3	10.2
Depreciation and amortization	8.9	9.1
Return on sales	26.0%	21.8%
Return on assets	22.2%	17.3%
Number of employees	1054	1052

sion/subsidiary president of the year, and the Chairman, Bob Koontz, hands you a $500,000 stock bonus.

As you are flying home with your spouse from the annual conference in Madrid, Spain, you wonder whether you and MedTech can keep it up. Already you have begun to anticipate your next major strategic decision: Should MedTech pursue a strategy of total quality management or a strategy of time-based competition? Having committed MedTech to producing lower-cost products, you must now augment that commitment by creating an environment at MedTech that is geared to total quality management or time-based competition. One strategy preaches best value and least cost, while the other promotes quickest time (which may also produce best value and least cost). The real difference boils down to an emphasis on *speed-to-market* versus an emphasis on *continuous improvement.*

While the time-based competition approach does offer promise, given MedTech's rapidly changing industry, the total quality management approach could benefit every aspect of the organization. Neither track poses any serious downsides; both represent the best and latest thinking of business leaders and professionals throughout the world, and you know that either one will be readily embraced by your management team.

By the time your Delta flight touches down in Atlanta, an interim stop before you reach home, you're tempted to toss a coin to decide the matter, but you resist the temptation and keep probing for a more logical reason for choosing one track over the other. After getting settled in your first-class seats aboard a new Boeing 757 for the last leg of your flight, you commit to making up your mind before you land again.

If you choose to pursue the total quality management strategy, turn to Chapter 18.

If you favor the strategy of time-based competition, turn to Chapter 19.

12
Sequencing Strategies

Having decided to proceed with sequencing the two strategies, you must set the order of sequencing: industrywide then underserved niches or vice versa. It's such a close call in your own mind, you put this one to a vote of the management team, which unanimously elects pursuit of the industry-wide strategy first in preparation for launching the underserved niche strategy later. Concurring with the consensus, you invite your marketing head Kate DaVaeno and outside consultant John Carbiggs to continue the second phase of their study aimed at pinpointing exactly how to implement a micromarketing strategy based on a number of customized variations in product packaging, pricing, distribution channels, and service offerings.

When Yankelovich Clancy Shulman completes its study three months later, Kate DaVaeno and her department begin administering the changes over a critical 90-day period. Some interesting and exciting ideas have been incorporated into the new micromarketing approach, including the introduction in selected metropolitan areas of MedTech Temps, groups of qualified staff that will go into large research labs and medical centers to assist during peak loads or crises; a MedTech Quick-Lease program that will allow midsized hospitals and emergency facilities to lease a sophisticated blood analysis, collection, and monitoring system by the week or month; and a sales team approach for all MedTech products that will send one wave of salespeople after another into the field to keep the medical staff, health-care administrators, and other buyers continuously abreast of the evolution of MedTech products and services.

As the new strategy builds steam, customers respond slowly, but favorably, giving MedTech a positive outlook for the future, until rival BBX Systems introduces their new line of blood analyzers in June. Almost overnight the new competition cuts MedTech's sales by close to 40 percent, and MedTech's new micromarketing approaches can do little to counter BBX's major product improvements. As everyone at MedTech scrambles to assess the damage and regroup for the future, it becomes painfully clear that things will get worse before they get better. You realize, in retrospect, how vulnerable MedTech was to such a move by BBX. How could you have been so blind to such a possibility? And, what's worse, the micromarketing strategy really was working. In time it would have paved the way for focusing on the underserved niche of small health-care providers. Now, the whole game has changed. Increasingly paranoid about what Benton executives are thinking, you desperately search for ways to combat MedTech's eroding performance. You become so discouraged and depressed, you visit your doctor to find ways to reduce the mounting stress. Ironically, your doctor prescribes an antidepression drug made by Benton Pharmaceuticals. You feel your self-image, confidence, and judgment seeping away as BBX's sales continue to grow and MedTech's micromarketing strategy founders. As morale at MedTech drops to new depths, you feel that no one in the whole organization any longer respects you.

Emotionally distraught, you conclude that your marketing background biased you toward pursuing a marketing and sales-oriented strategy at MedTech, which, in this industry, never could stand up long under pressure from a rival quality-improvement or product-innovation strategy, or so you tell yourself. Because the idea of sequencing strategies has been on your mind for the past few months, you think of your current predicament in those terms, concluding that a product quality or innovation strategy should almost always precede a marketing and sales strategy in the medical products industry. As you watch BBX rack up sales with their new line of blood analyzers, you come to believe that Benton Pharmaceuticals' overarching corporate strategy should begin with quality or innovation. However, when you share this insight with your boss, the president of the Medical Products and Systems Group, he takes a dim view of your desire to enlighten him and seizes the opportunity to chastise you for trying to pass the buck.

Eventually, Benton brings in a corporate marketing and finance group to assess MedTech's near-term prospects. Their report estimates sales and profits will decline at least 20 to 30 percent for the year, with a further decline anticipated for the following year. Their projections for this year are shown in the accompanying table.

After the report circulates throughout corporate headquarters, you find it hard to get through to your immediate boss at Benton and conclude that your future at MedTech and Benton looks bleak. No one will talk to you, and you feel your grip on the helm slipping. Thirteen months after arriving at MedTech and three months before the end of your first full fiscal year, you resign.

Selected Financial Information
(Dollars in Millions)

	Year ended September 30	
	This year (projected)	Last year
Operations		
Net sales	$115.0	$147.3
Cost of sales	40.0	52.7
R&D	13.0	15.2
Marketing	25.0	31.5
G&A	15.0	15.8
Operating profit	22.0	32.1
Financial position		
Current assets	65.0	81.3
Current liabilities	55.0	45.4
Working capital	10.0	35.9
Other assets	20.0	24.5
Property and equipment	90.0	79.8
Total assets	175.0	185.6
Other data		
Capital expenditures	10.0	10.2
Depreciation and amortization	10.0	9.1
Return on sales	19.0%	21.8%
Return on assets	13.0%	17.3%
Number of employees	1055	1052

If this were real life you would be attempting to rebuild your self-esteem and your career, but this book gives you a chance to redeem yourself by going back and trying again.

If you want to go back to your last strategic decision, return to Chapter 6.

If you want to start again from an earlier point, return to Chapter 3 or Chapter 1.

If you're still feeling the sting of defeat and believe you could have made your last strategic choice work in real life, you may be right. After all, this is just a game. However, if you return to your last strategic decision (the first option above) and select the other alternative, you will learn why the author considers it a better choice.

13
Separating Strategies

This decision does not come easily because separating MedTech into two divisions will present quite a few thorny problems, but nonetheless, you see no viable alternative. Of course, your management team supports your decision, but their lack of real enthusiasm makes you feel uneasy. Still, you remain convinced that such a separation makes the most strategic sense and can, in the long term, best ensure MedTech's growth.

To the surprise of your management team, you appoint marketing head Kate DaVaeno and finance head Amos Gill as the two new division presidents. Kate will manage the division geared to the underserved niches of small health-care providers, and Amos will oversee the division serving all customer segments industrywide. It had been tough gaining the approval of Benton executives for this move, and you had to lay your reputation and future on the line before they would go along with such radical reorganizing, but they finally agreed that your track record argued for giving you a free hand in resolving MedTech's situation.

During the next several weeks you work closely with DaVaeno and Gill to create two separate divisional structures within the company. First, you divide the R&D, production, marketing, sales, and technical service functions into two separate divisional groupings, while keeping finance, management information, and human resources reporting directly to you. Most of your management team remains in Gill's division, the larger of the two, with lower-level directors and managers in various functions staffing DaVaeno's new division.

During the second stage of separating, you will divide the finance function between the two divisions and complete a physical relocation of DaVaeno's group to a new building vacated by another of Benton's subsidiaries. However, these second-stage changes must wait until next year because you must set your immediate sights on improving this year's performance. You simply can't afford to do it all at once.

With stage one of the reorganization complete, you charge DaVaeno and Gill with boosting this year's sales and profits. As the dust settles over the massive reorganization, you are pleased to see a lot of energy and excitement pervade both divisions. In particular, you love the speed with which Kate DaVaeno and her new division bring a new, scaled-down version of the midpriced line of blood analyzers into production. Their advance sales of the new line to doctors' offices, clinics, and small health-care facilities doubles your original estimates.

When competitor BBX Systems introduces a new and improved blood analyzer line in June, MedTech is perfectly positioned to respond to it. Although sales in Gill's division, named MedTech–Industrywide until you can come up with a better name, decreases by 20 percent under the BBX onslaught, sales in DaVaeno's division, temporarily called MedTech–Small Providers, continue to grow. In only four months the MedTech–Small Providers division posts sales of over $50 million.

By the end of the fiscal year MedTech records an overall 16 percent sales increase to $169 million, with profits up 11 percent to $37 million, as shown in the accompanying table.

Selected Financial Information
(Dollars in Millions)

	Year ended September 30	
	This year	Last year
Operations		
Net sales	$169.3	$147.3
Cost of sales	60.3	52.7
R&D	13.5	5.2
Marketing	38.6	31.5
G&A	19.5	15.8
Operating profit	37.4	32.1
Financial position		
Current assets	83.9	81.3
Current liabilities	48.2	45.4
Working capital	35.7	35.9
Other assets	26.1	24.5
Property and equipment	82.6	79.8
Total assets	192.6	185.6
Other data		
Capital expenditures	12.3	10.2
Depreciation and amortization	9.2	9.1
Return on sales	22.1%	21.8%
Return on assets	19.4%	17.3%
Number of employees	1058	1052

Given this overall picture and the expectation of even greater increases in sales and profits next year, the morale at MedTech's two divisions soars so high that Benton executives choose MedTech as one of the lead stories in Benton's annual report.

Still not fully satisfied, however, that next year will turn out as well as predicted, you continue your reorganizational plan, with Amos Gill countering the challenge of BBX's new product line and DaVaeno strengthening her group's independence by relocating. Now you find yourself faced with another strategic decision: Should you extend MedTech's decentralization by creating even more divisions or should you focus on making micromarketing work even better at MedTech? While both options stress marketing and sales, one represents an organizational and management emphasis and the other constitutes a skills and capabilities emphasis. Which does MedTech need most? More decentralization, which had such a positive effect on MedTech's performance, will prevent any growing bureaucracy and help MedTech people create and adapt to more change. Expanded and improved micromarketing will build on MedTech's segmentation efforts and extend recent gains to other underserved market segments while encouraging MedTech people to grow ever more skillful at discerning customer needs. You consider combining the two alternatives by incorporating micromarketing into multiple divisions, but you quickly realize that improved and expanded micromarketing will require substantial sharing of capabilities and resources across all targeted niches, something further decentralization beyond the existing two divisions could hinder.

After lengthy discussions with Kate DaVaeno and Amos Gill, you discover that both remain rather ambivalent, with DaVaeno slightly favoring more emphasis on micromarketing and Gill leaning a bit more toward increased decentralization. In the end, they toss the decision back to you, pledging their support of either choice. Now, you must decide.

If you decide to pursue more decentralization, turn to Chapter 20.

If you prefer to expand and improve micromarketing, turn to Chapter 21.

14

Returning to a Product-Based Strategy

Still feeling somewhat stunned by last year's poor results, you find your confidence sagging, and you wonder whether you should have made a more forceful commitment to service. The past is the past, however, and this is no time for second-guessing. To kick off the new year, Mitch Cavanaugh, your group president, invites you to lunch, where he reemphasizes his belief that an excessive preoccupation with superior service can cause a manufacturing organization to lose sight of the basic elements of its business, namely costs and quality. Although you disagree with Cavanaugh and believe that even manufacturing organizations must pay attention to service and that service really will become a centerpiece of strategies in the future, you decide your point of view is ahead of its time and turn your attention to more traditional aspects of product manufacturing and marketing.

In a major regrouping effort, you involve each member of your management team in one of three major thrusts: product improvement, cost reduction, and revenue enhancement, all aimed at turning MedTech around quickly. However, after a few weeks, you realize your management team does not share your views. Perhaps they detect your forced optimism over the new thrust. You attempt to spur them on, but your enthusiasm wanes as MedTech continues struggling with its identity and fails to achieve much real progress. Convinced that the new "survival" imperative remains your only hope for improving MedTech's situation, you wield it like a club on your management team to keep them moving forward.

After months of grueling effort, you see a glimmer of improvement, but it still lacks the pace or magnitude you feel it must attain to effect a full turnaround. Weary and frustrated, you decide to start looking for another job rather than face an inevitable termination at the end of the year. After all, Benton prevented you from continuing your service emphasis, which you firmly believe would have borne fruit in time.

Eight months into the year, you announce your plans to join another pharmaceutical and medical products firm as president of an $80 million division. Not surprisingly, your announcement prompts little resistance from corporate headquarters, and you leave MedTech and Benton Pharmaceuticals within 30 days.

In real life, your work at MedTech would come to an end, but this book lets you rethink and remake some of your past choices.

If you want to return to your most recent strategic decision, return to Chapter 7.

If you would rather start with an earlier decision point, return to Chapter 3 or Chapter 1.

If you're still feeling the sting of defeat and believe you could have made your last strategic choice work in real life, you may be right. After all, this is just a game. However, if you return to your last strategic decision (the first option above) and select the other alternative, you will learn why the author considers it a better choice.

15
Holding Firm to a Service -Based Strategy

Confident that service activities will become more and more important in adding value and satisfying customers in your industry, eventually eclipsing the old way of producing value by focusing strictly on production processes, costs, or product quality, you doggedly hang on to the idea of improving service levels at MedTech. Your management team stands solidly behind you, particularly vice president of sales Bob Shay, vice president of marketing Kate DaVaeno, and vice president of technical service Victor Gomez.

You state your service mission this way: "Over the next 10 years all competitors in this industry will possess more or less the same product manufacturing capabilities. The winners will be those companies that stress nonmanufacturing, knowledge-based services, such as understanding the technical needs of customers, developing new and useful product concepts, customizing product offerings and features to meet special needs, or maintaining active interaction with customers. If MedTech begins preparing itself now for that inevitability, it will become and remain stronger than its competitors." You ask Benton executives for time to implement this service-based strategy and petition employees to work hard to meet Benton's expectations for revenue and profit growth this year.

In staff meetings with your senior team you promote nonmanufacturing, knowledge-based services as the ultimate strategic weapon and the only way to gain and keep loyal customers. It's like preaching to the choir, because your key people already agree that nothing drives business costs higher than losing customers and having to replace them with new ones, a reality that particularly affects the intensely competitive medical instrument industry. By focusing on service activities, MedTech can save the costs of replacing lost customers and pursue the much more effective and efficient course of retaining customers. Moreover, you can learn a great deal about customer needs from long-term customers; you are therefore better positioned to meet customer needs more fully and more quickly than your competitors. Finally, you remind your management team, loyal customers buy more products than moderately loyal or new customers.

After three months of championing your ideas to the senior executives at Benton Pharmaceuticals and to MedTech employees in every department and office, you and your management team grow exceptionally lucid and articulate in describing the importance of service activities for MedTech's future success. At midyear Benton executives finally begin believing you, as sales and profits show a year-to-date increase over the previous year and customers eagerly respond to MedTech's new services emphasis. However, while this progress brings encouragement, you realize that MedTech cannot sustain relatively superior service in all areas of the company's operations as competitors begin following your lead by improving nonmanufacturing service levels. You and your management team must identify those core service areas where MedTech enjoys unique capabilities and sustainable long-term advantage. Then, over time, you must eliminate, limit, or outsource (contract with an outside supplier to provide a service or services) all other service activities, allowing MedTech to focus only on those core service areas where it can develop and maintain "best in world" capabilities.

During the next two weeks nonstop discussions between you and your management team reduce MedTech's options to a few viable core service areas where the company enjoys comparative strength: identifying unusual customer needs, finding unique customer solutions from inside or outside MedTech, designing innovative product concepts, responding to sticky customer complaints, and maintaining superb customer relations.

However, debate reaches a crescendo when you attempt to bring consensus to your management team. You realize that a fundamental difference of opinion lingers within your management team. After more discussion, two conceptual alternatives emerge: narrowing the scope of core service areas to ensure uniqueness and superiority, or broadening the scope of core service areas to achieve greater control over all nonmanufacturing, knowledge-based services. Narrowing the scope to core services would mean outsourcing various activities such as manufacturing of components, aspects of R&D, and warehousing

---

and distribution to suppliers and affiliate companies. Broadening the scope of core service areas would eliminate most, if not all, outsourcing in an effort to maintain greater control over all service variables. Members of your team advance strong arguments for and against each of these alternatives as you guide them through a lengthy discussion in an effort to create harmony before moving forward.

On one side of the debate, Kate DaVaeno argues that pursuing a more narrow scope of core services sharpens strategic focus on core competence. A business should, she insists, focus on only a few things that it does extremely well while outsourcing other activities to suppliers or affiliates. "This is the wave of the future," she says.

On the other side, Victor Gomez argues that embracing a broader scope of core service areas supports a total customer service strategy that controls all nonmanufacturing, knowledge-based services without awarding priority to a few. Developing a solid reputation for total customer service, he insists, will require keeping under careful control all of the variables that affect MedTech's ability to meet customer needs.

Personally, you believe MedTech should narrow its scope of core services. To support your position you cite the example of Apple Computer, which chose to focus on its intellectual and knowledge capabilities to develop user-friendly personal computer products, along with key software, and not on microprocessors, chips, networking, and a lot of other related activities. Apple, you emphasize, purposely manufactures as little as possible, entering into relationships with suppliers and other outsourcing partners, such as MicroSoft, Hitachi, Texas Instruments, and Motorola. It turns over promotion to Regis McKenna and delegates distribution to ITT and Computerland, all of which allows Apple to continue focusing on those core services that make the company strong.

You also argue that given the intense and growing competition in your own industry, it would be foolish for MedTech to believe that it could gain superior performance in all nonmanufacturing, knowledge-based service areas. To back up your point, you quote from James Brian Quinn's book, *Intelligent Enterprise*: "Service-based strategies are most effective when companies develop 'best in world' capabilities around a few selected competencies that are important to customers, and then conscientiously maintain preeminence in those areas against all comers." The broad-scope alternative, you conclude, would be extremely difficult and very unwise to implement at this time. Even Victor Gomez seems convinced by your arguments.

However, a few days later, just when you feel ready to make the decision, you read another *Harvard Business Review* article that promotes the value of a broader definition of core competencies in business organizations. The article seems to run counter to Quinn's earlier work and your own intuition and confuses you, but it persuades you to tell your management team that you now feel less sure about which course to follow. When a new round of debate erupts among your senior executives, all of the arguments for a broader scope of core services come back to the table. You make copies of the *Harvard Business Review* article, "The Core Competence of the Corporation," by C. K. Prahalad and Gary Hamel, professors from the University of Michigan and the London Business School, respectively, and ask Kate DaVaeno and Vic Gomez to prepare new summaries of the pros and cons of each alternative. Once again, they offer strong arguments for each strategy. Now it seems you've come full circle and can do little more than flip a coin.

Desiring harmony and consensus among your management team, however, you discuss the alternatives for hours, listening intently to strong arguments from both DaVaeno and Gomez. Finally, your management team defers to your intuition and judgment. Once again, you find yourself ruing the loneliness of leadership as you, and you alone, must make your decision.

If you choose to pursue a narrow scope of core services, turn to Chapter 22.

If you prefer to expand the scope of core services by defining MedTech's core competence more broadly, turn to Chapter 23.

16
Creating a New R&D Division

In the early summer, almost 12 months after you assumed the reigns at MedTech, your major competitor, BBX Systems, introduces an improved blood analysis and collection system that cuts monthly sales of MedTech's midpriced line by over one-half. However, because you chose to combine FutureMed and MedTech's R&D functions to create a new, separate division headed by Jack Suhler, one of the founders of FutureMed, he has already been able to speed up the final development stages of the FutureScan and FutureStar systems, getting them ready for production by March 31, three months ahead of schedule.

The separation also enables you to direct your full attention to MedTech's production, marketing, and sales of the new products. Working closely with production vice president Ed Yates, you are able to begin production of FutureScan and FutureStar systems within days of receiving the green light from Suhler. As a result, marketing head Kate DaVaeno and sales head Bob Shay get FutureScan and FutureStar systems into medical labs, clinics, and doctors' offices by mid-spring, much more quickly and with greater penetration than anticipated. The FutureScan cardiopulmonary system offers its customers a more reliable line of instruments for pumping, oxygenating, and monitoring a patient's blood when routed outside the body during open-heart surgery; the FutureScan cell sorter system fully outperforms all your competitors' systems for sorting and analyzing different types of blood cells during diagnosis, particularly in medical crisis situations. In both the United States and abroad, the pace of sales for the FutureScan cardiopulmonary system and the FutureStar cell sorter far exceed expectations.

In addition, the separation of R&D into an autonomous division speeds up the development of FutureMed's new blood culturing system and the line of prepared plated culture media that goes along with it. Based on your current estimates, increased concentration and efficiency in R&D efforts has cut the original introduction schedule for the blood culturing system by six months, which should give MedTech an enormous boost in sales next year. Advance orders for the blood culturing system are already beginning to come in, as word of the accelerated timetable for introduction reaches industry media. In addition, the new blood culturing system should do extremely well in Japan, where MedTech's marketing and sales unit in Tokyo believes it can triple MedTech's sales within three months of the product's introduction.

The sales increase from FutureScan and FutureStar over the last six months of the year easily covers the sales decline caused by BBX's advancement. By year-end MedTech has produced an astonishing 30 percent increase in sales to $191 million and a 67 percent increase in profits to $54 million. The table below summarizes selected financial data for the year just ended and the previous year.

Even before the year-end numbers become widely known throughout the Benton organization, you are being heralded as a turnaround

Selected Financial Information
(Dollars in Millions)

	Year ended September 30	
	This year	Last year
Operations		
Net sales	$191.0	$147.3
Cost of sales	63.0	52.7
R&D	20.6	15.2
Marketing	38.6	31.5
G&A	15.3	15.8
Operating profit	53.5	32.1
Financial position		
Current assets	98.6	81.3
Current liabilities	51.1	45.4
Working capital	47.5	35.9
Other assets	30.2	24.5
Property and equipment	90.7	79.8
Total assets	219.5	185.6
Other data		
Capital expenditures	13.3	10.2
Depreciation and amortization	10.6	9.1
Return on sales	28.0%	21.8%
Return on assets	24.4%	17.3%
Number of employees	1070	1052

artist and a brilliant strategist. You have even been dubbed as the heir apparent to the presidency of the Medical Systems and Products Group by several corporate staff officers at Benton; even though such a move lies four or five years downroad, you have clearly solidified your reputation as a key Benton executive. To reward you for your performance, Bob Koontz, chairman and CEO of Benton Pharmaceuticals, personally delivers a stock option worth over $500,000.

The Wall Street Journal runs a front-page article, complete with an artist's sketch of you, which glowingly describes the alliance of MedTech and FutureMed and your creative approach to combining the two companies. Several business reporters dog you for interviews over the next several weeks, and although the media attention distracts you from business at hand, you love every minute of it.

Congratulations. After 15 months your strategic decision making has certainly reaped impressive results. However, you have not even begun to tackle the real test of long-term strategic viability. Can you keep up this track record or will it all end up looking like a short-lived flash of brilliance or just plain dumb luck?

After some of the hoopla surrounding MedTech's year-end results subsides, you realize you're facing yet another critical strategic decision. Should you build on the early success of the new R&D division, which you have officially named FutureMedTech, by stressing pioneering innovation or by pursuing more acquisitions? As you mull over these two options, you come to recognize that you've received equal praise for the divergent tasks of making a successful acquisition *and* focusing on breakthrough innovation. Now that you must stress one or the other, which route most likely guarantees MedTech's future? The pioneering innovation track might allow you to develop FutureMedTech into the technology leader in the industry and tap MedTech's production, marketing, distribution, and sales capabilities more fully. Clearly, the successes of FutureScan and FutureStar have motivated the people both at MedTech and FutureMedTech so much that they're projecting the introduction of another five breakthrough products over the next 18 months. The working relationship between the two entities has become phenomenally successful.

However, *The Wall Street Journal* lauded MedTech's acquisition of FutureMed as a model for strategic alliances, and you know you could engineer that same kind of successful acquisition again and again. The acquisitions track could provide enormous growth for MedTech and Benton Pharmaceuticals, not to mention increased visibility for you and your people. With Jack Suhler at the helm of FutureMedTech and

Ed Yates, Kate DaVaeno, Bob Shay, and the other vice presidents guiding MedTech, you can afford the time to pursue acquisitions.

As much as any strategic move you've made in the past, the decision you make here will greatly determine MedTech's future and your own. Confronting the challenge, you find yourself exhilarated by the responsibility for making such a momentous choice. After discussing both options with Jack Suhler, Ed Yates, Kate DaVaeno, Bob Shay, and the rest of your management team, you take the long Thanksgiving weekend to probe your own inner thoughts and feelings. By Sunday evening, you've made up your mind.

If you want to rely most heavily on acquisitions to grow and develop MedTech, turn to Chapter 24.

If you prefer to focus on pioneering innovation through FutureMedTech, supported by effective production, marketing, distribution, and sales through MedTech, turn to Chapter 25.

17
Integrating FutureMed

The task of uniting FutureMed and MedTech has taken longer than expected, diverting all your attention inward and away from the marketplace. While you have made measurable progress, you have suffered a delay in the introduction of FutureScan and FutureStar into medical labs, clinics, and doctors' offices. During the twelfth month of your tenure as CEO these delays become a major problem because your chief competitor, BBX Systems, has introduced a new and improved blood analysis system that has cut MedTech monthly sales by over one-half. You have been so deeply involved with office politics and hand-holding in order to effect a smooth integration of the two companies that you have taken your eye off the ball. Now you're paying for it. The BBX introduction couldn't have come at a worse time, but it does shock you into action.

To compensate for the lost sales you immediately speed up the introduction of FutureScan and FutureStar. Your quick and decisive action transforms the organization, shifting concerns from internal issues to the marketplace. Even Jack Suhler, a founder of FutureMed, and Ed Yates, vice president of production, who had been warring over turf, quickly bury their differences to address the outside threat.

It takes superhuman effort by everyone, but, with a short three months to go in the fiscal year, MedTech manages to bring the FutureScan cardiopulmonary system and the FutureStar cell sorter to market. The FutureScan cardiopulmonary system offers its customers the very best technology for pumping, oxygenating, and monitoring a patient's blood when routed outside the body during open-heart surgery, and the FutureStar cell sorter provides a superior method for sorting and analyzing different types of blood cells. Customers greet both products with enthusiasm.

By the end of the year MedTech neutralizes the impact of the BBX onslaught with new sales from FutureScan and FutureStar compensating for sales lost to BBX. There is an overall 2 percent sales increase to $150 million. Profits remain level at $32 million for the year, as shown in the accompanying table.

You've made some smart strategic decisions so far, but you have also put yourself and your company at risk by underestimating the time it would take to integrate FutureMed and MedTech and by getting bogged down in a lot of internal disputes and turf battles. It does not surprise you when Benton CEO Bob Koontz observes that corporate management will be watching you closely and that your next strategic move will make or break your future. Benton has decided to hang onto your strategy a little longer only because you've promised such strong projections for FutureScan and FutureStar sales for the coming year.

In the midst of this turmoil you begin looking for a new paradigm that can guide your future strategic decision making and help you avoid mistakes like the last one. You strongly believe that business organiza-

Selected Financial Information
(Dollars in Millions)

	Year ended September 30	
	This year	Last year
Operations		
Net sales	$150.4	$147.3
Cost of sales	53.1	52.7
R&D	16.2	15.2
Marketing	32.0	31.5
G&A	16.7	15.8
Operating profit	32.3	32.1
Financial position		
Current assets	82.1	81.3
Current liabilities	46.8	45.4
Working capital	35.3	35.9
Other assets	23.2	24.5
Property and equipment	81.2	79.8
Total assets	186.5	185.6
Other data		
Capital expenditures	9.4	10.2
Depreciation and amortization	9.3	9.1
Return on sales	21.5%	21.8%
Return on assets	17.3%	17.3%
Number of employees	1059	1052

tions must find new paradigms for operating if they expect to move beyond their current plateaus. You read Peter Schwartz's book, *The Art of the Long View*, which spurs you on to read all the latest management books and articles and attend four state-of-the-art management seminars, searching desperately for new perspectives and possible future scenarios.

Twenty-five books, thirty-seven articles, and four management seminars later, you boil your choice of new perspectives down to two: a liberation-management paradigm that encourages the ongoing creation of new approaches, or a learning-organization paradigm that stresses the importance of constant individual and organizational learning.

The liberation-management gambit appeals to you because it promises to create a climate of constant change and revolution that calls upon every employee to seek and develop new solutions to problems. By nature, the liberation-management paradigm provides a loose and open structure for revolutionary change and liberates people to initiate new ways of thinking about business, management, and everything else.

The learning-organization paradigm also appeals to you, though in a different way, because it provides a more holistic approach to organizational and individual learning. The learning-organization paradigm promises to create a climate for new ways of learning that could produce unprecedented productivity, innovation, and results.

After discussing the options with a few of your closest associates at MedTech, you decide that before you can make this decision, you need a few days away from the turmoil of daily pressures. You make plans for a week's ski vacation at Deer Valley, Utah, after which you will announce your decision.

If you decide to employ a liberation-management paradigm, turn to Chapter 26.

If you prefer adopting a learning-organization paradigm, turn to Chapter 27.

18
Implementing Total Quality Management

You immediately begin reading as much as you can on the subjects of total quality management (TQM) and continuous improvement and talking to other division presidents, people at headquarters, consultants, and associates in the industry to determine exactly how you're going to implement TQM at MedTech. Benton Pharmaceuticals has always stressed the notion of continuous improvement in general terms, and the philosophy has greatly helped your industry to grow faster than its Japanese and European counterparts. However, you feel that implementing total quality management more consciously and meticulously in your own MedTech unit will help you achieve your major long-term goals, among them reduced manufacturing costs.

During your search for ideas, you come across *The Goal* by Eliyahu M. Goldratt and Jeff Cox, a business novel that an executive of Benton has recommended highly. Not much of a fiction reader, you begin the book with some skepticism, but, unexpectedly, you find it highly stimulating, as Goldratt and Cox detail the process of ongoing improvement. The story dramatically illustrates how people in organizations can and must learn to face organizational problems head-on, solving them and then moving to the next set of challenges. The book strikes a chord for you because you see yourself and your own management style in its pages.

Subsequently, you urge each member of your management team to read the book. And you plan for a series of discussions about how MedTech can best implement a stronger, more deliberate ongoing improvement agenda. To bring additional focus on total quality and continuous improvement, you move Ed Yates from vice president of production to vice president of continuous improvement, giving his former job to one of his aggressive and bright directors, Sean Worthy.

To prepare for the upcoming series of discussions, you ask your senior management team to research current business literature dealing with total quality management, continuous improvement, total employee involvement, and the linkage between quality improvement and decreased costs. At a staff meeting, you make your intentions quite clear:

"We've been focusing on R&D and existing-product improvement around here for the past year and a half, and some of you have had this focus even longer than that. But it's time for us to buckle down and go beyond where we are now. We must strengthen our commitment to total quality and continuous improvement at MedTech. We all know that such a commitment can stimulate further cost reduction, innovation, productivity, customer loyalty, and, ultimately, higher profits. And although our company and industry may be ahead of many others in this regard, we cannot afford to rest on our laurels. We must find new ways to improve. I don't know exactly what the next few years will bring—surprising changes in our industry, bad economic news—but I do know that we must continue to improve every facet of our operations today, tomorrow, and the next day, or we will lose the momentum we've gained over the last year and a half.

"I've scheduled a series of discussion meetings after the first of the year to chart our total quality management course into the future. Between now and then, I'm asking each of you to become as knowledgeable as possible by reading the literature, talking to people in the industry, observing what competitors are doing, and gleaning everything you can from top companies in other industries. Remember, we're not looking for theory and philosophy—we already believe the theory—we're looking for the nitty-gritty, the nuts and bolts, that can make total quality management and continuous improvement a reality at MedTech."

Over a 10-day holiday vacation, you sequester yourself in your study at home for several hours a day to read books and articles and to contact friends and associates in a number of industries. You review Motorola's Six SIGMA Quality Program, Emerson Electric's Best Cost Analysis Program, Xerox's Systematic Benchmarking Program, and General Electric's Work-Out Program as well as their techniques called "Best Practices" and "Process Mapping."

You also scan the works of several total quality and continuous-improvement gurus: W. Edwards Deming, the best known of the quality experts with his 14 points for bringing about total transformation in organizations; Phillip Crosby, proponent of four absolutes of quality management; Armand Feigenbaum, master of the four jobs of quality control—namely, new design control, incoming material control, product control, and special process studies; Joseph Juran, advocate of the correlation between quality improvement and cost reduction; and Kaoru Ishikawa, recipient of the Deming Prize in Japan and the American Society of Quality Control's Shewhart Medal for his contribution to the understanding of total quality control.

Finally, you practically memorize the application instructions for the Malcolm Baldrige National Quality Award. By the time you return to work the first week of January, you have logged close to 70 hours of reading and telephone conversations, and you feel fully prepared for the upcoming discussions. To your delight, your senior management team also comes prepared with a staggering number of possible approaches to total quality and continuous improvement. As you try to sort out all the information over the next six weeks, you see the group's mood swing from exhilaration to bewilderment. There are, it seems, as many approaches to implementing total quality management as there are quality gurus, consultants, authors, and institutes. In order to bring the discussion sessions to some concrete conclusions, you charge Ed Yates, your new vice president of continuous improvement, with the job of summarizing all the input and discussion into a set of recommendations for immediate action.

One month later, you and your management team adopt four basic principles as the first step to implementing total quality management at MedTech:

1. Design quality into all products and services.

2. Improve every system continuously.

3. Create a supportive work environment.

4. Innovate constantly.

As your vice presidents implement these continuous-improvement principles over the next several months in each of their areas of responsibility, you begin to see measurable gains in innovation, cost reduction, product and service quality, and customer satisfaction. By the end of the fiscal year, MedTech reports a 43 percent revenue increase to $251 million and a 46 percent profit increase to $67 million, as shown in the accompanying table.

Soon after the close of the year, an idea that has been simmering in

Selected Financial Information
(Dollars in Millions)

	Year ended September 30	
	This year	Last year
Operations		
Net sales	$250.9	$175.8
Cost of sales	85.3	59.2
R&D	23.2	18.1
Marketing	52.7	37.1
G&A	22.6	15.7
Operating profit	67.1	45.7
Financial position		
Current assets	84.1	93.6
Current liabilities	43.7	53.7
Working capital	40.3	39.9
Other assets	25.2	27.3
Property and equipment	81.0	84.9
Total assets	190.3	205.8
Other data		
Capital expenditures	10.4	8.3
Depreciation and amortization	12.1	8.9
Return on sales	26.7%	26.0%
Return on assets	35.3%	22.2%
Number of employees	1212	1054

the back of your mind comes to a boil. Given MedTech's convincing performance, why not apply for the Baldrige Award? Although everything you've read about total quality management and continuous improvement suggests that you must remain vigilant and patient when transforming traditional management into total quality management because a brief lapse in concentration can set you back tremendously, you think that the positive reinforcement of a major prize could do wonders for MedTech's people.

What are the pros and cons? The more patient and persevering course could keep you on a relatively safe and sure road to slow but constant improvement. Seeking the Baldrige could cost your people thousands of hours of nonproductive busywork assembling the reams of data the Baldrige judges require. However, becoming too cautious and patient could bog down the efforts of the past year, making it difficult to bring about a genuine transformation. Seeking the Baldrige could provide the intense focus necessary to effect the full transformation sooner rather than later.

Ed Yates, your continuous-improvement vice president, favors the patient, persevering path toward transformation, but more than half of your senior team feels that seeking the Baldrige would put real life into the total quality and continuous-improvement effort at MedTech. However, after a lengthy discussion every member of your management team promises to back your choice. Which course do you favor?

If you want to apply for the Baldrige award, turn to Chapter 28.

If you would rather work more patiently toward transformation, turn to Chapter 29.

19
Adopting a Time-Based Competition Strategy

In a world of accelerating change, time represents one of the surest competitive advantages. Therefore, you commit to providing the most value for the lowest cost in the least amount of time, a decision you feel will contribute more than anything else to MedTech's success in the years to come. You have always considered yourself an action-oriented competitor, able to muster the available resources to defeat an opponent, and since your realistic sense of expediency has always helped you seize and exploit the moment, you feel especially well-suited to implement a strategy based on speed and timing.

As you probe more deeply into time-based strategies, you contact a close friend at The Boston Consulting Group who helps you understand that many of the old assumptions about how costs and customers behave no longer hold true. She offers to send you *Competing Against Time: How Time-Based Competition Is Reshaping Global Markets* by George Stalk and Tom Hout, two of her colleagues at The Boston Consulting Group, and reads a few sentences from the preface to whet your appetite: "Instead of costs going up with greater investment in quality, they decrease. And, finally, instead of costs going up with increasing variety and decreasing response time, they go down. Further, instead of customer demand being only marginally affected by expanded choice and better responsiveness, it is astoundingly sensitive to this better service—with the company that is able to set customer's expectations for choice and response very quickly dominating the most profitable segments of demand."

Further convinced that you made the right strategic decision after reading Stalk and Hout's book, you begin implementing a time-based competition approach at MedTech by asking your friend from The Boston Consulting Group to conduct a few sessions with your management team. During these sessions she emphasizes that initiating and executing a program to improve time responsiveness will not come easily. Such a program, she points out, demands the complete focus of senior management because improving responsiveness depends on a thorough shift in focus throughout the organization from cost to time. MedTech, like most other organizations, has customarily stressed the traditional financial measurements of sales, costs, and profits and has spent scant time monitoring the consumption of time, a practice that must now change. For a time-based competition approach to succeed, flexibility and responsiveness must become the two predominant elements of MedTech's culture.

Despite the difficulties involved, your management team respects your enthusiasm for this approach and pledges their full support in shaping a new vision for offering greater varieties of low-cost blood analysis, collection, and monitoring products in less time.

During the ensuing months, you find yourself frustrated with the paradox that implementing a new time-based strategy within MedTech takes an inordinate amount of time, and you come to appreciate just how massive a shift it will take to make time consumption your organization's primary focus. Fortunately, sales of last year's new economy line of blood analyzers continues to increase through the final months of the year, encouraging you to project a strong second year with the economy line. That optimistic projection wins strong support among Benton executives for allowing MedTech to pursue its new time-based strategy.

Before the year comes to an end, you ask Kate DaVaeno and Bob Shay to identify opportunities for using time as a strategic weapon in MedTech's marketing, sales, and distribution areas. You also request Richard Riley and Ed Yates to do the same for R&D and production and you assign Ken Matsumori, your vice president of management information systems, to coordinate the planning for all three arenas. You give them three weeks to come up with concrete recommendations.

As shown in the accompanying table, MedTech ends the year with sales increasing 29 percent to $227 million, and with profits increasing 40 percent to 64 million, a level of performance that gives you the leeway in the coming year to complete MedTech's shift to time-based competition.

Selected Financial Information
(Dollars in Millions)

	Year ended September 30	
	This year	Last year
Operations		
Net sales	$226.8	$175.8
Cost of sales	73.4	59.2
R&D	21.1	18.1
Marketing	48.5	37.1
G&A	20.3	15.7
Operating profit	63.5	45.7
Financial position		
Current assets	75.1	93.6
Current liabilities	39.0	53.7
Working capital	36.0	39.9
Other assets	22.5	27.3
Property and equipment	81.4	84.9
Total assets	178.9	205.8
Other data		
Capital expenditures	10.7	8.3
Depreciation and amortization	12.1	8.9
Return on sales	28.0%	26.0%
Return on assets	35.5%	22.2%
Number of employees	1173	1054

Now, at the start of a new year, after reviewing recommendations from your management team, you must choose whether to authorize a sudden, massive spending surge for developing and manufacturing products on a crash basis, with the goal of shocking your organization into accelerated change, or to create structurally different methods for developing, manufacturing, and selling new products with the goal of establishing a new time-based paradigm of providing the most value for the least cost in the least amount of time. Authorizing a sudden crash spending surge offers the advantage of stimulating the MedTech organization toward immediate action, making time consumption the top priority of the entire organization, but it could also prove highly chaotic and extremely expensive. Creating structurally different methods would not create as much chaos or expense, but it would take longer to implement and could fail to produce results in sufficient time to keep MedTech on the new track.

The dilemma comes down to how best to move MedTech permanently away from a traditional strategy of making lower-cost products by relying on lower wages and economies of scale to a time-based competition approach that employs flexible factories and operations, expands product varieties, and speeds innovation to respond to customers' needs faster and more cost effectively than competitors. The crash alternative would force MedTech to act as if it were already a time-based competitor and allow ad hoc work methods to grow out of that environment. The structural alternative would require MedTech to first redesign the way work gets done. Both paths appeal to your management team, and they tell you they will support the decision you make. Now you must decide.

If you choose the crash alternative, turn to Chapter 30.
If you prefer the structural alternative, turn to Chapter 31.

20
Pursuing More Decentralization

Long enamored by the ideas of George Gilder, as spelled out in his books *The Spirit of Enterprise* and *Microcosm,* and by the stirring story of human achievement detailed in Tracy Kidder's classic, *The Soul of a New Machine,* all of which argue that smaller is better when attempting to gain efficiency and effectiveness, you choose to decentralize MedTech even further into strategic business units. You also plan to employ the idea of strategic leverage to maximize the freedom and maneuverability in each of the new divisionalized units, thus creating work environments that can quickly adapt to and create change. In an effort to convince your management team of the rightness of this course, you go to great lengths describing how large firms naturally restrict their strategic leverage and strategic choices, as their very size prevents them from remaining flexible to change prices, raise or lower advertising expenditures, redesign products, or otherwise alter the ways in which they compete in the marketplace. "On the other hand," you argue, "small organizations can gain efficiency, remain flexible, and constantly alter the ways in which they conduct business."

Given MedTech's recent success and the reputations of George Gilder and others who promote the idea of smallness as a key to organizational flexibility, your management team quickly lends their full support to further decentralization. As a first step, you hire a well-known Chicago-based consultant Milind Lele, author of *Creating Strategic Leverage,* to develop a strategic map for MedTech that shows how industry participants cluster into specific groups, how economic forces separate the different groups, and how barriers might restrict maneuverability or influence return. After several weeks, the strate-

gic-mapping process enables you to visualize opportunities for strategic leverage in several areas within the blood analysis, collection, and
monitoring market, and you and your management team divide the
MedTech Industrywide division into six new divisions that can seize
these opportunities. Within 60 days you reorganize MedTech into
seven strategic business divisions, including the small health-care
providers division created a year earlier: low-end blood analyzers,
high-end blood analyzers, blood collection systems, blood monitoring
devices, blood testing kits, and peripheral instruments.

Although you meet some resistance from Benton executives, you so
persuasively argue that the wave of the future lies in smaller, more
flexible business units with strategies that foster accelerated growth
and development that they finally approve the appointment of general managers for the new divisions. Kate DaVaeno continues as head of
the division for small health-care providers, Amos Gill takes over the
high-end blood analyzers, and five other MedTech executives take
over the remaining divisions. You encourage the new division managers to create their own divisional hierarchies as quickly as possible,
and you immediately begin revising MedTech's compensation systems to allow for more incentive-based pay for the divisional general
managers and their key people.

As the year unfolds, sales remain stagnant and profits decline,
prompting Mitch Cavanaugh, your group president, to accuse you of
empire building at the expense of business building. From that day
on, you realize that you've lost Mitch Cavanaugh's support, but you
respond by intensifying your efforts to make sure MedTech's decentralized structure works and becomes a model for Benton
Pharmaceuticals' other divisions.

During the last half of the year, each of the seven divisions within
MedTech creates such brilliant strategic plans that MedTech's future
looks brighter and brighter. However, the short-term picture worsens.
At the end of the year MedTech reports sales of $171 million, a 1 per-
cent increase, and profits of $32 million, a 14 percent decrease, as
shown in the accompanying table.

When Mitch Cavanaugh and other Benton executives ask you to justify MedTech's performance and detail its prospects for the future,
you respond by giving them copies of your divisions' seven strategic
plans and again argue eloquently that smaller organizations can maximize their strategic leverage in the marketplace. However, Benton
executives, pressured by an unfolding recession, insist that within six
months MedTech must demonstrate its ability to make the new decentralized structure work in terms of sales and profits growth.

Selected Financial Information
(Dollars in Millions)

| | Year ended September 30 | |
	This year	Last year
Operations		
Net sales	$171.2	$169.3
Cost of sales	61.3	60.3
R&D	18.1	13.5
Marketing	33.9	38.6
G&A	25.8	19.5
Operating profit	32.1	37.4
Financial position		
Current assets	75.1	83.9
Current liabilities	39.0	48.2
Working capital	36.0	35.7
Other assets	22.5	26.1
Property and equipment	80.6	82.6
Total assets	178.1	192.6
Other data		
Capital expenditures	9.9	12.3
Depreciation and amortization	12.1	9.2
Return on sales	18.8%	22.1%
Return on assets	18.0%	19.4%
Number of employees	1182	1058

Unfortunately, sales remain stagnate over the next few months, and profits plummet further as each of the new divisions struggles to gain enough organizational mass to operate efficiently and effectively. The infrastructure development and systems modification necessary to allow each of the divisions to operate autonomously cut deeply into profits and hinder sales growth.

Although you still believe that smallness represents the wave of the future, you gradually acknowledge that you underestimated the time and resources required to make your new divisions functional and miscalculated the need for coordination and infrastructure sharing among the divisions. Given another one to two years, you feel that MedTech could make the concepts of smallness and strategic leverage really pay off, but in the face of a deepening recession, you know Benton executives will not give you a chance to prove your case. Discouraged by the short-sightedness of Benton executives and your own miscalculations, you tender your resignation and accept a position as a consultant with SLC Consultants, the Chicago-based firm that conducted the strategic-mapping project for MedTech almost a year earlier.

You look forward to your new career as a consultant, hoping that you can help other executives avoid the mistakes you made in the last 18 months. In the final analysis, you realize that managerial revolutions like the one you attempted at MedTech cost a lot in terms of time and money and don't always constitute successful change. You vow to teach your clients to avoid drastic, revolutionary courses of action by finding ways to implement the principles of smallness and strategic leverage in existing operations without excessive stress and upheaval.

If you would like to continue making strategic decisions at MedTech, select one of the options below.

If you want to revisit your most recent strategic decision, return to Chapter 13.

However, if you would prefer starting over, return to Chapter 6 or Chapter 3.

If you're still feeling the sting of defeat and believe you could have made your last strategic choice work in real life, you may be right. After all, this is just a game. However, if you return to your last strategic decision (the first option above) and select the other alternative, you will learn why the author considers it a better choice.

21
Expanding and Improving Micromarketing

Although marketing gurus have long predicted a form of micromarketing, the concept has received a lot of attention lately from business writers and thinkers who champion such wrinkles as *micromarketing, database marketing, maximarketing,* or simply the *new marketing.* Regardless of the lingo, you decide that micromarketing represents the wave of the future. Rather than organize new divisions within MedTech, you ask Kate DaVaeno, who heads MedTech–Small Providers, and Amos Gill, who oversees MedTech–Industrywide, to organize all of MedTech's marketing systems along niche or customer segment lines. Doing so will require utilizing the earlier segmentation study to examine the marketplace more carefully, gather data more scrupulously, differentiate among products and services more precisely, and analyze all discrete customer segments. Then MedTech must muster its resources to develop more products and services, establish more channels of distribution, launch more advertising campaigns, create more sales presentations, and bring to bear more strategic marketing to meet the needs of those segments.

As a first step toward marshaling the necessary resources to make micromarketing really work for MedTech, you hire a new vice president of marketing strategy and charge her with taking MedTech to a higher level of micromarketing proficiency. Your new marketing strategy vice president, Cam Cardon, began her career with the consulting firm of Arthur D. Little, working for three years as a management consultant, after which she spent five years at Procter & Gamble, then two at Colgate Palmolive, a company that during her stay invested an enormous amount of time and money in database-driven micromarketing. As Cam smoothly adapts to her new environment, you pride yourself in having made a great selection.

Over the next few months, you spend most of your time with four executives, Amos Gill, Kate DaVaeno, Cam Cardon, and management information vice president Ken Matsumori. Together you develop a micromarketing-oriented organizational structure for each of MedTech's two major divisions, renamed the Large-Scale-Provider and the Small-Scale-Provider Divisions. As part of the restructuring, 30 new market-niche managers, who function somewhat like product managers in the consumer-goods industry but with a "market product" rather than a "product market" orientation, represent a striking departure from business as usual. By midyear, the number of MedTech's product variations triples in response to market-segment demands. Five new models of blood analyzers are introduced before the end of the year, each one with fairly minor product adjustments designed to meet the unique needs of a given niche, and over a dozen new blood collection and monitoring devices come on-line in response to the unique needs of customers in targeted segments.

A new set of strategic marketing questions preoccupy your executives and managers: Who are MedTech's heavy users? Who are its light users? Which customers are expanding or decreasing their purchases? What do customers really value? How frequently do they purchase? What promotions and advertising campaigns appeal best to various customer segments? Who makes the purchasing decision? Which customers buy a full line of products and services, and which don't? MedTech's marketing personnel have posed similar questions in the past, but now, with the new orientation toward micromarketing, these questions are always uppermost in their minds.

As momentum behind the micromarketing program builds, you ask Ken Matsumori, vice president of management information systems, to help the 30 market-niche managers establish separate but linked marketing databases that can facilitate effective niche management. *Customizing,* tailoring products and services to meet customer segment needs, becomes MedTech's new operating style, and you encourage your management team to tackle even more regional and local marketing considerations in order to expand the company's number of targeted segments. Aware of the pitfall that MedTech might become a hodge-podge of autonomous niche markets, you stress the advantages of spreading overhead costs across the niches, sharing valuable information, cooperating on R&D projects, and creating efficiencies with expansion funding. Finally, in the midst of all this activity, you realize the need for a common purpose or conceptual theme that can guide and link all of MedTech's market niches, and, as the fiscal year ends, that looms as your next major strategic decision.

As a result of all your micromarketing efforts, sales for the year increase over 30 percent to $225 million, with profits rising similarly to $50 million, as shown in the accompanying table.

These numbers prompt congratulations from Benton executives and an invitation from *Business Week* to speak at its annual conference about MedTech's accomplishments. Despite all the hoopla, you find yourself struggling to determine what overriding theme, principle, or purpose should drive the micromarketing emphasis in the year ahead.

While you pride yourself on your ability to analyze facts and apply logic to all your decisions, you feel less comfortable moving into the realm of philosophy and theory, a weakness shared by your action-oriented management team. To compensate, you seek the help of an outside strategy consultant, Pamela West, who has a flair for conceptual and theoretical thinking. After several sessions with West, you identify two possible unifying themes: creating value is one possible

Selected Financial Information
(Dollars in Millions)

	Year ended September 30	
	This year	Last year
Operations		
Net sales	$224.7	$169.3
Cost of sales	76.4	60.3
R&D	17.9	13.5
Marketing	58.9	38.6
G&A	22.0	19.5
Operating profit	49.5	37.4
Financial position		
Current assets	75.3	83.9
Current liabilities	39.1	48.2
Working capital	36.1	35.7
Other assets	22.6	26.1
Property and equipment	92.7	82.6
Total assets	190.6	192.6
Other data		
Capital expenditures	15.6	12.3
Depreciation and amortization	13.0	9.2
Return on sales	22.0%	22.1%
Return on assets	26.0%	19.4%
Number of employees	1150	1058

theme and avoiding head-on competition is another possible theme. The theme of creating value would drive MedTech's market-niche managers and their people toward activities that maximize value for customers in every targeted customer segment. The theme of avoiding head-on competition would cause MedTech's market-niche managers to focus on products or services that avoid existing or potential direct competition. The more you think about these two choices, the more you recognize their fundamental differences: creating value represents a customer-driven strategy that depends on MedTech's capabilities and its customers' needs; avoiding head-on competition represents a competitor-driven strategy that centers on competitors' choices and how they meet customer needs.

West calls avoiding head-on competition the "classic" strategy, citing Sun-Tsu's *The Art of War* and McKinsey & Company's competitive-interaction doctrine as prime sources; and she refers to creating value as the "new wave," citing Michael Porter's *Competitive Advantage* and the Harvard Business School's emphasis on value as key proponents of that approach. In summary, West argues that avoiding head-on competition may reap short-term rewards but could lack sufficient steam to drive long-term results, whereas creating value may provide long-term strength but lack short-term clout. Now, having systematically organized the facts and carefully listened to Pamela West's theories, you must make your own decision.

If you choose creating value as MedTech's unifying theme, turn to Chapter 32.

If you favor avoiding head-on competition as MedTech's central principle, turn to Chapter 33.

22
Narrowing the Scope to Core Services

This decision proved a particularly nettlesome one; you respect your initial intuition that a narrow scope of core services will better position MedTech to meet customers' needs and sustain competitive advantage. During the next few months you and your management team, and particularly Kate DaVaeno, work hard to narrow MedTech's focus to two core services: (1) identifying unmet customer needs and (2) finding unique product solutions in the area of blood analysis, collection, and monitoring.

With the benefit of this narrower focus, you begin outsourcing non-core services and you zero in on the unmet customer need of identifying viruses rather than just the antibodies they produce, because such identification would facilitate earlier diagnosis and treatment, as in the case of AIDS.

A few weeks after you mobilize MedTech employees in all functions to look for possible solutions, Vic Gomez, vice president of technical service, tells you he's discovered a small company, Genemed, outside of Boston, which has already developed a new blood test for identifying viruses rather than antibodies. Genemed's researchers have been waiting to publish their findings until after they've conducted expensive verification, which they cannot do because of limited funding.

You immediately enter into a licensing arrangement with Genemed that gives MedTech the exclusive right to manufacture and market the virus identification testing process internationally in return for the necessary funding to complete all necessary tests and gain FDA approval. Genemed will also receive a 15 percent royalty on all sales of the new virus identification test. Six months later MedTech introduces the new virus identification testing package complete with the necessary reagents, control materials, and software compatible with MedTech's blood analyzers.

The new virus identification test spurs MedTech's sales upward by 18 percent to $160 million for the year, with an even greater increase of 32 percent in profits to $37 million, as shown in the accompanying table.

While these numbers are not earth-shattering, they are sufficiently attractive, particularly in light of expected future sales from the virus identification testing package, to give you and your management team the green light from Benton to proceed with your current strategic direction.

With a home run under your belt, you now face the more subtle strategic decision of how to develop and strengthen MedTech's narrower focus on core services even further. Essentially, the issue boils down to this question: Should you emphasize the external monitoring of customer expectations or the internal building of employee com-

Selected Financial Information
(Dollars in Millions)

| | Year ended September 30 | |
	This year	Last year
Operations		
Net sales	$160.2	$135.2
Cost of sales	56.0	48.0
R&D	12.8	12.8
Marketing	37.3	32.2
G&A	16.8	14.0
Operating profit	37.3	28.2
Financial position		
Current assets	54.1	78.5
Current liabilities	28.1	46.1
Working capital	25.9	32.4
Other assets	16.2	24.1
Property and equipment	78.2	85.2
Total assets	148.5	187.8
Other data		
Capital expenditures	7.6	5.6
Depreciation and amortization	12.1	9.2
Return on sales	23.3%	20.9%
Return on assets	25.1%	15.0%
Number of employees	1003	1066

mitment? Better monitoring of customer expectations would improve MedTech's ability to identify various unmet customer needs, whereas building stronger employee commitment would improve MedTech's ability to find unique product solutions. It's a chicken-or-egg question. You realize that you'll need to do both well in years to come, but which one deserves your priority attention at the moment? Which one should precede and then drive the other? Though either emphasis could get results, and though one will spring naturally from the other, your intuition tells you the right choice might make a bigger difference than at first seems apparent, especially in the short term.

With little discussion among your management team, you decide to make this subtle strategic decision on your own. No one seems to care much, one way or the other, so you might as well get on with it.

If you choose monitoring customer expectations to discover unmet customer needs as MedTech's driving force in strengthening its core services, turn to Chapter 34.

If you feel that building employee commitment to find better product solutions should propel MedTech's strengthening of its core services, turn to Chapter 35.

23

Expanding to a Broader Definition of Core Competence

Acting against your intuition, you decide to focus on broadening the scope of core services in an expanded definition of MedTech's core competence. You take some solace in the fact that no competitor has pursued such a course. Your management team trusts you so much, they support your decision and move quickly to get the entire organization thinking in terms of core competence.

You spend significant resources and several months developing a companywide strategic architecture that establishes objectives for building a core competence based on nonmanufacturing, knowledge-based services, and you send every member of your senior management team to customer service and core competence seminars around the country. Drawing upon the seminar experiences of your senior team, Susan Carter, your vice president of human resources, develops and conducts an in-house training program for middle managers, first-line supervisors, and workers throughout the company, which indoctrinates every MedTech employee in a short 90-day period.

The employees learn about core competencies from Prahalad and Hamel's work, wherein the two authors outline three tests of core competence: "First, a core competence provides potential access to a wide variety of markets....Second, a core competence should make a significant contribution to the perceived customer benefits of the end product....Finally, a core competence should be difficult for competitors to imitate." Employees also learn how to operate within a hierarchy of core competencies and core products, which brings excitement and freshness to the MedTech organization.

However, while you expect your efforts to pay off eventually, the end of the fiscal year produces only a 7 percent increase in revenues to $145 million and only a slight increase in profit to $29 million, as shown in the accompanying table.

When you pick up on rumors circulating among corporate staffers that MedTech's performance has convinced headquarters to form a halt to your present course, you begin looking for another job outside of MedTech and Benton Pharmaceuticals. Group president Mitch Cavanaugh confirms the rumors, and you resolve to leave the company.

After a brief search, you accept a job offer from an old family friend who wants to retire from a small medical supply distribution business but has no interested heirs or capable managers who can take over. You become executive vice president of Bruden Medical Supply with the promise that you will assume the presidency within two years.

Selected Financial Information
(Dollars in Millions)

	Year ended September 30	
	This year	Last year
Operations		
Net sales	$144.7	$135.2
Cost of sales	55.0	48.0
R&D	11.8	12.8
Marketing	31.9	32.2
G&A	17.4	14.0
Operating profit	28.6	28.2
Financial position		
Current assets	49.9	78.5
Current liabilities	26.0	46.1
Working capital	24.0	32.4
Other assets	15.0	24.1
Property and equipment	77.5	85.2
Total assets	142.4	187.8
Other data		
Capital expenditures	6.8	5.6
Depreciation and amortization	12.1	9.2
Return on sales	19.8%	20.9%
Return on assets	20.1%	15.0%
Number of employees	1028	1066

In real life, your strategic decision making at MedTech would cease as you leave for your new job, but in this book you can continue the adventure, if you'd like to do so.

If you would like to return to your most recent strategic decision, go back to Chapter 15.

If you want to go back to an earlier decision point, return to Chapter 7 or Chapter 3.

If you're still feeling the sting of defeat and believe you could have made your last strategic choice work in real life, you may be right. After all, this is just a game. However, if you return to your last strategic decision (the first option above) and select the other alternative, you will learn why the author considers it a better choice.

24
Playing the Acquisition Game

You feel confident that MedTech can successfully build on its recent track record with the FutureMed acquisition. Given so many explosive opportunities taking shape in the health-care industry, an aggressive acquisitions strategy makes a lot of sense because it will allow you to seize those opportunities quickly. Your management team supports your decision enthusiastically, but you hear through the company grapevine that a few people in your organization have expressed fears that you've let MedTech's recent success go to your head. According to the rumor, one of your vice presidents thinks that your proposed "acquisitions binge" represents nothing but a personal ego trip. Undaunted by the internal stirrings, however, you move forward with firm resolve to complete at least three additional acquisitions by the end of the fiscal year. You also make note of the need for more cheerleading to keep any stirrings of doubt from growing into rumbles of disapproval.

You appoint Amos Gill, vice president of finance, and Ken Matsumori, vice president of management information systems, as the official merger and acquisition specialists for MedTech, and they, in turn, seek out the assistance of two people *Fortune* magazine has called "the merger mavens," Philip Mirvis and Mitchell Marks. With the help of these consultants and their book, *Managing the Merger: Making It Work,* your two vice presidents, Gill and Matsumori, identify the five most common reasons why acquisitions and mergers fail:

1. Price (Acquiring companies paid too much.)

2. Purpose (Despite careful prepurchase analysis, many acquisitions and mergers simply didn't make sense in the first place.)

3. Partnership (Companies found it impossible to combine two separate entities.)

4. Timing (Things never came together to meet the precise demands of the marketplace.)

5. Management (merger and acquisition mismanagement stifled the blending of the two companies.)

Since none of these common mistakes occurred during the FutureMed acquisition, you ask Gill and Matsumori to make sure MedTech incorporates into its strategy the processes and systems needed to avoid all these common mistakes during future acquisitions. Then, out of the blue, during a senior management staff meeting, Kate DaVaeno, your vice president of marketing, confronts you with this question: "I've been doing a little homework. Data from the FTC, the SEC, and the business media indicate that two-thirds to three-fourths of all mergers and acquisitions don't work out. Maybe we were lucky with FutureMed, but based on the historical odds, our next three acquisitions could be duds. How do you plan to beat the odds?" The dead silence that greets this question tells you that a lot of people in the room share DaVaeno's skepticism.

You respond, "Some of you may wonder whether the FutureMed deal has gone to my head, that our new acquisition strategy is just an ego trip, but I want to tell you how I really feel. I strongly believe two things: First, we have the ability to manage the merger and acquisition process as well as or better than anyone ever has; second, we're going to see a hurricane of change in this industry over the next 10 years, particularly in blood analysis and related markets. I honestly think that if we can pinpoint the best companies out there and link up with them, we can turn into a major player faster than if we try to do it all by ourselves." Your management team seems to accept your explanation and agrees to give your strategy wholehearted support. Even DaVaeno seems satisfied.

Over the next several months, you fortify your mergers and acquisitions group by hiring a new vice president of mergers and acquisitions, Meg Daniels, a former Morgan Stanley investment banker. You elevate Amos Gill, Ken Matsumori, and Jack Suhler to senior vice presidents and ask the group of four to lead MedTech's merger and acquisition attack, with Daniels identifying and evaluating prospective candidates, Gill arranging and negotiating financing, Matsumori monitoring and guiding assimilation of the new entities into MedTech, and Suhler coordinating R&D efforts throughout the expanding company.

After looking at over 500 possible targets MedTech acquires four companies by the end of the fiscal year—Immucorp, BP Data, Maxima, and Teva-Yavne.

Immucorp, acquired for $56 million, manufactures a complete line of reagents used in procedures to type and group blood, to identify blood-borne antibodies, and to screen donor blood for various infectious diseases such as AIDS and hepatitis. Although MedTech also produces a line of reagents, you expect Immucorp will provide important access to a new market, blood banking. BP Data, acquired in a $24 million transaction, manufactures ambulatory devices that allow doctors to monitor their patients' blood pressures over a 24-hour period. Although these devices for ambulatory monitoring of blood pressure still spark some controversy over need and usefulness, your team sees them as an important wave of the future. Experts such as Arthur Gainesworth, professor of medicine at Cornell University, has said, "Ambulatory monitoring will become the new gold standard for evaluating blood pressure problems." Maxima, acquired for $12 million, distributes medical supplies and instruments, mainly in the European blood analysis market. Headquartered in Brussels, Belgium, Maxima will greatly expand MedTech's markets internationally. The Teva-Yavne plant, acquired for $9 million, produces blood analysis, collection, and monitoring instruments in Yavne, Israel. This plant, which

Selected Financial Information
(Dollars in Millions)

	Year ended September 30	
	This year	Last year
Operations		
Net sales	$336.0	$191.0
Cost of sales	116.1	63.0
R&D	36.2	20.6
Marketing	65.9	38.6
G&A	33.8	15.3
Operating profit	84.0	53.5
Financial position		
Current assets	113.0	98.6
Current liabilities	58.8	51.1
Working capital	54.3	47.5
Other assets	33.9	30.2
Property and equipment	92.1	90.7
Total assets	239.0	219.5
Other data		
Capital expenditures	16.6	13.3
Depreciation and amortization	13.0	10.6
Return on sales	25.0%	28.0%
Return on assets	35.1%	24.4%
Number of employees	1301	1070

was easily converted within a 90-day period to produce MedTech's products, now augments MedTech's manufacturing capacity for Europe and Asia. MedTech's sales soar, with the newly acquired entities adding over $80 million in sales. By year-end, sales have increased 76 percent to $336 million, and operating profits have risen 57 percent to $84 million, as shown in the accompanying table.

For several weeks after the end of the fiscal year, you continue receiving accolades from corporate headquarters and requests from the business press for interviews. Many reporters, watching the successful integration of MedTech's recent acquisitions, think you may have figured out the secret to the enigmatic acquisition game. However, a new strategic question looms on the horizon, and you know you'll have to make another critical decision soon. Should MedTech focus on assimilating current acquisitions or on initiating aggressive global expansion?

With the health-care industry booming around the world, savvy competitors serving Third World populations can gain strong positions and global franchises for years to come. Initiating aggressive global expansion also offers a much more rapid growth track, but one that requires swift action to stay ahead of the pack. On the other hand, assimilating MedTech's current acquisitions would allow the company to integrate all of its operations, thus strengthening its technological base and market leadership, particularly in the United States. Once again, you face a crucial judgment test. What will you decide?

If you want to initiate aggressive global expansion as the next major step in MedTech's development, turn to Chapter 36.

If you favor assimilating current acquisitions as the preferred focus, turn to Chapter 37.

25
Pioneering Innovation

Agreement between Russian economist Nikolai Kondratiev and German economist Joseph Schumpeter that technological innovation has occurred in 50-year cycles ever since the beginning of the industrial revolution in the 1790s convinces you that the electronics innovation of the "fourth wave," which began in the 1940s, has run its course. Now, you anticipate the beginning of a "fifth wave" in the fields of medicine and biotechnology. You're not alone. Scores of trend trackers, industry experts, and business analysts predict incredible innovation in these fields over the next few decades. Having made a strategic decision to pursue pioneering innovation, you totally commit yourself and MedTech to riding the crest of this gathering wave.

With FutureMedTech, the new R&D division working so smoothly, you believe your company's exploration of the frontiers of medical science will achieve major breakthroughs. To your mind, FutureMedTech's current projects represent just an initial ripple in what you know will build into a flood of innovations. Of course, that won't happen unless you continue to make pioneering innovation a perpetual reality at FutureMedTech, with support from the rest of MedTech.

After innumerable discussions with Jack Suhler, now head of the new FutureMedTech R&D Division, and with other members of your management team, you decide to divide FutureMedTech into four separate groups: Hematology, Flow Cytometry, Retrovirology, and Scientific Instruments. Hematology, the largest group, would continue to focus on blood analysis, collection, and monitoring; Flow Cytometry would explore autoimmune disorders and new laser-based equipment for examining cells and their makeup; Retrovirology would strive to apply the new laser-based equipment and graphics to the study of cancer and virus cells; and Scientific Instruments would tackle various kinds of particle counters MedTech can sell to such diverse organizations as Coca-Cola, Sherwin Williams, and NASA. While Hematology would continue to receive the lion's share of FutureMedTech's R&D attention, the other three areas would also enjoy substantial funding. MedTech's long history in blood analysis, collection, and monitoring combined with FutureMed's superior R&D, you believe, continue to give FutureMedTech an edge in unlocking the mysteries of many diseases.

To finalize MedTech's reorganization you combine all non-R&D operations into a second division named MedTech Operations, and you convince Benton headquarters that it makes sense to promote Jack Suhler to senior vice president of MedTech and president of the FutureMedTech division and Kate DaVaeno to senior vice president of MedTech and president of the MedTech Operations division. With MedTech, Inc., becoming a corporate entity with two operating divisions, you also make a basic change in your operating style, shifting the burden of daily decision making to Jack Suhler and Kate DaVaeno and giving more attention to your own personal staff of scientists, analysts, and planners. Suhler and DaVaeno should, you insist, develop their own management teams and challenge them to maintain superb coordination between the two divisions.

Months later, you feel your confidence in Jack Suhler and Kate DaVaeno was well-placed. Their actions prove that both executives share your deep devotion to pioneering medical innovation, and they have done a superb job of pushing MedTech to explore and exploit the most promising breakthrough possibilities. In April their hard work and commitment pay off when the hematology and retrovirology R&D groups achieve a major breakthrough in blood analysis, developing a revolutionary blood analyzer that uses small lasers to sort individual blood cells automatically. The genius of the new instrument lies in the way the lasers align with a video camera and remove the need for microscopes. This allows for rapid transfer of test results to other computer software programs for greater in-depth analysis than anyone in the field ever imagined. Kate DaVaeno's division works furiously in the final quarter of the fiscal year to introduce the new blood analyzer, which, bearing a list price of $225,000, will initially serve high-end research lab customers. Sales of the new blood analyzer in the final two months of the year boost MedTech's sales for the year to $386 million, a 102 percent increase, and profits to $118 million, a rise of 121 percent, as shown in the accompanying table.

The business press, particularly reporters interested in medical and biotechnology stories, dog you for more detailed information about

Selected Financial Information
(Dollars in Millions)

	Year ended September 30	
	This year	Last year
Operations		
Net sales	$386.2	$191.0
Cost of sales	123.6	63.0
R&D	57.9	20.6
Marketing	50.0	38.6
G&A	36.6	15.3
Operating profit	118.1	53.5
Financial position		
Current assets	127.5	98.6
Current liabilities	66.3	51.1
Working capital	61.2	47.5
Other assets	38.2	30.2
Property and equipment	93.4	90.7
Total assets	259.1	219.5
Other data		
Capital expenditures	18.0	13.3
Depreciation and amortization	13.0	10.6
Return on sales	30.6%	28.0%
Return on assets	45.6%	24.4%
Number of employees	1340	1070

the new instrument, but you decide to severely limit your exposure to the media in order to protect your people from undue outside scrutiny. Even though one reporter quotes you as saying, "We're not interested in PR, we're interested in innovation," the media keeps pestering you for interviews.

Benton headquarters lavishes praise on you for MedTech's performance, and Mitch Cavanaugh, your group president, encourages you to spend whatever money you wish on new R&D projects. He also gently requests that you open FutureMedTech's R&D projects to review and participation, wherever possible, so other Benton divisions, particularly those in the diagnostic products group, can further exploit the advantages your company is creating. You reluctantly agree but inform Cavanaugh that you will shut the door quickly if such openness jeopardizes progress in any of FutureMedTech's R&D projects.

A short time later you discover that Charles Doan, group president of the Diagnostic Products Group, wants MedTech to become part of the Diagnostic Products Group, a move you resist because you fear Doan will force MedTech to diffuse its focus in the coming years. Ironically, while FutureMedTech's focused concentration on pioneering innovation has created an R&D powerhouse now heralded throughout the Benton organization, that very success is placing considerable pressure on FutureMedTech to water down its R&D activities by molding them with those of other divisions. Although both you and Jack Suhler take some pride in all the praise for your skills as managers of scientists and engineers, you both begin to feel somewhat embarrassed by all the fawning because you know the situation could reverse itself overnight if you do not keep on making sound strategic decisions. A major one now looms on the horizon: Should MedTech maintain its focus on blood and cell R&D, or should the company expand to accommodate other areas of medical, biotechnical, and pharmaceutical research and development in conjunction with other Benton divisions?

You discuss this strategic question with Jack Suhler, Kate DaVaeno, and your personal staff, trying to grapple with the pros and cons of each alternative. Sticking with blood and cell R&D provides clarity of focus, builds on past successes, and offers the greatest potential for major breakthroughs in the future. However, the rest of the Benton organization would probably view such a course of action as myopic and self-centered. Conversely, the major advantage to expanding beyond blood and cell R&D lies in the application of what many consider MedTech's "enlightened R&D management" to a wider scope of opportunities in the overall field of medicine and biotechnology. Of course, expanding MedTech's R&D focus would undoubtedly diffuse the company's current emphasis on blood and cell research, where you see so much continuing promise for further breakthroughs. After thinking about these two options for a few weeks, you feel quite frustrated because what at first seemed like an easy choice has now taken on mammoth political implications. What will you do?

If you choose to remain focused on blood and cell R&D, turn to Chapter 38.

If you decide to expand beyond blood and cell R&D, accommodating other medical, biotechnical, and pharmaceutical areas, turn to Chapter 39.

26

Creating a Liberation- Management Paradigm

The added sales of FutureStar and FutureScan prove invaluable as the year progresses, allowing you and your management team the time and security to install a new liberation-management paradigm that will shape the company's destiny. Confident that the most successful companies in the future will continually develop their own unique ways of operating, you strive to position MedTech to reinvent itself before some competitor beats you to it. "We must," you tell your management, "question every existing principle, practice, or procedure. Nothing is sacred. In your minds, I want you to knock everything apart and rebuild it from scratch." Drawing from Tom Peter's new book, *Liberation Management,* which he almost entitled "Create and Destroy," you tell your team to watch out for the false prophets of comprehension and quote from Peters, "Instead of the frantic pursuit of total comprehension (via central-control schemes), let's revel in our very *lack* of comprehension. While less successful businesspeople retain consulting chaoticians to construct ponderous models aimed at explaining what went wrong yesterday, the champion entrepreneur gets in another 10 tries, one of which just might click." You then exclaim, "I want this organization liberated so we can make things happen."

Together, you and your team identify the trends and fashions that will most likely affect MedTech in the future, trends such as globalization, the worldwide health-care crisis, the environment, the quality revolution, increasing diversity, biotechnology breakthroughs, and, of course, the increasingly "fickle, ephemeral, impermanent, fleeting" nature of everything. You know that all of these trends and more will affect MedTech's future, but exactly how and when should MedTech respond?

Over the next several months, ideas flourish in the company as members of your management team and ambitious middle managers use their own unique problem-solving approaches to identify and propose several paradigm shifts within MedTech. These ideas include a new organizational structure that would decentralize MedTech into very small regionally based units; strategic partnerships with medical centers, hospitals, and clinics; a holistic focus on innovation in blood analysis; a new service center that would analyze blood long-distance through computer networking with labs across the country; new marketing concepts that would educate consumers in the multiple uses of blood analysis; and an expanded role for blood analysis in preventative health care in anticipation of a new national health-care policy that Congress may soon adopt.

In order to test out some of these ideas and to invite even more creative ones from the field, you make a point of attending industry association meetings around the country. As the year unfolds, you learn a lot about what hospital administrators, doctors, government officials, consumer advocates, and ordinary citizens expect from companies like yours. The experience is as humbling as it is enlightening. In a particularly touching incident, you visit an experimental retirement community in Arizona that has integrated progressive levels of medical care into standard living quarters. An 84-year-old retired professor tells you from his bed that you should come up with a blood test diabetics can administer on the golf course. He means it as a joke, but his words set your imagination running. Never before have you felt so in tune with the needs of your real customers.

Sales of FutureStar and FutureScan continue to increase through the third quarter, but when they fall off in the fourth quarter, that turn of events exposes MedTech's biggest weakness: too little attention to new sources of sales. At year-end, the company reports an increase of sales to $165 million, a climb of 10 percent, and profits of $35 million, an increase of 8 percent, as shown in the accompanying table.

Too late, you realize that MedTech has become expert at identifying tomorrow's opportunities at the expense of tending to today's sales. The thought of focusing on near-term sales depresses you because it will sidetrack your longer-term pursuit of new product and service solutions.

Selected Financial Information
(Dollars in Millions)

	Year ended September 30	
	This year	Last year
Operations		
Net sales	$165.3	$150.4
Cost of sales	51.8	53.1
R&D	19.8	16.2
Marketing	33.6	32.0
G&A	24.7	16.7
Operating profit	35.4	32.3
Financial position		
Current assets	54.1	82.1
Current liabilities	28.1	46.8
Working capital	25.9	35.3
Other assets	16.2	23.2
Property and equipment	80.6	81.2
Total assets	150.8	186.5
Other data		
Capital expenditures	9.9	9.4
Depreciation and amortization	12.1	9.3
Return on sales	21.4%	21.5%
Return on assets	23.5%	17.3%
Number of employees	1053	1059

As you consider your options, you recognize yourself as much more of a revolutionary than a realist. You also know that it will take a hard-nosed realist to boost MedTech's sagging sales and profitability. Can you set aside your search for extraordinary transformation, which has been so exhilarating this past year? Not without a lot of regret. Therefore, you reluctantly decide that the time has come for you to leave MedTech and redirect your career. In a matter of weeks you accept a position as Ad Hoc Chief of Customerizing for the Tom Peters Group, which had recently engaged you to speak at an important industry conference.

As you leave MedTech, you briefly wonder if you're just ducking reality. You try hard to convince yourself that you've made the right career decision, even though you'll miss the substance of the strategic decision making that you so enjoyed at MedTech. Perhaps you would like to travel back in time and remake some of those decisions.

If you want to revisit your last strategic decision, go back to Chapter 17.

If you would rather go back to an earlier strategic decision, return to Chapter 8 or Chapter 4.

If you're still feeling the sting of defeat and believe you could have made your last strategic choice work in real life, you may be right. After all, this is just a game. However, if you return to your last strategic decision (the first option above) and select the other alternative, you will learn why the author considers it a better choice.

27
Adopting a Learning-Organization Paradigm

Believing that too much concentration on change can create an extreme environment of disjointed development in an organization, you decide to structure MedTech's evolution by adopting a philosophy of principle-based learning, which you hope will provide the impetus for continual yet orderly growth. However, you suspect that this strategy will require going far beyond notions of total quality management, continuous improvement, or renewal to get at the very core of how human beings learn, progress, and improve their performance. Thus, you continue searching for a perspective that will help MedTech create a new kind of learning organization for the twenty-first century and, at the same time, ensure necessary near-term sales.

Although you recognize yourself as more of an idealist than a realist, you know that you cannot concentrate on MedTech's long-term success and well-being at the expense of annual growth. Therefore, you ask your management team to focus on developing MedTech's existing products, with particular emphasis on FutureStar and FutureScan, and on further integrating FutureMed into the organization. This then affords you time to search out a specific paradigm for turning MedTech into a learning organization.

You study Royal Dutch Shell, a global oil company dedicated to learning and growing as an organization, and Xerox, the copier manufacturer that reinvented itself in the late 1980s. Former Xerox CEO David Kearns and his consultant David Nadler chronicled that achievement in their book *Prophets in the Dark*, which you find particularly revealing. You also read again *The Fifth Discipline* by Peter Senge, director of the systems thinking and organizational learning program at MIT's Sloan School of Management, and *The 7 Habits of Highly Effective People* by Stephen Covey, chairman of the Covey Leadership Center and the nonprofit Institute for Principle-Centered Leadership, who together make perhaps the best case for creating a learning organization.

At midyear you conclude that the ideas in *The Fifth Discipline* and *The 7 Habits of Highly Effective People* should shape MedTech's framework for becoming a learning organization. Over the next several months you begin slowly introducing the concepts of Senge and Covey to your management team. First, you expose the crippling "learning disabilities" suffered by many organizations, including the delusion of learning from experience, the fixation on events, and the myth of teamwork. By discussing these stumbling blocks, you help your management team recognize that people and organizations can learn better and faster by avoiding trial-and-error experiences, deemphasizing events as indicators of success or failure, overcoming the inherent mediocrity that characterizes teamwork, and placing principles over circumstances.

By carefully managing the short term, while conscientiously preparing for the long term, you keep MedTech on track with Benton's growth standards, reporting a 15 percent growth in year-end sales and profits of $173 million and $37 million, respectively, as shown in the accompanying table.

After a good deal of soul-searching, you take an unprecedented step within the Benton organization, asking for a three-year period in which to build a learning-organization environment at MedTech. Specifically, you ask Mitch Cavanaugh, your group president, and Bob Koontz, chairman and CEO of Benton Pharmaceuticals, to suspend all growth expectations for three years, allowing MedTech to implement a learning-driven and principle-centered culture without the fear stimulated by quarterly and annual growth expectations. In return for such an unprecedented dispensation, you promise Benton executives that MedTech's sales and profit growth will far exceed a compounded 15 percent growth rate at the end of three years. The three-year reprieve will, you argue, create just the right psychological conditions among employees that will allow you and your management team to create the beliefs and behavior you feel must drive your organization into the twenty-first century. After sharing your own deep feelings about how organizations must change in the coming years, you give Koontz and Cavanaugh copies of *The Fifth Discipline*

Selected Financial Information
(Dollars in Millions)

	Year ended September 30	
	This year	Last year
Operations		
Net sales	$173.2	$150.4
Cost of sales	63.0	53.1
R&D	17.2	16.2
Marketing	38.0	32.0
G&A	18.1	16.7
Operating profit	36.9	32.3
Financial position		
Current assets	93.6	82.1
Current liabilities	53.7	46.8
Working capital	39.9	35.3
Other assets	27.3	23.2
Property and equipment	84.9	81.2
Total assets	205.8	186.5
Other data		
Capital expenditures	8.3	9.4
Depreciation and amortization	8.9	9.3
Return on sales	21.3%	21.5%
Return on assets	17.9%	17.3%
Number of employees	1133	1059

and *The 7 Habits of Highly Effective People.* "Read these books," you urge your superiors. "They'll open your eyes."

Ten days later during a follow-up meeting, you walk Koontz and Cavanaugh through the concepts and principles contained in these two books, which prepares them for a workshop conducted by Peter Senge and Stephen Covey for all key Benton executives four weeks later. Finally, Koontz and Cavanaugh give you permission to experiment and grant MedTech a three-year hiatus from the usual growth expectations. Nevertheless, Koontz cannot resist reminding you that you've put your career on the line.

At a special management meeting for MedTech's top 100 officers, directors, and managers you announce Benton's three-year reprieve and outline the laws of *The Fifth Discipline* according to Peter Senge:

1. Today's problems come from yesterday's solutions.
2. The harder you push, the harder the system pushes back.

3. Behavior grows better before it grows worse.

4. The easy way out usually leads back in.

5. The cure can be worse than the disease.

6. Faster is slower.

7. Cause and effect are not closely related in time and space.

8. Small changes can produce big results, but the areas of highest leverage are often the least obvious.

9. You can have your cake and eat it, too, but not at once.

10. Dividing an elephant in half does not produce two small elephants.

11. There is no blame.

Then, you review the 7 Habits identified by Stephen Covey:

1. Be proactive.

2. Begin with the end in mind.

3. Put first things first.

4. Think Win/Win.

5. Seek first to understand, then to be understood.

6. Synergize.

7. Sharpen the saw.

In the early stages of the MedTech 36-month program, you draw upon the expertise of Peter Senge and Stephen Covey to ingrain these principles into the people at MedTech, and you watch with delight as they enable your people to begin forming the company into a learning organization. You stimulate early progress by focusing heavily on the five learning disciplines which stress the whole as opposed to the parts: systems thinking, personal mastery, mental models, building shared vision, and team learning. Within this context, every MedTech employee reevaluates his or her place within the organization. Systems thinking helps them embrace holistic interconnectedness; personal mastery teaches them to respect being and connectedness; mental models reinforce the value of truth and openness; building shared vision instills commonality of purpose and partnership; and team learning emphasizes collective intelligence and alignment. You also stress the importance of each employee's moving from dependence to independence to interdependence.

Slowly but surely, month by month, the learning-organization concepts of Senge and Covey manifest themselves in the daily lives of
MedTech people. You marvel as the organization develops new channels of distribution that bring MedTech products to the far corners of
the globe; installs a new manufacturing process that lops 25 percent
off the cost of producing MedTech's most expensive blood analyzers;
introduces a new miniblood analyzer that patients can easily operate
and that requires very little blood to conduct 12 major blood tests;
develops a host of new blood monitoring and collection products;
increases customer responsiveness in the midst of a recession; and
responds to a new national health-care policy by reeducating physicians in the multiple uses of blood tests, thereby eliminating other
tests that drive up medical costs. Psychologically, the three-year
reprieve helps engender a widespread belief throughout MedTech
that the company really can implement the principles and practices of
a learning organization.

Intuitively, but without empirical data or experience, you knew that
MedTech people could climb to much greater heights if you could
only guarantee their security while they did so. You were right. Over
the three-year period people have reached higher levels of productivity than you imagined possible, and, to your absolute delight, they
have actually begun eliminating the conflict between work and family. A side effect of the program has been a lesson that people must
view their professional lives within the larger context of life, making it
possible for them to coordinate and integrate professional, personal,
and family values with a host of new work practices. This interaction
includes business and vacation trip combinations, personalized work
shifts, four-day work weeks, project-employees, competence networks, home and company telecomputer links, and incentives for
reaching work, personal, and family goals.

At the end of the third year, MedTech reports sales of $1.7 billion, a
10-fold increase in three years, and profits of $430 million, a 12-fold
increase, as shown in the accompanying table.

This incredible performance wins you a $3 million cash bonus and
$7 million in stock options, distinction as the CEO of the year in your
industry, and an interview with Bob Koontz, who informs you that he
and the Benton board of directors have picked you to succeed him as
chairman and CEO within the next few years. The media hounds you
for interviews, and you appear on *Today, Sixty Minutes, The
MacNeil/Lehrer Newshour, 20/20,* and *Nightline.* The business press hails
you as one of the foremost architects of the learning organization and
a person with the management vision it will take to guide American

Selected Financial Information
(Dollars in Millions)

	Year ended September 30	
	This year	Three year earlier
Operations		
Net sales	$1711.1	$173.2
Cost of sales	538.7	63.0
R&D	178.1	17.2
Marketing	359.3	38.0
G&A	205.3	18.1
Operating profit	429.7	36.9
Financial position		
Current assets	510.5	93.6
Current liabilities	249.9	53.7
Working capital	260.6	39.9
Other assets	144.2	27.3
Property and equipment	198.6	84.9
Total assets	853.3	205.8
Other data		
Capital expenditures	112.5	8.3
Depreciation and amortization	21.0	8.9
Return on sales	25.1%	21.3%
Return on assets	50.4%	17.9%
Number of employees	3001	1133

business back to a position of dominance in the world. *Time, Newsweek, Fortune, Business Week, Forbes, People, Life,* and scores of other publications write feature-length and cover-story articles on how you and MedTech have reinvented American business.

As you look back, you realize that your idealistic vision, Peter Senge's and Stephen Covey's concepts, and Benton's three-year commitment made all the difference, but, then, so did the people of MedTech, who rose to the challenge to become more and do more than they dreamed possible. In the final analysis MedTech accomplished what David Kearns and David Nadler described would happen at the end of *Prophets in the Dark:* "The 1980s witnessed the financial restructuring of much of corporate America. If we are to succeed, the 1990s will need to witness the strategic, managerial, and organizational restructuring of our firms, and the development of new architectures for the enterprise. That's our challenge."

Congratulations! You met the challenge facing American business with an unwavering vision that has produced a great success for you, MedTech, and Benton Pharmaceuticals. Now you can apply your strategic thinking to new challenges by selecting one or more of the options below.

If you want to compare how the results of your last five years of strategic decision making stack up against the other positive outcomes in The Strategy Game, turn to Chapter 68.

If you desire a look at the outcome of the liberation-management paradigm choice, turn to Chapter 26.

If you want to consider the outcomes of other choices you could have made on this track, turn to Chapter 16 or Chapter 9.

If you would like to apply your strategic thinking to a new decision-making track, turn to Chapter 5.

28
Seeking the Baldrige

You immediately spend a couple of hours with Ed Yates, vice president of continuous improvement, to obtain his support for an all-out effort to apply for and win the Malcolm Baldrige National Quality Award next year. Yates commits to the project enthusiastically and promises to marshal all the necessary people and resources behind it.

After garnering the full support of your management team, you assign Yates the job of assembling a Baldrige task force, which will include representatives from all of MedTech's major functions. You also hire the consulting group that helped Motorola recently apply for and win the Baldrige prize.

Having already laid the necessary groundwork, you discuss your plans with Benton executives, who also promise their support. Although your own group president, Mitch Cavanaugh, expresses mild concern that this undertaking could turn into a costly distraction at a time when Benton needs strong earnings growth from each of its divisions, you push forward, making "Win the Baldrige" a rallying cry throughout the organization.

With help from experienced consultants, Yate's Baldrige task force identifies several major initiatives that MedTech must implement in seven different categories prior to completing the Baldrige application process later next year: leadership, information and analysis, strategic quality planning, human resource utilization, quality assurance of products and services, quality results, and customer satisfaction.

By March, MedTech sales have fallen off substantially as a worsening recession takes a big bite out of the capital and operating budgets that labs, hospitals, clinics, and doctors' offices had previously set aside for purchasing new blood analysis, collection, and monitoring instruments and supplies. Predictably, you begin receiving additional pressure from Benton to increase sales. Mitch Cavanaugh, your group president, keeps reminding you that the time-consuming Baldrige application process is distracting people from a focus on immediate business concerns, but you reassure him that the Baldrige application process will enhance MedTech's commitment to total quality and continuous improvement and thus help all employees better deal with problems brought on by the recession.

During the next several months, you devote most of your own attention to the Baldrige application process while your management team attends to the sales problem with, among other tactics, a discount program across all product lines. While customers respond favorably to the discount program, at least temporarily halting the sales decline, MedTech's profits predictably suffer. Informing Benton executives of MedTech's status, you argue that this year's reduced profit constitutes only a short-term setback, which will be offset long-term by a strong application for the Malcolm Baldrige Award that will provide great strength for the company in the years ahead. You know that group president Cavanaugh does not agree with your judgment and decision making, but you move forward, confident in your organization's course. To waiver now would compromise MedTech's future growth and development while offering little relief to the current profit squeeze.

At one point, Cavanaugh asks you to consider disbanding the task force, putting Ed Yates back to work on product improvement, and cutting all consulting fees in order to shore up profits for the last quarter of the year. Though you argue vehemently against such a course of action, Cavanaugh's concerns about your judgment and strategic decision making deepen. The rift becomes irreconcilable.

As the fiscal year comes to a close, MedTech submits its application for the Malcolm Baldrige Award, even though profits have temporarily declined 29 percent from the previous year to $45 million on a 13 percent sales increase to $283 million, as shown in the accompanying table.

Headquarters greets the numbers with a deafening silence, and Mitch Cavanaugh remains curiously quiet during the weeks following the close of the fiscal year, but you remain hopeful that winning the Baldrige will ultimately vindicate your decisions.

A few months later, when the judges announce the results of the Malcolm Baldrige National Quality Award, you are shocked to find out that MedTech received only 476 points out of a possible 1000. In a detailed report and subsequent conversation with members of the review committee, you discover that MedTech had received high marks for its many initiatives in each of the seven categories but had

Selected Financial Information
(Dollars in Millions)

| | Year ended September 30 | |
	This year	Last year
Operations		
Net sales	$283.2	$250.9
Cost of sales	104.1	85.3
R&D	30.6	23.2
Marketing	65.3	52.7
G&A	38.1	22.6
Operating profit	45.1	67.1
Financial position		
Current assets	95.6	84.1
Current liabilities	49.7	43.7
Working capital	45.9	40.3
Other assets	28.7	25.2
Property and equipment	80.4	81.0
Total assets	204.6	190.3
Other data		
Capital expenditures	13.0	10.4
Depreciation and amortization	11.6	12.1
Return on sales	15.9%	26.7%
Return on assets	22.0%	35.3%
Number of employees	1281	1212

lost points for not demonstrating sufficient evidence of the positive impact of those initiatives. Most of MedTech's penalty resulted from a recent modification in the Baldrige evaluation process to include an opinion poll of company employees aimed at detecting gaps between what the CEO of an applying organization says and believes, and what the employees actually see and live with every day. MedTech received a high rhetoric gap rating, exposing a serious discrepancy between activities and results. To your dismay, the majority of MedTech's employees express doubt that the company's recent initiatives for total quality and continuous improvement will last beyond the application period.

When word of the Baldrige evaluation results arrives at Benton headquarters, it takes little more than a week for your group president, Mitch Cavanaugh, to step into your office and ask for your resignation. In the real world, you'd be out of a job, but, happily, this book gives you another chance to go back to earlier strategic points and improve your choices.

If you want to go back to your most recent strategic decision, return to Chapter 18.

If you want to revisit an earlier strategic decision, return to Chapter 11 or Chapter 5.

If you're still feeling the sting of defeat and believe you could have made your last strategic choice work in real life, you may be right. After all, this is just a game. However, if you return to your last strategic decision (the first option above) and select the other alternative, you will learn why the author considers it a better choice.

29
Working Patiently
Toward
Transformation

As an action-oriented person, you naturally distrust theories and abstract concepts. But on the basis of your recent reading and experience, you recognize that the idea of patient perseverance has gained substantial acceptance as an accurate description of how total quality management actually gets implemented and how lasting organizational change really occurs. You still wonder, however, whether that approach doesn't sometimes mask a lot of risk taking and bold initiative. You find yourself searching for a metaphor that will somehow communicate to every single person within the MedTech organization that patient perseverance, not to be confused with halting hesitance, really works and can bring about a true total quality transformation. Quite by accident, you come across an article by Norm Smallwood and Lee Perry in the periodical *Executive Excellence* titled "Strategic Improvising," in which the authors use two metaphors for describing traditional and dynamic organizations: symphony orchestras and jazz bands. Traditional organizations, the article argues, operate like symphony orchestras that require a high degree of coordination between instruments to attain perfect harmony. In today's competitive world, however, situations change so rapidly that the symphony orchestra approach no longer works. The dynamic organization, the article points out, functions like a jazz band in which accomplished musicians play together harmoniously but improvise rather freely. A string melody line may give direction to the performance, but each individual musician can add inventive detail and texture to the music, thus taking control of the end product into their own hands. Symphony orchestra conductors rely on centralized direction and control, whereas jazz band leaders identify a melody line and then give freedom within that broad context to every individual.

You like that idea so much, you begin communicating it to everyone in the MedTech organization through memos, speeches, and meetings, encouraging every MedTech employee to become a jazz virtuoso.

You marvel as people quickly respond to the jazz metaphor by exhibiting a new feeling of empowerment and injecting their own personal creative contribution into MedTech's transformation toward a dynamic total quality organization.

As a worsening recession exerts more pressure for performance on MedTech and other Benton divisions, the improvisational style pays big dividends by allowing individual employees to create personalized visions of how they can invent new ways to increase sales and reduce costs despite customer budget cuts. A flurry of innovations emerge in the early months of the year as employees devise extended-pay programs, new leasing arrangements, expanded-rental policies, and new terms for purchasing to help customers and fuel sales. In addition, continuous-improvement efforts unfold in every one of MedTech's blood analysis, collection, and monitoring product lines as "jazz combos" produce a wide variety of cost reductions and quality improvements, ranging from new single-supplier contracts for blood analyzer components that immediately reduce costs and enhance quality, to a restructured manufacturing process that cuts the waste in MedTech's blood reagent manufacturing operation by 50 percent.

As a reward to Ed Yates, who has become a hero in the organization because of his strong advocacy of patient and persevering transformation into a total quality management company, you promote him to executive vice president and chief operating officer. You also receive word from Mitch Cavanaugh, your group president, that you should start preparing a successor for yourself because new responsibilities in the Benton organization will soon be coming your way. The news greatly boosts your confidence in your own strategic decision-making ability and further convinces you of the rightness of MedTech's current course.

By the end of the fiscal year, you have prevented MedTech from falling into the hole dug by the recession that has sucked in so many other Benton divisions. Revenues have reached $312 million, a 24 percent increase, and profits have hit $79 million, an 18 percent increase. MedTech shines as one of only five of Benton's over sixty divisions that has managed to remain above Benton's 15 percent growth expectations for the year, as shown in the accompanying table.

While you and your people take home slim bonuses for the year owing to the recession and Benton's attempt to bolster earnings, you have earned a bright future with the company and an almost assured

Selected Financial Information
(Dollars in Millions)

	Year ended September 30	
	This year	Last year
Operations		
Net sales	$312.4	$250.9
Cost of sales	106.2	85.3
R&D	30.2	23.2
Marketing	65.6	52.7
G&A	31.2	22.6
Operating profit	79.2	67.1
Financial position		
Current assets	104.7	84.1
Current liabilities	54.4	43.7
Working capital	50.2	40.3
Other assets	31.4	25.2
Property and equipment	80.4	81.0
Total assets	216.4	190.3
Other data		
Capital expenditures	13.0	10.4
Depreciation and amortization	11.6	12.1
Return on sales	25.4%	26.7%
Return on assets	36.6%	35.3%
Number of employees	1331	1212

promotion within the next three years. At the annual corporate conference of division presidents and senior Benton executives, you describe how MedTech's strategy evolved from an R&D focus to an emphasis on improving existing products and reducing costs, and then to a total quality management and continuous-improvement philosophy. As you describe the impact upon MedTech people of the simple, yet powerful jazz band metaphor, the other division presidents bombard you with questions that delay the next presentation for over two hours.

However, in the midst of all the congratulations for MedTech's impressive performance, both you and Ed Yates share a growing concern: a mounting demand from middle managers throughout MedTech for more specifics, structure, and systems to support the company's commitment to total quality management. Simply stated, middle managers want more tangible guidelines, more detailed instructions, and more specific training in order to become even more accomplished jazz musicians.

Together, you and Ed review the voluminous notes and materials on total quality and continuous improvement you had amassed 18 months earlier, and you update yourselves on new ideas and programs other companies are currently implementing around the country. After a few weeks of analysis and discussion you and Ed and your management team boil it all down to a choice between W. Edwards Deming's 14 points of management, best described in his book *Out of the Crisis*, and a modified Deming approach that would incorporate the ideas of Crosby, Juran, Feigenbaum, Ishikawa, Schonberger, and others. The advantage to a pure Deming approach lies in its proven track record—tried, tested, and heralded by many organizations as the best way to provide the discipline and specificity middle managers and frontline supervisors need to create environments for total quality and continuous improvement. On the other hand, the advantage of a modified Deming approach lies in the combination of many variations on Deming's theme that have bolstered such American companies as Motorola, Emerson, Xerox, Disney, General Electric, and AT&T. A modified Deming approach would allow you to tap the best of all approaches, while a strict Deming approach would give you a depth and consistency that a combination approach might lack. Once again, MedTech's future, as well as your own, rides on your decision. To stumble now, after making so much progress toward creating a genuine commitment to total quality and continuous improvement within MedTech, would be worse than never having come this far.

Some members of your management team advocate a modified Deming approach, but Ed Yates argues for following a pure Deming model. Ed was right last time, but is he right this time? If he's wrong, you need to help him broaden his thinking as a key step in his preparation for taking the reins at MedTech. If he's right, you don't want to stand in his way, especially since you and Benton executives expect a smooth succession.

You look forward to making this tough decision as you leave the office for a long weekend, confident that you'll make the right decision by Monday morning.

If you decide on a modified Deming approach, turn to Chapter 40.
If you opt for the pure Deming model, turn to Chapter 41.

30
Undertaking a Crash Course

Not wishing to incur any further delays, you announce at a Monday morning staff meeting that you have authorized a massive spending surge to develop, manufacture, and sell products on a crash basis. Your management team seems taken aback by your impulsiveness. While Kate DaVaeno and Ken Matsumori indicated they would support your decision, they now argue that such a course could create far too much chaos within the organization and actually impede MedTech's evolution into a time-based competitor.

For the next two hours you justify your decision and fiercely defend your strategic choice as the best way to proceed. By the end of the meeting, an emotional Ken Matsumori accuses you of impatience in a situation that demands prudence. Although you counter that impulsiveness epitomizes time-based competition, some members of your management team remain unconvinced. Heated discussion fills the next few days as your senior executives characterize your decision as everything from reckless and impulsive to responsive and brilliant. As you prepare for your next management meeting, you wonder whether you should reconsider, but you decide that any indecisiveness at this stage would seriously undermine your leadership. You simply must move forward on a crash course.

At your next meeting, you issue a challenge to your management team to develop and introduce a second, even less expensive, economy line of blood analyzers targeted at doctors' offices, as well as an economy line of reagents. You also challenge them to develop a new higher-end blood analyzer that can handle up to 200 blood samples at a time, a new line of blood vials, tubes, and containers, and at least one new diagnostic test for viruses. To accomplish these crash objectives, you promise that all projects will receive full funding so that results can be obtained within six months. You further insist that all performance appraisals within the organization stress individual and group responses to these challenges. While your challenge positively stimulates several members of your management team, Ken Matsumori confronts you again, questioning the wisdom of your program, at which point you calmly inform Ken that he may find himself happier working for another organization. At that, Ken storms out of the meeting.

A week later you issue your challenges to all employees at MedTech headquarters with a video presentation, copies of which you express to all 36 MedTech locations throughout the world. In the ensuing weeks, MedTech explodes in a burst of activity as the most action-oriented and competitive people within the organization rush forth with bold new ideas for achieving MedTech's new objectives, reducing manufacturing cycle times and expanding product varieties to satisfy newly identified customer needs. You take heart from this lightning response, and for the next 90 days you believe the crash-course experiment will really work.

However, as a number of promising projects move into prototype development and testing phases, chaos within the organization becomes a major impediment as too many product champions, too few supporters, and unresponsive systems force the company into a virtual gridlock. To overcome the confusion, you ask every employee to help define the new work methods needed to turn ideas into reality more quickly and to get the products demanded to market faster, but too many people charging down too many paths with insufficient coordination only exacerbate the problem.

During this period of rising frustrations, Kate DaVaeno decides to take a job with another division within Benton Pharmaceuticals after blasting your crash course to Mitch Cavanaugh, your group president. You carefully select replacements for DaVaeno and Matsumori, making sure you hire people willing to work within MedTech's crash-course environment, but, as the months wear on, you observe deepening frustration throughout the company. On the plus side, many employees are devising new work methods for getting new products to market more quickly, although progress is so painfully slow, you fear it may have come too late. The year ends with sales increasing only 12 percent to $254 million and profits declining to $58 million, a 9 percent decrease, as shown in the accompanying table.

Disappointment over what many now call your blatant recklessness spreads throughout the Benton Pharmaceuticals organization and some of your management team members predict that in the months ahead conditions will get worse. Thirty days later, your group president, Mitch Cavanaugh, asks for your resignation in return for a severance package worth $200,000. You accept the offer and resign a week before a vice president of The Boston Consulting Group who

Selected Financial Information
(Dollars in Millions)

| | Year ended September 30 | |
	This year	Last year
Operations		
Net sales	$254.0	$226.8
Cost of sales	86.6	73.4
R&D	22.7	21.1
Marketing	58.4	48.5
G&A	28.2	20.3
Operating profit	58.1	63.5
Financial position		
Current assets	85.2	75.1
Current liabilities	44.3	39.0
Working capital	40.9	36.0
Other assets	25.5	22.5
Property and equipment	79.7	81.4
Total assets	190.4	178.9
Other data		
Capital expenditures	12.0	10.7
Depreciation and amortization	11.6	12.1
Return on sales	22.9%	28.0%
Return on assets	30.5%	35.5%
Number of employees	1235	1173

had recently been working with companies in the pharmaceutical and medical products industries replaces you.

In the real world your decision-making days at MedTech would have ended here, but in this book you can try your hand again, if you'd like.

If you would like to revisit your most recent strategic decision, return to Chapter 19.

If you would rather go back and review an earlier strategic decision, return to Chapter 11 or Chapter 5.

If you're still feeling the sting of defeat and believe you could have made your last strategic choice work in real life, you may be right. After all, this is just a game. However, if you return to your last strategic decision (the first option above) and select the other alternative, you will learn why the author considers it a better choice.

31

Changing the Structure of Work

Some rather strong concerns expressed by a few members of your top management team convince you to check your initial urge to pursue a crash course. The structural approach, you conclude, offers the best and longest-lasting alternative for creating a time-sensitive environment.

Under the tutelage of your friend at The Boston Consulting Group, you learn about two core concepts upon which an organization must base the rethinking and restructuring of its work: main sequence and continuous flow. The main sequence includes all organizational activities that directly add value for customers in real time; everything else you categorize as a support or off-line activity. Time-based companies must identify direct value-adding activities and then organize those activities into a clear, consistent sequence separate from support functions. Once you isolate the main sequence, you can concentrate on orchestrating the continuous flow of work through the main sequence to reduce cycle times in R&D, manufacturing, marketing, sales, distribution, and service.

To install these concepts at MedTech, you formally engage a consulting team from The Boston Consulting Group to guide development and implementation of a major work-restructuring plan aimed at reducing cycle times, increasing responsiveness, cutting costs, improving quality, and gaining greater customer loyalty. Imbuing your management team with your own sense of expediency, you ask each of them to work closely with the consulting team. They do so with much enthusiasm. Soon an inevitable battle cry of time-based competition gets the whole organization fired up over a new vision of work.

It takes a full eight months to sort out all the details involved in designing new work structures for MedTech, but the results quickly prove astonishing. In the manufacturing area, shortened production runs triple the variety of blood analysis, collection, and monitoring products offered a year ago, causing customers to increase their orders dramatically over last year.

Buyers in doctors' offices, who always desire different combinations of blood collection bags, tubes, and vials, love the fact that MedTech can now deliver their ideal orders. Clinics rejoice that orders for blood reagents and other control materials for diagnostic tests can now arrive overnight in any quantity desired, and hospitals delight in MedTech's wider variety of blood analyzers. Clearly, your company's new work structure, which emphasizes adding value for customers over products or processes, has made it possible to satisfy more customers' needs more often. You've made time your strongest ally.

At the same time, coordination between R&D and manufacturing reaches new levels as people in both functions find new ways to interact with and respond to customers. This enables MedTech to develop five different versions of the economy line of blood analyzers, each of which fulfills unique customer needs. As the company moves from its old habit of central scheduling to a new one of local scheduling, employees begin making more decisions on the factory floor, further increasing MedTech's responsiveness to customers.

At the point of customer contact, MedTech salespeople easily increase orders by 25 to 30 percent because of the rapid delivery of the right mix of reagents, collection gear, monitoring devices, and blood analyzers to their customers. Reports from customers indicate that your competitors are suggesting that MedTech has compromised quality to meet unrealistic delivery schedules, but your own analysis proves that quality has actually increased during MedTech's work-restructuring program.

By the end of the fiscal year, even in light of the eight-month work-restructuring program and despite a deepening global recession, MedTech sales increase by 39 percent to $315 million, with profits rising by almost 50 percent to $95 million, as shown in the accompanying table.

MedTech's dramatic success with its work-restructuring program prompts a number of other Benton division presidents to come to you for advice on how they, too, can create strategies for time-based competition. Within a few weeks, the Boston Consulting Group enters into consulting arrangements with more than a dozen Benton divisions, and Bob Koontz, Benton's CEO, asks you to chair a corporatewide

Selected Financial Information
(Dollars in Millions)

	Year ended September 30	
	This year	Last year
Operations		
Net sales	$315.2	$226.8
Cost of sales	88.0	73.4
R&D	32.1	21.1
Marketing	69.5	48.5
G&A	31.0	20.3
Operating profit	94.6	63.5
Financial position		
Current assets	100.8	75.1
Current liabilities	52.4	39.0
Working capital	48.4	36.0
Other assets	30.2	22.5
Property and equipment	82.6	81.4
Total assets	213.6	178.9
Other data		
Capital expenditures	14.9	10.7
Depreciation and amortization	11.6	12.1
Return on sales	30.0%	28.0%
Return on assets	44.3%	35.5%
Number of employees	1337	1173

steering committee for implementing time-based competition, a prelude, he hints, to bigger and better things for you at Benton.

Two weeks later you receive a tempting offer to join The Boston Consulting Group as a senior vice president at double your current salary and with a lucrative ownership incentive, but you turn down the offer because you so thoroughly enjoy your current situation. When senior executives at Benton find out about the offer from The Boston Consulting Group, you receive a 75 percent increase in your salary, from $200,000 to $350,000, making you the highest-paid division president in the organization's history.

Knowing that, in business, you're only as good as last year's triumph, you quickly come down out of the clouds to face another tough decision. With MedTech's basic work flow restructured, you must decide how to handle the company's growing organizational needs. To incorporate MedTech's new work methods and accommodate the recent growth, should you reorganize the company from the top down, or should you let reorganization emerge from within the heart of the company?

You find that your management team splits evenly on the issue of whether to force a reorganization or to let the reorganization evolve at its own pace. Ed Yates, vice president of production, and Susan Carter, vice president of human resources, most clearly articulate the two opposing views. Yates favors taking a strong initiative because he believes senior management must impose a definitive structure upon MedTech that can integrate all of the gains the company has won with the new work methods. People, he says, need clarity, tight organization, and a strong institutionalization of the new work flow. While Yates acknowledges MedTech's progress, he feels uneasy that nothing seems tied down or finished, a situation that could eventually hurt the organization. "I will be the first to admit," he concludes, "that moving away from traditional management methods has worked brilliantly here, but now it's time to take everything we've learned and put it into a well-conceived organizational structure everyone understands."

In opposition to Yates' view, Susan Carter points out that people at all levels in the organization have taken responsibility upon themselves to do whatever it takes to reduce cycle time and better meet customer needs, creating an organizational flexibility that could easily disappear if management tries to impose too rigid a structure on it. Susan argues, "We must continue motivating our people to remain time-based competitors by emphasizing responsiveness to customers and flexibility of work approaches, even if that means perpetually redefining the main sequence of work within MedTech. The last thing we should do is dictate a reorganization from the top."

Rather heated discussions among the management team convince you that this will not be an easy decision. A mistake here could jeopardize all the progress MedTech has made during the past year. Even your friend at The Boston Consulting Group admits that she is still undecided on this issue herself because it represents new ground for many time-based competitors. Some of her clients have moved to institutionalize their new time-based work structures, while others have kept their organizations as open and flexible as possible. "Where does the optimum solution lie?" she asks. "I honestly don't know."

Now you must decide.

If you favor letting the reorganization emerge naturally, turn to Chapter 42.

If you believe in taking the initiative to reorganize, turn to Chapter 43.

32
Creating Value

In your heart you know that nothing drives a business more than creating value for the customer. Given that fact you and your senior management team, Kate DaVaeno, president of the Small-Scale-Provider division, Amos Gill, president of the Large-Scale-Provider division, Cam Cardon, senior vice president of marketing strategy, and Ken Matsumori, senior vice president of management information, confer to establish creating value as the guiding theme for MedTech's micromarketing strategy. Drawing from Michael Porter's concept of value-chain analysis, described in his book *Competitive Advantage,* you convince your senior executives that MedTech must develop a systematic way of examining all activities within the company to identify and analyze the ways in which they create value for customers and contribute to competitive advantage. This value-chain approach will, the four of you believe, keep the company ahead of the pack.

Based on Pamela West's recommendation that you hire another outside consultant to guide MedTech's value-chain analysis you retain the services of Mary Updike from Monitor, a consulting firm built upon the conceptual frameworks and principles espoused in Michael Porter's work. She will help you manage the expectations of your senior management team by making it clear that the process of value-chain analysis will take most of the year to complete. In a management meeting you stress that during the analysis MedTech must continue to capitalize on the micromarketing gains achieved last year, exploiting them to the fullest possible extent, thereby buying the company the necessary time to prepare for longer-term competitive positioning based on a clear understanding of the real value of MedTech's products and services to its customers. Happily, Mary Updike relates well to members of the senior team and to managers in both of MedTech's divisions, and you marvel as she unthreateningly takes charge of the value-chain analysis, showing your senior team how to methodically scrutinize MedTech's own value chain as well as those of suppliers, distributors, and buyers.

As this year of analysis creeps along, the most demanding responsibility for you and your senior team revolves around identifying the technologically and strategically distinct "value activities" within MedTech. Everyone in both of MedTech's divisions works hard to avoid thinking about the company the old way, as Mary makes it clear that new, fresh thinking—looking at MedTech with a new set of eyes—must drive this process forward. Using Porter's conceptual framework, Mary guides the analysis through each of the division's primary value activities: (1) inbound logistics; (2) operations; (3) outbound logistics; (4) marketing, sales, and service; (5) support activities such as procurement, technology development, and human resource management; and (6) firm infrastructure. The analysis differentiates between direct activities that involve creating value for the buyer, indirect activities that make it possible for the direct activities to occur, and quality assurance activities that ensure that both direct and indirect activities center on quality.

After six months of intense analysis, carefully balanced with a continuing emphasis on current sales and profitability, Mary Updike and your senior management team have identified and evaluated 53 different value activities within the value chains of MedTech's two divisions. To your delight, you now find it very easy to identify which specific activities within the value chains offer cost or differentiation advantages. You also begin to understand your customers' value chains better than ever, zeroing in on exactly how and why MedTech's products or services create value for your customers.

During the second half of the year everyone in the entire MedTech organization continues analyzing the information, absorbing it, communicating it, and using it to reorient the way they think about business. As you watch the concept take hold throughout both divisions, you become more convinced than ever that this effort will affect the growth and particularly the profitability of MedTech for decades to come. Never before have you understood the economic logic of a business as well as you now understand MedTech, thanks to the help of Michael Porter, Mary Updike, a committed senior management team, and two adaptive division cultures.

By the end of the year, you have proved your ability to undertake a major analytical project affecting the entire organization and at the same time increase sales and profits. MedTech reports a 41 percent increase in sales for the year to $317 million and a 66 percent increase in profits to $82 million, as shown in the accompanying table.

Selected Financial Information
(Dollars in Millions)

| | Year ended September 30 | |
	This year	Last year
Operations		
Net sales	$316.8	$224.7
Cost of sales	107.1	76.4
R&D	30.6	17.9
Marketing	63.4	58.9
G&A	34.7	22.0
Operating profit	82.0	49.5
Financial position		
Current assets	104.7	75.3
Current liabilities	54.4	39.1
Working capital	50.2	36.1
Other assets	31.4	22.6
Property and equipment	81.2	92.7
Total assets	217.2	190.6
Other data		
Capital expenditures	14.1	15.6
Depreciation and amortization	11.5	13.0
Return on sales	25.9%	22.0%
Return on assets	37.8%	26.0%
Number of employees	1340	1150

Now that MedTech has exploited its previous micromarketing gains to the maximum, it must marshal its new understanding of creating value behind new growth initiatives. With the value-chain analysis complete, you can now see that MedTech's market-niche managers are vacillating between creating cost-based and differentiation-based value. Luckily, vacillating between the two has not caused severe problems at this point because the industry has grown so rapidly. However, in the midst of a major recession, which could damage MedTech's momentum the coming year, and in the light of increased competition, you know MedTech must now settle on one or the other of these generic approaches for creating value.

Right now, MedTech's two divisions have fairly well mastered an equal number of value activities in both cost advantage and differentiation advantage across all their more than 80 different market niches, so choosing one or the other for primary emphasis poses a genuine dilemma. You firmly believe Michael Porter's dogma: "While stuck-in-the-middle competitors can allow a firm to achieve both differentiation and low cost, this state of affairs is often temporary. Eventually a competitor will choose a generic strategy and begin to implement it well, exposing the tradeoffs between cost and differentiation. Thus a firm must choose the type of competitive advantage it intends to preserve in the long run. The danger in facing weak competitors is that a firm will begin to compromise its cost position or differentiation to achieve both and leave itself vulnerable to the emergence of a capable competitor."

Therefore, rather than depend on facing stuck-in-the-middle competitors or risk getting stuck-in-the-middle yourself, you conclude that one or the other must become dominant this coming year. You briefly consider whether each division should pursue a different path, but you immediately realize that such a course would demand total separation of the two divisions into autonomous companies, something you do not want, at least not in this time of economic recession.

After weighing which advantage to pursue in both divisions and across all niches, you realize that each carries potential risks. If you pursue the cost advantage, competitors can imitate you or target subniches where they can achieve lower costs; evolving technology can change the whole cost picture at any time. By the same token, if you pursue the differentiation advantage, competitors can imitate the advantage or focus on a subniche that offers greater differentiation; any differentiation selected by MedTech can become less important to customers over time.

While Mary Updike and Cam Cardon urge you to pursue the differentiation advantage, Kate DaVaeno, Amos Gill, and Ken Matsumori favor the cost advantage. Their differing views make this decision even more difficult for you. What will you do?

If you choose to pursue the differentiation advantage, turn to Chapter 44.

If you prefer the cost advantage, turn to Chapter 45.

33
Avoiding Head-On Competition

After again reading Sun-Tsu's *The Art of War*, a 2500-year-old treatise on strategy, you conclude that the Chinese general's ideas make a lot of sense in the modern world of dog-eat-dog competitive warfare. According to Sun-Tsu, "To fight and conquer in all your battles is not supreme excellence; supreme excellence is breaking the enemy's resistance without fighting." These words convince you, beyond the shadow of a doubt, that the age-old rules of warfare apply perfectly to competitive business interaction. MedTech will, you decide, avoid head-on competition at all possible costs. Aware, however, that battlefield metaphors offend many people, you weave several recent business articles and books into a short essay supporting the theory that avoidance of head-on competition represents a wise strategic position. This six-page document, which you title "The Art of Business," will provide MedTech managers with both a philosophy and an agenda for the future.

After giving your senior management team time to read your essay, you explain how avoiding head-on competition simply means targeting niches that competitors have overlooked or neglected, thus allowing MedTech to claim and dominate those niches without having to battle competitors for them. Further, you advise, "This approach actually benefits our customers, who have an increasingly wider variety of needs and exhibit a growing frustration with suppliers who drive up prices through wasteful head-on competition." Gill, DaVaeno, Cardon, and Matsumori agree and pledge their help in preparing a presentation of the new philosophy to MedTech's market-niche managers.

Drawing on the philosophy of The Boston Consulting Group's founder, Bruce Henderson, McKinsey & Company's gameboard concept for competitive interaction, the books of Al Ries and Jack Trout,

Positioning and *Marketing Warfare*, and stacks of micromarketing literature that preach "niche or be niched," you and your senior management team assemble a convincing case for avoiding head-on competition as MedTech's guiding theme in years to come. During a special meeting with MedTech's senior executives, management teams from both divisions, and more than 40 market-niche managers, you lay out the rationale behind the new theme. Then marketing strategy senior vice president Cam Cardon introduces a new strategic planning process that requires all niche business plans to include avoiding head-on competition as a key component. The market-niche managers respond enthusiastically to the presentation and express eagerness over incorporating the new theme into all their micromarketing efforts.

As the year unfolds, MedTech market-niche managers find a wealth of opportunities where competitors have neglected, overlooked, or underestimated customer needs in certain niches. In one case, a niche manager discovers that research laboratories conducting extensive blood testing and analysis rely heavily on computer graphics to report results, but no competitors have paid full attention to this need and have therefore left laboratories underserved in this regard. In response to this underserved need, MedTech's software engineers work with market-niche managers to design a computer graphics package that allows research laboratories to provide far superior reports to their customers. As a result, MedTech quickly becomes the dominant player in the blood analysis–computer graphics game, capturing many new research laboratories as customers.

In another case, MedTech market-niche managers determine that competitors have ignored the need for a less expensive method of continually monitoring blood clotting in patients after surgery. MedTech scientists and engineers, identifying this as a niche the company could own, work feverishly to design a small blood-clotting management device that a patient can take home after surgery to monitor and guide the dosage of various medications and therapies required during recovery, without the aid of a nurse or physician.

In yet another case, a market-niche manager identifies rural health-care facilities with their sporadic need for blood reagents as a niche the company could dominate by simply adding extra services such as quick delivery of small orders. When combined with the lower-end, economical blood analyzers, these services quickly allow MedTech to serve and dominate a market niche that had previously been serviced by medical jobbers, wholesalers, and intermediaries, who usually failed to provide the superior and timely service now provided by MedTech.

With these and other stories of success spreading throughout the

MedTech organization, further fueling the commitment to find new ways to avoid head-on competition and better meet the needs of a growing number of niches, MedTech's sales soar to $345 million, a 54 percent increase, and profits jump to $86 million, a whopping 74 percent increase, as shown in the accompanying table.

Selected Financial Information
(Dollars in Millions)

	Year ended September 30	
	This year	Last year
Operations		
Net sales	$345.1	$224.7
Cost of sales	110.4	76.4
R&D	27.6	17.9
Marketing	82.9	58.9
G&A	37.9	22.0
Operating profit	86.3	49.5
Financial position		
Current assets	113.9	75.3
Current liabilities	59.2	39.1
Working capital	54.7	36.1
Other assets	34.2	22.6
Property and equipment	99.9	92.7
Total assets	247.9	190.6
Other data		
Capital expenditures	24.0	15.6
Depreciation and amortization	13.0	13.0
Return on sales	25.0%	22.0%
Return on assets	34.8%	26.0%
Number of employees	1351	1150

Of course, Benton executives love these numbers and lavish you with bonuses and assurances of promotion. An editorial writer from *The Chicago Tribune,* intrigued by your interest in ancient Chinese military strategies, writes a feature article for the Sunday business section in which she nicknames you "Son of Sun-Tsu." Although you relish the praise and recognition, all this increased visibility alerts your competitors to your strategy. With all this notoriety, how long can MedTech continue to avoid head-on competition? Almost overnight, competitors go on the offensive, attempting to duplicate MedTech's moves in the marketplace and thereby capture business in the newly identified niches.

While you do not regret choosing and communicating the theme of avoiding head-on competition to focus all of MedTech's micromarketing efforts, you now recognize the need to stay ahead of your increasingly savvy competition by identifying new ways to avoid head-on battles. Figuring out just how to do that leads you to your next strategic choice: Should MedTech avoid head-on competition by continuing to rely on its relative superiority in identifying and serving neglected market niches or by creating fundamentally new approaches to doing business? In other words, should MedTech play the same game it's been playing in the marketplace, avoiding head-on competition by carefully managing its relative superiority in targeted niches, or should it play a new game, radically changing how it avoids head-on competition?

The advantage of playing the same game, continually redefining market niches in accordance with company strengths and competitor positions, lies in the fact that the company already knows how to play that game and can thus employ its resources behind it most efficiently. The disadvantage lies in the fact that knowledgeable competitors can overtake or duplicate MedTech's superiority in a specific market niche with relative ease. Consequently, such a course of action would require MedTech to become even more vigilant in identifying new market niches and new applications of its strengths vis-à-vis its competitors.

On the other hand, creating a fundamentally new approach to doing business could propel MedTech years, rather than months, ahead of the competition. Under such a scenario you avoid head-on competition by playing with a set of rules so fundamentally different from the old rules that it will take competitors a long time to duplicate or overtake your position. The disadvantage of such a course comes from its higher risk and the greater resources required to implement it.

A deepening recession that caused little disruption in the past six months at MedTech could make competitors extremely anxious to duplicate MedTech's successful "competition avoidance strategy" in the coming year, so you must waste no time in making up your mind.

If you choose to pursue a new game strategy and invent fundamentally new approaches to doing business, turn to Chapter 46.

If you favor a same-game strategy, continuing to exploit MedTech's relative superiority and its competitors' relative weaknesses, turn to Chapter 47.

34
Monitoring Customer Expectations

While you still believe that identifying unmet customer needs and finding unique product solutions will propel MedTech forward, you conclude that monitoring customer expectations will fuel that engine. The metaphor of "fueling the engine" inspires your management team who all seem anxious to carry out your latest strategic decision.

As the first crucial step, you ask Bob Shay, your vice president of sales, to develop a comprehensive system to monitor customer expectations. Immediately Shay dives into the assignment, enlisting the help of every member of the senior team, as well as several middle managers and first-line supervisors to define how to develop a sort of customer expectations fuel gauge the whole organization can use. Over the next three months, Shay puts in 14-hour days because he must not only develop his system but also increase sales of the new virus identification testing package MedTech introduced last year. Nonetheless, he pushes forward and, together with other members of the management team, presents his ideas at a two-day retreat. At the outset he defines "cardinal sin" as the belief that there's nothing more to learn from customers. "Cardinal virtue" is defined as the attitude that you cannot pay too much attention to customers' ideas, opinions, and feelings. Drawing on the ongoing work of *Service America* authors Ron Zemke and Carl Albrect, Shay and the management team recommend eight practices to ensure superior monitoring of customer expectations: face-to-face communication, formal research, frontline contact, customer hot lines, complete customer comment analysis, consumer advisory panels, mutual education sessions, and competitor intelligence.

Delighted with these concrete recommendations, you ask your management team to implement the eight practices throughout the organization. What occurs in the next few months surprises even you, as customers enthusiastically respond to the way MedTech listens to their concerns, opinions, ideas, and expectations regarding needs and services. You not only keep your old customers, you acquire a flood of new ones anxious to buy MedTech's virus identification tests and other blood analysis, collection, and monitoring products.

As a result of the new monitoring practices, MedTech introduces a second package of virus identification tests that pinpoint the existence of a half dozen viruses not identified in the first package. This second package attracts even more new customers, who not only buy this product but also other blood analysis, collection, and monitoring products. At a time when many competitors are suffering from a deepening recession, MedTech seems to have immunized itself from the effects of the weak economy, and by fiscal year's end, the company reports 40 percent increases in both sales and profits to $221 million and $53 million, respectively, as shown in the accompanying table.

Although Benton executives applaud your performance, they seem somewhat skeptical, as if they're still waiting for the big payoff from

Selected Financial Information
(Dollars in Millions)

	Year ended September 30	
	This year	Last year
Operations		
Net sales	$221.4	$160.2
Cost of sales	75.2	56.0
R&D	17.7	12.8
Marketing	52.4	37.3
G&A	23.0	16.8
Operating profit	53.1	37.3
Financial position		
Current assets	74.2	54.1
Current liabilities	38.6	28.1
Working capital	35.6	25.9
Other assets	22.2	16.2
Property and equipment	75.5	78.2
Total assets	171.9	148.5
Other data		
Capital expenditures	10.5	7.6
Depreciation and amortization	11.2	12.1
Return on sales	24.0%	23.3%
Return on assets	30.9%	25.1%
Number of employees	1141	1003

your new core services strategy. In fact, Mitch Cavanaugh, your group president, tells you he thinks you struck it lucky with the virus identification testing packages. "Can you," he asks, "follow up with even stronger results next year, when the real gauge of MedTech's new strategy will come?" You guarantee that you can and will.

To deliver on that promise, you must ensure that the newly acquired customers find no reason to go elsewhere, and that means further internalizing and institutionalizing MedTech's core services strategy and its newly implemented customer expectations monitoring practices. Now, it's time to increase employee commitment.

Scouring the literature, you confirm two basic approaches to increasing commitment and solidifying MedTech's uniquely focused core services strategy and culture: either fine-tune the company's "infrastructure and design" (systems, practices, structures, processes, etc.), or focus on "people and leadership." MedTech's need for concrete standards of "superior service" in the core service areas and measurement mechanisms to guard against merely "acceptable service" argues for creating an infrastructure that will establish reward and recognition systems, increase employee involvement, and renovate physical facilities all geared to supporting MedTech's core services and customer-monitoring thrusts. On the other hand, MedTech's need for a clear vision of "best in world" core services and customer monitoring argues for focusing on people and leadership. Hiring, training, and developing the right kind of people who can really deliver superior service in the core areas also argues the latter focus. It all boils down, once again, to which variable should drive the other.

Because of your penchant to maintain harmony with your management team, you openly discuss the issues with them, but they again defer to your judgment. However, this time you ask them to gather input from middle managers and first-line supervisors throughout the company. What comes back frustrates you because the feedback almost equally supports both the infrastructure and design side as well as the people and leadership side of the equation. You resist the temptation to implement both because the principle of focus and sequencing has served you so well in the past. Unable to reach a decision in your office, where the usual interruptions make it so hard to think clearly, you leave early to wrestle with the dilemma at the health club.

If you choose to focus on infrastructure and design, turn to Chapter 48.

If you prefer to emphasize people and leadership, turn to Chapter 49.

35
Building Employee Commitment

Drawing ideas from the book *Commitment: The Dynamic of Strategy*, by Pankaj Ghemawat, a former McKinsey & Company consultant and current professor of business administration at the Harvard Business School, you tell your management team that commitment—above and beyond all other generic strategies regarding market entry or exit, vertical or horizontal integration, product expansion or innovation—determines the difference between winners and losers in the marketplace. According to Ghemawat, and you believe him, commitment, which perpetuates a persistent purpose in an organization, offers the most accurate measure of differences in performance among companies over time. MedTech's recent focus on a narrow scope of core services represents what Ghemawat calls *commitment intensive choices* that lock you into a track, lock competitors out, make the lag factor an advantage, and capitalize on inertia. "We have made some important strategic choices at MedTech," you conclude, "but now, we must strengthen our commitment to 'best in world' performance in our selected core services and then motivate everyone in the company to do the same."

Over the next several months, you throw yourself into the task of making commitment the key to MedTech's future, urging every employee you encounter in more than 40 MedTech offices and facilities around the world to commit 110 percent to the core services: identifying unmet customer needs and finding unique product solutions in the blood analysis, collection, and monitoring market.

By midyear, sales show a small decline from last year-to-date figures; however, you inform your management team and employees that Benton executives have promised to give MedTech the necessary time to build a high-commitment environment and gain competitive prominence in its core services. Your constant encouragement and commitment aimed at identifying unmet needs and finding unique solutions finally pay off as two new product solutions, engineered through arrangements with a small U.S. computer graphics firm and a well-positioned European distributor, provide enhanced visual displays of blood test results and boost worldwide sales in the third quarter.

Unfortunately, Mitch Cavanaugh, your group president, doesn't share your optimism and expresses his concern that too much focus on commitment can actually create a false sense of well-being within an organization. Offended by his criticism, you argue heatedly that commitment offers the only general explanation for sustained differences in performance among organizations. "Don't pull the plug on us now," you plead. "We're just about to turn the corner." Cavanaugh listens to your plea, but withholds his full support and cautions you to not get too philosophical or theoretical about what accounts for business success. In parting, he says, "The problem with all these academic strategists is that they try to identify the single overriding factor that leads to business success, but what they never come to grips with, in practical terms, is that business success depends on a hundred variables you must control or overcome. You have convinced me that you made the right decision to focus on a narrow scope of core services, but this recession is putting a lot of pressure on all of us for results, and I'm not sure you're going to get them if you fool yourself into believing commitment is the only answer."

Cavanaugh's words sting, and as you reflect on your recent experience with Benton executives, who discouraged you from focusing on service, you pride yourself in having stuck to your guns because it worked. Eventually, you convince yourself that you must continue harping on commitment to "best in world" core services because you really do believe it will make the biggest long-term difference.

In succeeding months, a spirit of commitment spreads like wildfire throughout the MedTech organization as your management team and middle managers spend a lot of time explaining the role commitment plays in building "best in world" competence at identifying hidden customer needs and satisfying them with unprecedented product solutions. At the end of the fiscal year, MedTech reports sales of $156 million, a decline of 3 percent over the previous year, and profits of $34 million, a decline of 8 percent, as shown in the accompanying table.

Not surprisingly, it doesn't take long for Mitch Cavanaugh to invite

Selected Financial Information
(Dollars in Millions)

	Year ended September 30	
	This year	Last year
Operations		
Net sales	$156.2	$160.2
Cost of sales	53.5	56.0
R&D	11.1	12.8
Marketing	35.0	37.3
G&A	22.7	16.8
Operating profit	33.9	37.3
Financial position		
Current assets	54.1	54.1
Current liabilities	28.1	28.1
Working capital	25.9	25.9
Other assets	16.2	16.2
Property and equipment	80.6	78.2
Total assets	150.8	148.5
Other data		
Capital expenditures	9.9	7.6
Depreciation and amortization	12.1	12.1
Return on sales	21.7%	23.3%
Return on assets	22.5%	25.1%
Number of employees	1020	1003

you to his office for a meeting. You arrive the night before, and, after a sleepless night, you enter Cavanaugh's office first thing in the morning. You're amazed to see a copy of Ghemawat's book on Cavanaugh's desk. As you sit down, he reiterates his earlier caution that academic strategists are only interested in conceptual generalizations that have little to do with the real world. He then picks up Ghemawat's book on commitment, shakes it, and says, "Because of this book you have ignored some important factors critical to MedTech's success, and, as a result, sales have declined at a time when they should have been increasing." Cavanaugh then reminds you that Benton has recently combined two divisions in the Medical Products and Systems Group, leaving Claude Randall, president of one of the divisions, without a job. You feel tension spreading from your head to your toes as Cavanaugh informs you that Randall will become the new president of MedTech, effective immediately. He explains that you can remain at MedTech as executive vice president and that, in fact, both he and Randall want you to stay. Stunned, you hardly hear him say, "I really think you can learn a lot from Randall, and, of course, vice versa. Think about it, and let me know your decision by Friday."

You leave Cavanaugh's office, deeply discouraged that you won't be guiding MedTech into the future, but you decide to stay with the company for the time being. In the following weeks, Claude Randall quickly reverses your focus on commitment and installs a sophisticated program to monitor customer expectations, designed to support and sustain MedTech's core services of identifying unmet customer needs and finding unique product solutions. Randall reassures you that your help and support is vital to the company's success, but you're not sure you can continue playing second fiddle in an organization you once led with enthusiasm and pride.

In real life, you would have to decide whether to remain on as executive vice president of MedTech or look for another job, but in this book you can go back and try to correct any mistakes you made.

If you wish to rethink your latest strategic decision, return to Chapter 22.

If you prefer to go back to an earlier strategic decision, return to Chapter 15 or Chapter 7.

If you're still feeling the sting of defeat and believe you could have made your last strategic choice work in real life, you may be right. After all, this is just a game. However, if you return to your last strategic decision (the first option above) and select the other alternative, you will learn why the author considers it a better choice.

36
Initiating Aggressive Global Expansion

After securing the necessary approvals from Benton for your strategic decision, you promote Meg Daniels to senior vice president and solidify your core team composed of Gill, Matsumori, Suhler, and Daniels to help you mastermind and implement MedTech's global expansion. Immediately the team begins mapping out a global acquisition strategy, paying particular attention to the differences between domestic and global deal making, namely, foreign negotiating environments, cultures, ideologies, bureaucracies and organizations, laws and government, currencies, and social and political instability. Despite the greater complexity that surrounds global deals, you feel that developing a network of competitive entities with technological advantages and distribution channels throughout the world will reap enormous dividends for MedTech.

The rapid growth of the entire health-care and medical industry coupled with a deepening recession make the timing of MedTech's global strategy all the more advantageous. Many companies throughout the world with genuine breakthroughs are failing to develop, produce, introduce, or market those breakthrough products to their full potential because of lack of capital. Your vision for MedTech takes further shape through a series of intense, offsite strategy sessions with your core team.

You agree that, depending on a host of variables, acquired companies must play their own unique roles in the different countries but still crank out new products and function within the framework of MedTech's overall emphasis on R&D. To create that overarching strategy, you use a global expansion model developed by Harvard and

INSEAD business school professors Christopher Bartlett and Sumantra Ghoshal, which identifies four basic types of national subsidiaries the global company encounters:

1. *The strategic leader,* a highly competent national subsidiary located in a strategically important market, becomes a partner with corporate headquarters in developing and implementing strategy.

2. *The contributor,* a national subsidiary operating in a small and strategically unimportant market, offers a distinctive capability that the rest of the organization can use.

3. *The implementer,* a national subsidiary in a less strategically important market, maintains enough competence to serve the local market.

4. *Black holes,* national subsidiaries with strategically nonviable positions, offer no opportunities to the global corporation.

Your core team agrees to look for *strategic leaders* in Western Europe, Australia, and Israel; *contributors* in Japan, India, and Eastern Europe; and *implementers* in Latin and South America, Russia, Africa, and the less-developed portions of Asia. Of course, you will avoid black holes like the plague.

Over the next several months, with the help of Merrill Lynch, Morgan Stanley, Salomon Brothers, and a number of smaller international investment banking firms, you acquire nine companies and enter into four strategic partnerships. Of the thirteen deals, you classify five as strategic leaders, two as contributors, and six as implementers. You hope none of them turn into black holes. Two of the strategic leaders, both Israeli companies, manufacture inexpensive, but extremely accurate, blood testing kits. The other three strategic leaders, located in France and Germany, manufacture instruments and devices that greatly broaden MedTech's range of blood analysis, collection, and monitoring products. The contributors include an innovative plastics manufacturer in Czechoslovakia and two medical software developers in India and Japan. The six implementers comprise manufacturing, marketing, and distribution companies in Malaysia, Brazil, Mexico, Russia, and Egypt.

The recession takes its toll on Benton Pharmaceuticals, but MedTech's acquisition strategy produces one of the corporation's few bright spots for the year with sales of $510 million, an increase of 52 percent over the previous year, and operating profits of $124 million, a 48 percent increase, as shown in the accompanying table.

Selected Financial Information
(Dollars in Millions)

	Year ended September 30	
	This year	Last year
Operations		
Net sales	$510.7	$336.0
Cost of sales	172.1	116.1
R&D	56.0	36.2
Marketing	97.0	65.9
G&A	61.3	33.8
Operating profit	124.3	84.0
Financial position		
Current assets	170.7	113.0
Current liabilities	88.8	58.8
Working capital	81.9	54.3
Other assets	51.2	33.9
Property and equipment	97.4	92.1
Total assets	319.3	239.0
Other data		
Capital expenditures	20.8	16.6
Depreciation and amortization	13.2	13.0
Return on sales	24.3%	25.0%
Return on assets	38.9%	35.1%
Number of employees	1523	1301

You and your core team of senior vice presidents log over 1.5 million miles in the air during the year, leading some Benton executives to refer to you as "the flying tigers." You pride yourself on having carried off a brilliant strategic coup: a global expansion perfectly timed to coincide with a global recession that made acquired companies willing and anxious to affiliate with a growing, visionary company.

However, as you and your senior team analyze the year's activities, you visualize another strategic decision on the near horizon: Should the mix of MedTech's external affiliations favor acquisitions (purchase of another business entity) or alliances (affiliation of two business entities for a common purpose)? Your year-end analysis has identified that traditional acquisitions take two to three times longer to consummate than strategic alliances. However, strategic alliances demand more intensive, ongoing coordination and management. Traditional acquisitions, easier to control and direct, can lose steam and initiative, while strategic alliances, harder to control and direct, can increase motivation and creativity. Traditional acquisitions can rely on specific and proven approaches to combining businesses, whereas strategic alliances represent a relatively new and less precise form of business combinations. While traditional acquisitions epitomize the traditional pattern of global growth, strategic alliances symbolize the future of global growth. Since MedTech has achieved success with both traditional acquisitions and strategic alliances, you see this decision as one more close judgment call. Daniels argues for a mix emphasizing traditional acquisitions, Gill and Suhler express ambivalence, and Matsumori favors more strategic alliances. Now you must decide.

If you conclude that innovative strategic alliances should dominate the mix of MedTech's affiliations, turn to Chapter 50.

If you decide that more traditional acquisitions and mergers should dominate the mix, turn to Chapter 51.

37

Assimilating Current Acquisitions

On the basis of unacceptably high failure rate or mediocre performance of acquisitions in general, you decide to halt MedTech's flurry
of mergers and acquisitions for a time and turn your attention to
assimilating all your acquisitions and alliances before launching
another wave of activity.

Although the executives at Benton Pharmaceuticals view your strategy as a bit too prudent and overly conservative, they support it in
light of the threatening recession. You immediately hire a human
resources consulting firm to help you restructure the organization and
establish consistent career path and compensation opportunities
across the 16 entities that now comprise MedTech. With their help you
actively and candidly communicate with all MedTech employees that
the coming year will emphasize assimilating and solidifying the
growth of recent years.

As the focus turns inward to MedTech's organization, management
processes, and operating systems, you grow concerned about
decreased attention to customers and the marketplace. Your concern
deepens when several large customers take their business elsewhere
and the recession causes some employees to turn even more inward,
worrying about their jobs as a general state of economic sluggishness
afflicts the entire world. A growing number of fearful and anxious
middle managers fan your concern, which escalates to serious worry
when Meg Daniels leaves MedTech for a competitor that has
remained on a fast-acquisition track. Losing a key person so instru-
mental to MedTech's successful acquisitions sends an alarming message across the organization that you may have made a strategic error
by slowing down your M&A activity.

The next blow comes from Jack Suhler, head of FutureMedTech and another member of your core team, who wants to scale down his involvement and become a half-time manager. Jack asserts that he doesn't need the money and can't muster the motivation to work full-time. By the end of the year, you realize the full impact of your strategic mistake, and while you take some consolation from the fact that other Benton divisions have also posted poor to mediocre results in a recessionary year, you feel you should have done better. MedTech sales for the year increase 2 percent to $343 million, and profits decline 28 percent to $39 million, as shown in the accompanying table.

Selected Financial Information
(Dollars in Millions)

	Year ended September 30	
	This year	Last year
Operations		
Net sales	$342.7	$336.0
Cost of sales	123.4	116.1
R&D	41.2	36.2
Marketing	81.2	65.9
G&A	58.3	33.8
Operating profit	38.6	84.0
Financial position		
Current assets	116.5	113.0
Current liabilities	60.6	58.8
Working capital	55.9	54.3
Other assets	35.0	33.9
Property and equipment	97.4	92.1
Total assets	248.9	239.0
Other data		
Capital expenditures	20.8	16.6
Depreciation and amortization	13.2	13.0
Return on sales	11.3%	25.0%
Return on assets	15.5%	35.1%
Number of employees	1314	1301

Resisting the temptation to take yourself off the hook by claiming to be a victim of circumstances beyond your control, you pledge to make the coming year a banner one by putting MedTech back on the merger and acquisition track. However, shortly after the close of the fiscal year, Benton Pharmaceuticals decides to sell MedTech. When you try to persuade Benton executives to change their minds, they argue that

MedTech is one of the few Benton units with sufficient promise to command a premium sales price in a sluggish market. Bob Koontz, Benton CEO, offers you a corporate staff position, vice president of mergers and acquisitions, but avoids promising you another operating position in the near future. He simply says, "Look, you've proven yourself in the acquisitions game, and Benton will need that expertise in the future." As you probe further with other Benton executives you discover that corporate headquarters respected your ability to identify, negotiate, and close deals, but not your ability to manage and build an enterprise.

Your strategic thinking and decision making may have come to an end at MedTech, but this book allows you a new lease on life, if you wish to take it.

If you want to revisit the last strategic decision you made, return to Chapter 24.

If you want to reconsider an earlier strategic decision, return to Chapter 16 or Chapter 8.

If you're still feeling the sting of defeat and believe you could have made your last strategic choice work in real life, you may be right. After all, this is just a game. However, if you return to your last strategic decision (the first option above) and select the other alternative, you will learn why the author considers it a better choice.

38
Remaining Focused on Blood and Cell R&D

Although people in other Benton divisions resent your stand against R&D joint ventures with them, Benton's CEO, Bob Koontz, supports your decision with the proviso that your focus had better pay off in a big way. The veiled threat does nothing to dampen the enthusiasm of Jack Suhler, Kate DaVaeno, their respective management teams, and your own personal staff for MedTech's continuing emphasis on blood and cell R&D.

Sales of the new high-end blood analyzer, introduced last year, continue growing, but because of the relatively small number of research laboratories, MedTech will soon saturate that market and must, therefore, develop less costly versions for other markets. Making matters worse, a deepening worldwide recession will surely hurt overall sales toward the end of this year and throughout most of next year.

To signal your sharpened focus on blood and cell R&D, you dramatically increase R&D spending at FutureMedTech, but as the recession wears on, Benton executives begin pressuring all divisions to freeze capital expenditures and selectively cut or postpone R&D and product introduction expenditures. Mitch Cavanaugh, your group president, believes you can easily reduce total R&D and product-introduction spending at MedTech because you have targeted the investment at such a narrow field. Even though you explain to him the critical nature of your research and development efforts in several related areas, he insists you obey the corporate edict. Reluctantly, you ask Jack Suhler and Kate DaVaeno to separate the R&D projects and product introductions that should receive priority attention from those you could possibly delay.

Your resentment of corporate authority grows as you scale back
MedTech's R&D spending and place three new product introductions
on hold. Discerning dampened spirits in Jack Suhler and Kate
DaVaeno, you reassure them that MedTech will return to its pioneering position in the industry as soon as the economy turns around.
Although they seem to accept your reassurances, you suspect that
both Suhler and DaVaeno, two close friends and key executives on
whose motivation MedTech's future depends, have lost some of their
earlier enthusiasm. As the fiscal year comes to an end, MedTech again
reports stellar sales and profit increases, an 82 percent increase in revenues to $703 million, and a 91 percent increase in profits to $225 million, as shown in the accompanying table.

Despite these strong numbers, the ongoing recession, coupled with
MedTech's saturation of the research laboratory market with its
newest product, will make it virtually impossible for MedTech to sustain anything close to the same kind of performance in the coming

Selected Financial Information
(Dollars in Millions)

| | Year ended September 30 | |
	This year	Last year
Operations		
Net sales	$702.8	$386.2
Cost of sales	217.9	123.6
R&D	112.4	57.9
Marketing	77.1	50.0
G&A	70.2	36.6
Operating profit	225.2	118.1
Financial position		
Current assets	230.2	127.5
Current liabilities	119.7	66.3
Working capital	110.5	61.2
Other assets	69.1	38.2
Property and equipment	102.0	93.4
Total assets	401.2	259.1
Other data		
Capital expenditures	24.2	18.0
Depreciation and amortization	13.3	13.0
Return on sales	32.0%	30.6%
Return on assets	56.1%	45.6%
Number of employees	1642	1340

year. In addition, the continuing pressure from Benton headquarters to reduce spending to maximize profits forces you to face new, tough, short-term choices in terms of which R&D projects to emphasize and which product introductions to push.

Suhler's and DaVaeno's new priority lists surprise you because for the first time the two executives express two very different views of the future. John Suhler believes R&D projects in the flow cytometry and retrovirology areas deserve priority funding because continued research and development in these areas could lead to cell transplant breakthroughs, making it possible for genetically altered cells to kill viruses or cancer cells right inside the body. In addition, Suhler argues, "with FutureMedTech's best biotechnologists, scientific instrument specialists, blood analysts, and software engineers working on these projects, we might even solve the mystery of the century by developing a genetic map to identify the mysterious sequencing of the DNA ladder and its genetic signposts, allowing for accurate reading of each piece of DNA." Showing his old fire as he stakes out his position, he paints a glowing picture of a future where projects in cell transplant and genetic mapping propel MedTech to the pinnacle of the industry.

In sharp contrast, Kate DaVaeno proposes that MedTech should stick to its hematology base, further refining its blood analyzing capabilities, introducing even more sophisticated instruments to the research laboratory market, and developing less expensive versions of existing blood analyzers for the medical center and hospital markets. She, too, displays her old enthusiasm as she argues that too much emphasis on cell transplant and genetic mapping R&D will cause MedTech to lose its historical dominance in the research lab market and its technological leadership in the field of blood analysis. Further improving MedTech's blood analyzers would allow the company to contribute indirectly to a myriad of medical and biotechnical R&D projects throughout the world, including Suhler's pet projects, cell transplant and gene mapping technology.

When Suhler rebuts DaVaeno's arguments, claiming that MedTech's future rests on applying its own blood analyzing technology to cell transplants and genetic mapping, DaVaeno responds that Suhler has spent too much time in the laboratory, not enough in the field. You are somewhat taken aback by the bickering because these two people have always worked so smoothly together. The situation, it seems, has taken an emotional toll on everyone.

After several days of discussions with Suhler and DaVaeno, you desperately wish the recession would go away so that you could pursue both strategies. Having already lost the battle with Bob Koontz and Mitch Cavanaugh at Benton headquarters for the application of more resources, you know that MedTech cannot afford both of Suhler's and DaVaeno's priorities, at least not next year. What a thorny dilemma! If you pursue cell transplants and genetic mapping, you could fall behind in the blood analysis technology field. But, if you pursue improved blood analysis technology, you could miss the opportunity of a lifetime by allowing someone else to make the big breakthroughs in cell transplants and genetic mapping.

When you seek counsel from Bob Koontz, Mitch Cavanaugh, and other senior executives at Benton, you receive mixed signals. Some argue for an emphasis on cell transplant and genetic mapping, while others favor blood analysis technology. But regardless of their preference, they all express confidence in your ability to make the right decision. You spend a long weekend in the Florida Keys to ponder your decision. Walking through the quaint streets of Key West with your spouse, you can't help reflecting on Robert Frost's poem, "The Road Not Taken": "Two roads diverged in a yellow wood, /And sorry I could not travel both...."

If you opt to pursue cell transplants and genetic mapping, turn to Chapter 52.

If you prefer emphasizing blood analysis technology, turn to Chapter 53.

39
Expanding Beyond Blood and Cell R&D

In response to a deepening worldwide recession, which limits Benton's overall spending on R&D, and mounting pressure from other Benton divisions that MedTech share its expertise, you and Jack Suhler begin a substantial expansion of FutureMedTech's R&D activities by creating four more R&D groups in the areas of blood and platelet, diagnostic testing, heart valve, and neurological research. You also organize a large R&D support staff at the MedTech corporate level that will coordinate each group's activities and monitor relationships with R&D groups from other divisions.

You expect your decision to play well with both Benton executives and stock analysts, who have been preaching R&D diversity in recent years as a means of managing risk, but you're not prepared for the intensity of the reaction. Benton's stock soars, and overnight you and your management team find yourselves buried under an avalanche of requests for joint R&D projects from other Benton divisions. Sorting out the priorities gridlocks the FutureMedTech division and your own staff for three months as it works feverishly to establish policies and develop a system for handling a quadrupling of R&D projects.

It doesn't take long before FutureMedTech's original hematology, flow cytometry, retrovirology, and scientific instruments groups claim that their vital projects are suffering from insufficient funding and overworked personnel. Similarly, people in the MedTech Operations division, saddled with coordinating an enormous number of product introductions with other divisions, find it impossible to keep on top of marketing the high-end blood analyzer. A weary Kate DaVaeno informs you that MedTech is selling fewer instruments than expected.

After several months of general upheaval within MedTech, a growing dissatisfaction at headquarters with MedTech's operations, coupled with concern over declining sales growth and reduced profits, causes Benton executives to take a careful look at you and your management practices. Earlier praise for your willingness to open up FutureMedTech's R&D to other Benton divisions turns to criticism as managers and executives throughout the Benton system cite mismanagement, rather than their own exaggerated expectations, to explain MedTech's turmoil and sagging performance.

As the year comes to a close, MedTech records a sales increase of 36 percent to $525 million, and a profit decrease of 35 percent to $77 million, as shown in the accompanying table.

In response to your argument that MedTech needs to get back to its primary business, Benton executives decide to remove the FutureMedTech division from MedTech, placing it at the corporate level under Jack Suhler as the new president of Benton Research and

Selected Financial Information
(Dollars in Millions)

	Year ended September 30	
	This year	Last year
Operations		
Net sales	$525.4	$386.2
Cost of sales	178.6	123.6
R&D	94.6	57.9
Marketing	91.2	50.0
G&A	84.1	36.6
Operating profit	76.9	118.1
Financial position		
Current assets	176.0	127.5
Current liabilities	91.5	66.3
Working capital	84.5	61.2
Other assets	52.8	38.2
Property and equipment	102.0	93.4
Total assets	330.8	259.1
Other data		
Capital expenditures	24.2	18.0
Depreciation and amortization	13.3	13.0
Return on sales	14.6%	30.6%
Return on assets	23.2%	45.6%
Number of employees	1518	1340

Development. Bob Koontz, Benton's CEO, rationalizes the move by
saying it will take a lot of pressure off MedTech, improve coordination of R&D projects across the company, and increase
FutureMedTech's clout by elevating it to the corporate level.

Left with no R&D division and a culture in disarray, MedTech's
morale plummets and several key people begin openly looking for
jobs elsewhere. When your own motivation hits bottom, you demand
a heart-to-heart talk with the Benton CEO, Bob Koontz, even though
you know doing so will inflame Mitch Cavanaugh, your group president. Two days later you angrily march into Koontz's office and proceed to tell him exactly how you feel about having FutureMedTech
ripped away from MedTech. The usually low-key Koontz becomes
furious, telling you in no uncertain terms that you mismanaged the
scope-expansion of MedTech's R&D. A heated argument ensues, but
you realize somewhere along the line that Koontz has stopped listening to you.

As you storm out of the CEO's office, he fires a parting salvo at
your back: "This session today only proves that I made a mistake
when I put so much confidence in you. For your own sake, you
should consider looking for opportunities outside Benton."

Oddly, his words don't fuel your anger, but, in fact, as you cool
down, you realize you have been moving toward the same conclusion
over the past few months. You enjoyed the ride while it lasted, but
you're ready for a change of scenery.

Your strategic decision making at MedTech will come to an end
within a few months as you move to a new company, but if you could
do it all over again, would you take a different road?

If you would like to remake your last strategic decision,
return to Chapter 25.

If you would like to revisit an earlier strategic decision,
return to Chapter 16 or Chapter 8.

If you're still feeling the sting of defeat and believe you
could have made your last strategic choice work in real life,
you may be right. After all, this is just a game. However, if
you return to your last strategic decision (the first option
above) and select the other alternative, you will learn why the
author considers it a better choice.

40
Taking a Modified Deming Approach

Despite some serious reservations about your decision, Ed Yates assures you that he will throw himself into the effort. Unfortunately, as you and your management team work to refine MedTech's approach to total quality management, you conclude that Ed has consciously or unconsciously put himself on the sidelines. When you raise the issue with Mitch Cavanaugh, group president, he confides that an opportunity may open up at corporate headquarters for Ed Yates to assist other divisions in their total quality management efforts. Together, you and Cavanaugh work out the details for Yates' transition to corporate headquarters, setting a schedule that should avoid any further delays in developing MedTech's more specific approach for guiding employees through a complete transformation into a dynamic total quality management organization.

Now, of course, you must identify a potential successor for yourself. In an unprecedented move, you appoint Susan Carter, vice president of human resources, as the new executive vice president and chief operating officer, charging her with the responsibility to coordinate and refine a modified Deming approach to total quality and continuous improvement. You settle on Susan for three simple reasons: she possesses strong communication skills, she represents a tempered view of Deming's ideas, and she has always displayed keen sensitivity to the human side of enterprise, attitudes you believe will provide the key to gaining the support of middle managers and frontline supervisors for the specific guidelines you expect will emerge under Susan's supervision. She has also told you many times that she longs to move into general management. Given her inexperience, however, you plan to monitor her performance closely.

Over the next several weeks, a six-point plan of continuous improvement takes shape for MedTech. The components are (1) philosophy, (2) planning, (3) prevention, (4) problem solving, (5) education, and (6) evaluation. The philosophy component, which comes from Deming and Juran, as well as from Motorola, expresses a clear commitment to constant improvement and recognizes quality as the key to product improvement, cost reduction, customer loyalty, and increased profits. The planning component draws upon Phillip Crosby's emphasis on goal setting and incorporates the Malcolm Baldrige process for strategic quality planning as well as elements of the TQM practices of Motorola, Corning, Xerox, Ford, and Hewlett-Packard. The prevention component stems primarily from Phillip Crosby's stress on preventing problems, rather than just finding and fixing them. The problem-solving component, in concert with prevention, utilizes General Electric's Work-Out Program and Juran's project approach to solving problems. The education component draws from successful training programs already in place in a number of leading corporations and from Deming's on-the-job training philosophy. Finally, the evaluation component incorporates Feigenbaum's concepts of quality information feedback and special quality studies, as well as Xerox's systematic benchmarking, General Electric's best practices, and a QEC (Quality-Efficiency-Cost) process incorporated by Globe Metallurgical, one of the early winners of the Malcolm Baldrige Award.

When you and Carter unveil the six-point plan to middle management, with all its details and specifics, it receives rave reviews. People throughout the organization seem increasingly eager to put it into practice as Susan Carter and her staff communicate all the details through video presentations, newsletters, staff meetings, question-and-answer sessions, and one-on-one discussions throughout the company. You feel confident that things are going well until a growing number of organizational and implementation problems begin to crop up because of perceived contradictions among the plan's various philosophies and concepts. As more and more people in the organization become preoccupied with the contradictions, you fear that MedTech's melody line is losing its clarity. Some employees do not appreciate the evaluation process emphasis on indicators (charts, graphs, reports, and meetings), while other employees believe the evaluation component constitutes the most critical part of the plan. Still others complain about too little individual responsibility for results and argue that Crosby's approach to prevention, demanding that people within the organization conform to the requirements of quality and continuous improvement, actually creates a great deal of fear within the organization, something the Deming philosophy absolutely abhors.

Although Susan Carter works diligently to resolve the disputes and attempts to eliminate apparent contradictions in the six-point plan, MedTech quickly develops a reputation within Benton Pharmaceuticals as a total quality experiment gone sour. Without really intending to, Ed Yates adds to the confusion inside MedTech by telling some people at other Benton divisions that he believes a total quality management approach cannot succeed without a unified set of specific and detailed techniques and procedures and that only a pure Deming model can deliver those internal consistencies. To your chagrin MedTech is being cited as an example of how drawing bits and pieces from the best TQM practices and leading continuous-improvement gurus can spell disaster.

Toward the end of the year, you, Susan Carter and your management team finally bite the bullet and eliminate two newly created quality-improvement departments, three levels of decision-making review, and several evaluation indicators. However, many groups within the company continue disputing the importance of one concept over another. The fiscal year grinds to an end and MedTech reports revenues of $345 million, an 11 percent increase, and a drop in profits to $59 million, an 18 percent decrease, as shown in the accompanying table.

Looking back over the turbulent year, you realize that MedTech's internal strife surrounding the six-point plan has actually blunted your response to a major event—the passage of a national health-care act by the United States Congress. Even customers have noticed the company's inward focus and several have begun complaining about sagging service levels and unresponsiveness. To make matters worse, one of MedTech's heralded product improvements, a new generation of blood analyzers for clinics and doctors' offices, was recalled in the fourth quarter for minor adjustments. Although the recall entailed only a minor adjustment, it contributed to increased costs and reduced profits for the year. The news also added another cloud over MedTech's image in the marketplace.

Shortly after the end of the fiscal year, you engage in an arduous review session with Mitch Cavanaugh, your group president, during which you stress how much you feel you've learned over the past 12 months and how a sharper focus can dramatically improve MedTech's future. About halfway through the four-hour session, Cavanaugh informs you that he thinks Ed Yates is ready to run a division and asks whether you think Ed could handle the presidency of MedTech.

Selected Financial Information
(Dollars in Millions)

| | Year ended September 30 | |
	This year	Last year
Operations		
Net sales	$345.0	$312.4
Cost of sales	131.1	106.2
R&D	34.4	30.2
Marketing	72.5	65.6
G&A	48.3	31.2
Operating profit	58.7	79.2
Financial position		
Current assets	119.0	104.7
Current liabilities	61.9	54.4
Working capital	57.1	50.2
Other assets	35.7	31.4
Property and equipment	83.1	80.4
Total assets	237.8	216.4
Other data		
Capital expenditures	16.2	13.0
Depreciation and amortization	11.5	11.6
Return on sales	17.0%	25.4%
Return on assets	24.7%	36.6%
Number of employees	1394	1331

Immediately, your mind flashes back to your conversation with Benton executives over a year ago in which Cavanaugh and others asked you to prepare a successor because you would soon be needed elsewhere in the company. Your uneasiness swells as you struggle to discern why Cavanaugh has raised the issue of Ed Yates' running MedTech before any mention of your own future. Your mind racing, you review the ugly reality of last year's difficulties, your confidence seeping out of you to the point where you'll jump at whatever Cavanaugh offers. You answer Cavanaugh's question by praising Ed Yates and expressing your confidence that he would do a good job running MedTech.

Perhaps sensing your underlying concern, Cavanaugh tells you that he would like you to take over as division president of a struggling $40 million subsidiary, Syntac, which desperately needs new leadership to implement a total quality management approach. "We need you to do for Syntac what you tried to do for MedTech," Cavanaugh says. "You're over the learning curve now, so the job should perfectly suit you."

You accept the offer, hoping to apply everything you learned to the new challenge. While you look forward to your new assignment, you wish you could turn back the clock and do things differently at MedTech. In the real world you would have to live with your earlier strategic decision making, but since this book allows you to turn back the clock, you may, in fact, revisit one of your earlier strategic decisions.

If you desire to reconsider your most recent strategic decision, return to Chapter 29.

If you would like to reconsider an earlier decision, return to Chapter 18 or Chapter 11.

If you're still feeling the sting of defeat and believe you could have made your last strategic choice work in real life, you may be right. After all, this is just a game. However, if you return to your last strategic decision (the first option above) and select the other alternative, you will learn why the author considers it a better choice.

41

Implementing the Pure Deming Model

When you tell Ed Yates of your decision, he seems quite pleased, saying, "You've made the right decision! The Deming model will give us the internal consistencies and specific techniques we'll need to complete the transformation of MedTech into a dynamic total quality management organization. By sticking close to Deming's approach, we can discard outmoded management practices such as quality inspections, minimum quality standards, and management by objectives." Clearly, Yates is the right person to begin developing recommendations for implementing the Deming model at MedTech.

With the help of outside consultants, Ed Yates discovers that MedTech has already done a lot to transform itself into a continuously improving organization. However, one team of consultants points out the need to help individual employees better function as jazz musicians, improvising and adding their own contributions to the basic melody line. Only then can MedTech people improve, continuously providing customers with better and less expensive products, top-quality service, and solutions to their tough blood analysis, collection, and monitoring problems. The stakes are high, not only for MedTech's future but also for millions of people throughout the world who will benefit from MedTech's transformation.

As soon as Ed Yates has pulled everything together for a thorough review of the differences between conventional organizations (including many "would be" total quality companies) and a pure Deming organization, you convene a meeting of your senior team. Ed concludes his opening remarks by saying: "Conventional companies view quality as expensive, believe that defects are caused by workers, buy at the lowest cost from suppliers, play one supplier off against another, use fear and reward to motivate people, and obtain profits by keeping revenues high and costs low. The Deming company, on the other hand, knows that quality itself leads to lower costs, believes that most defects are caused by faulty systems, buys from suppliers committed to quality, works with single suppliers to incorporate them into the continuous-improvement system, recognizes fear as a dangerous state of mind, and gains profits by creating loyal customers, who remain loyal because of continuously improving products, services, and costs."

Together, you and Ed then review in detail the famous 14 points of transformation from a conventional to a Deming company, setting the stage for an upcoming retreat for middle managers that will launch a companywide implementation of the Deming model.

At the middle management retreat, you form 14 cross-functional task forces to monitor each of Deming's 14 points. These task forces devote the balance of the first day developing and coordinating plans. On the second day of the retreat you tell the group that during the next 12 months you expect every employee to focus on constantly improving all products and services within MedTech, with an explicit goal of building strong customer loyalty through better quality and lower costs: "The Deming approach will guide us during the next phase of our total quality management transformation, and it will require that you give up more of your conventional notions of what constitutes good management. It won't be easy, but it will be worth it. Working together, we can change the fabric of this organization, finally getting rid of our old lockstep symphony and replacing it with a Deming-oriented jazz band."

At the end of your pep talk, you commit to making sure that MedTech's management system allows every individual employee to function as a seasoned jazz musician, able to make the necessary personal contributions that will create harmonious and lasting improvement at MedTech: "We'll remove the pressures for increased productivity from people who are already doing all they can do by eliminating work standards, quotas, management by objectives, and the barriers between departments that prevent coordination and cooperation. We'll revamp all our performance appraisal systems to focus on continuous improvement rather than on the old competitive approach that pits employee against employee. In return, I ask you to commit yourselves 100 percent to making MedTech a model Deming company." The response heartens you. Every manager at the retreat signs a large poster that pledges all-out support to the Deming transformation.

As the year unfolds, Ed Yates and a group of talented outside consultants provide so much daily guidance about implementing Deming's 14 points that an amazing constancy of purpose begins to permeate all of MedTech's operations, and you see more joy, pride, and happiness among your employees than you've ever experienced at MedTech or at any other organization. You owe it all to Dr. W. Edwards Deming, the mathematician and physicist who developed a statistical approach to quality control and then fashioned an entire management philosophy that enabled the Japanese to become world-class quality experts. Now MedTech, like other enlightened companies, has brought his breakthroughs back home, when they're sorely needed.

The most visible fruit of MedTech's efforts, a new generation of economical and technically sophisticated blood analyzers for the low end of the market, enters the marketplace three months before the end of the year with $5000 to $10,000 price tags, more than 30 percent lower than competitors' lowest-priced alternatives. Fortuitously, the product introduction coincides with passage by the U.S. Congress of a national health-care act guaranteeing a minimum level of health care to all American citizens. As doctors, clinics, hospitals, health maintenance organizations, and insurance companies desperately strive to cut costs in order to meet this new mandate, the new generation of blood analyzers quickly captures the market. A *Fortune* magazine cover story proclaims MedTech's accomplishment as a shining example of what companies can do to reduce costs through steadfast adherence to total quality and continuous improvement.

At the end of the year, MedTech posts record gains: $578 million in revenues, an increase of 85 percent, and $150 million in profits, an increase of 90 percent, as shown in the accompanying table.

In addition to awarding you compensation equivalent to $3.5 million, composed of cash income, deferred income, and stock options, Benton's chairman and CEO, Bob Koontz, informs you that you will be promoted to group president of the Medical Products and Systems Group at the end of the coming year. Mitch Cavanaugh, the current group president, will become president of the Pharmaceuticals Group, and will likely become Benton's next president and CEO. In addition to continuing as MedTech's president over the next year you will act as assistant group president, getting familiar with the other divisions within the group in order to effect a smooth transition. In no uncertain terms, Bob Koontz tells you that you can follow in Mitch Cavanaugh's footsteps if you continue to provide the leadership you have displayed at MedTech.

Selected Financial Information
(Dollars in Millions)

	Year ended September 30	
	This year	Last year
Operations		
Net sales	$578.3	$312.4
Cost of sales	190.8	106.2
R&D	63.9	30.2
Marketing	121.4	65.6
G&A	52.0	31.2
Operating profit	150.2	79.2
Financial position		
Current assets	192.3	104.7
Current liabilities	100.0	54.4
Working capital	92.3	50.2
Other assets	57.7	31.4
Property and equipment	83.1	80.4
Total assets	333.1	216.4
Other data		
Capital expenditures	16.2	13.0
Depreciation and amortization	11.5	11.6
Return on sales	26.0%	25.4%
Return on assets	45.1%	36.6%
Number of employees	1637	1331

As the congratulations and praises begin to die down after the close of the year, you work closely with Ed Yates to prepare him to take MedTech's helm at the end of the year. With the Deming approach securely in place, both you and Ed recognize the need for a final solidifying focus to complete MedTech's transformation.

Ed Yates boils MedTech's options down to two alternatives: (1) increase the individual accountability of every MedTech employee or (2) improve the leadership of all MedTech managers. Of course, both can fuel total quality and continuing improvement, but you must determine which one will play the most critical role in this final stage of MedTech's amazing transformation. Individual accountability rests at the core of any continuous-improvement environment and particularly in a Deming company. Strengthening the accountability of every individual for constantly improving everything (products, service, process, systems, etc.) could ensure completion of MedTech's transformation. However, you think to yourself, stressing individual accountability without putting in place the necessary leadership could burn out employees as they become more accountable for results but then bump up against lingering management system restrictions and inadequacies. Managers with underdeveloped leadership skills could undermine all that you've accomplished. Because of the subtleties involved in this strategic decision, you spend a lot of time wrestling with this difficult judgment call, but you relish the opportunity to make the right choice. Finally, you reduce it all to a question of principle: in the final stage of transformation into a total quality management company should you focus on the system or the individual?

If you choose to increase individual accountability, turn to Chapter 54.

If you would rather improve managerial leadership, turn to Chapter 55.

42
Letting the Reorganization Emerge

While you favor letting the reorganization emerge somewhat naturally, you do worry about the consequences of an instable organizational
environment. However, to impose too much stability and order on
MedTech too soon would undermine the spontaneity, flexibility, and
time-based orientation you've worked so hard to cultivate.
Attempting to quell the disagreement between Ed Yates and Susan
Carter, you encourage Ed to study ways in which MedTech might
institutionalize portions of what's been happening at the company
this past year, but you tell Susan Carter it's her job to encourage every
employee within the organization to experiment freely with the way
work gets done. You and Carter persuade the rest of your management team to get behind the idea of a naturally emerging reorganization with the promise that eventually you'll institutionalize the best
methods that emerge.

As a result of this freewheeling policy, a new wave of cycle-time
improvements occurs over the next several months. One group of
salespeople experiments with new data links and software for field
reporting, which allows them more time with customers and more
rapid communication with sales administration offices without
lengthy meetings or excessive travel. Another pilot program reconfig-
ures the manufacturing process for the low-end line of blood analyzers, cutting the already streamlined manufacturing cycle from four to
two days, with an outside chance it can be cut to less than 24 hours.

Though MedTech continues to make great strides forward, you
often find yourself having to resolve tensions that surface as experiments and pilot programs challenge established work methods, even
those introduced last year. Undaunted, you continue championing

experiments and pilots that continually modify every aspect of MedTech's work processes. Even though you know Tom Peters can be an extremist, you gain confidence from his new book, *Liberation Management: Necessary Disorganization for the Nanosecond Nineties,* in which he counsels CEOs: "The message is clear: (1) trust, (2) `they' can handle `it' (*whatever* `it' is), (3) you're only in control when you're out of control (`head' of a flat, decentralized `organization')."

Your unwavering vision uniquely prepares MedTech to respond to a new national health-care act passed by Congress that mandates changes to curb rising costs of medical care and guarantees every American a minimum level of care. Before any other competitor can react, MedTech develops a sophisticated new blood analyzer that incorporates a greater variety of testing capabilities less expensively than older models. This product helps satisfy the demand for reducing costs, without lowering the level of medical care. The new blood analyzer lets hospitals, clinics, and physicians get more information out of a single blood test.

More than anything else, this simple breakthrough demonstrates the value of MedTech's naturally emerging organization, and it comes at a time when many companies in the industry are suffering from stagnant sales because of all the uncertainty surrounding the new national health-care legislation. MedTech's sales skyrocket by the end of the year to $682 million, an increase of 116 percent, and profits reach $218 million, a 130 percent increase, as shown in the accompanying table.

When asked at the annual corporate retreat to recount the story of MedTech's success, you describe how becoming a time-based competitor requires vision and commitment at the top of the organization and a willingness, throughout the organization, to rethink and rework what's going on at every level, empowering those capable of bringing about short-term as well as long-term change. All along the way you must constantly monitor the experimentation, the pilot programs and the breakthrough teams, to make sure that none of them get bogged down or off track. Finally, the core concepts of main sequence and continuous flow enable the flexible organization to respond to customers with lightning speed, while providing more product variety, innovating more rapidly, reducing costs associated with longer cycle times, and improving quality.

In succeeding weeks you fend off numerous job offers from outside the company and decline an invitation to become president of the Medical Products and Systems Group. Instead, you ask Benton executives to give you one more year at MedTech to complete the process of

Selected Financial Information
(Dollars in Millions)

	Year ended September 30	
	This year	Last year
Operations		
Net sales	$682.3	$315.2
Cost of sales	184.2	88.0
R&D	75.8	32.1
Marketing	143.0	69.5
G&A	61.2	31.0
Operating profit	218.1	94.6
Financial position		
Current assets	216.6	100.8
Current liabilities	112.6	52.4
Working capital	104.0	48.4
Other assets	65.0	30.2
Property and equipment	100.9	82.6
Total assets	382.5	213.6
Other data		
Capital expenditures	32.2	14.9
Depreciation and amortization	11.8	11.6
Return on sales	32.0%	30.0%
Return on assets	57.0%	44.3%
Number of employees	1697	1337

turning the company into a time-based competitor. You know it will take at least one more year for the reorganization to emerge fully.

Once again you receive generous salary increases, bonuses, and stock options, and promises that a top job awaits you at headquarters whenever you're ready for it.

You feel you must answer one crucial strategic question before you'll feel comfortable moving on: How should you solidify the reorganization or institutionalize the new liberation at MedTech? What focus will ensure that MedTech never abandons its time-based philosophy for the old traditions? How can you solidify the reorganization without creating a deadening bureaucracy? How can a company remain a *perpetual* time-based competitor, providing the most value at the least cost in the least amount of time?

You conclude that your choices come down to attitude versus technique. The right attitude certainly provides the key to competing more quickly, more effectively, and more efficiently than anyone else. To instill the right attitude, you must attract, develop, and keep people who thrive on the thrill of competition and love responding faster and better to customer needs. On the other hand, would the right attitude alone carry the company forward, or would you need more technique and process?

If more process and procedure are needed, technique should take precedence, because you need it to benchmark the processes and procedures of the best time-based performers in the marketplace. To focus on technique, you must go even further to involve all key managers in pilot programs and breakthrough teams, spreading successful team members among fledgling pilots. You must create new measures and awards emphasizing cycle time, reorient the approval process for capital expenditure to promote time compression, and monitor customer satisfaction, particularly as it relates to time dimensions. However, would a focus on technique rob the company of its fighting spirit?

With only one year left at MedTech, you wrestle with the issue, knowing it will contribute greatly to the legacy you leave behind. While you believe MedTech will need both the right attitudes and the right techniques in the future, you realize that you must make one the primary focus during the coming year. What do you want to do?

If you prefer to stress attitude, turn to Chapter 56.
If you would rather emphasize technique, turn to Chapter 57.

43

Taking
the Initiative to
Reorganize

You announce that you've decided to undertake an immediate reorganization, institutionalizing all the new work flow processes that have occurred at MedTech. Your management team greets the news with mixed feelings. An elated Ed Yates assures you that you've done the right thing, while a skeptical Susan Carter expresses severe doubts and worries that this decision could hinder everything that MedTech has accomplished so far.

Although you work feverishly to unite your management team behind the reorganization, you cannot change Carter's mind. To minimize the tension mounting within the management team you make a strong case to your group president, Mitch Cavanaugh, and other Benton executives that they should transfer the talented Susan Carter to some other division within Benton. Not wanting to lose Carter, Benton executives make Susan an offer she quickly accepts, and you promote Casey Pinnock, who has championed the initiative to reorganize, to vice president of human resources. With your management team finally moving forward together, you act quickly to institutionalize all the improvements from the past years by organizing departments, solidifying relationships among departments, giving the authority to managers throughout the organization to continue a time-based focus, clarifying reporting relationships and establishing performance evaluation processes. You document the main sequence for adding value and the basic work flow within MedTech and use them as the basis for all organizational processes and management systems.

Unfortunately, after three months the company loses a good deal of last year's momentum. As MedTech employees emphasize institutionization over discovery, their enthusiasm for future refinements in work methods dies, though not without a fight from some. The confusion over what people now perceive as mixed signals from top management creates hesitation and uncertainty throughout the organization.

As you attempt to address the growing problems, you discover that the organization is actually reverting to many of its old ways. Where once people had shifted their focus to the main sequence of work activities for creating value, they are now falling back into their old functional habits. Instead of supporting a continuous work flow, you find departments once again erecting walls around their activities and assuming the batch-work mentality that characterized MedTech before the new time-based era. Bottlenecks begin clogging up the system, and managers beg for more investment to reduce costs instead of time.

Halfway through the year you realize you've made a strategic blunder, which you attempt to remedy by firing Ed Yates as vice president of production. However, your management team views the move as an effort to lay blame on someone other than yourself. As morale plummets, you can't believe how quickly a once-vibrant organization can disintegrate.

As a new national health-care act hurtles through Congress, giving every American the right to a minimum level of health care, you find it difficult to consider the implications of such a sweeping industry change because you're so preoccupied with regaining MedTech's lost momentum. By the beginning of the fourth quarter, you abandon all efforts to reorganize and attempt to recapture the spirit of time-based competition.

Your behavior does not please your group vice president, Mitch Cavanaugh, who takes you to task during a performance evaluation session at the end of the year. "Your actions have seemed almost spastic lately," he observes. "No one knows where you really stand strategically or organizationally."

Not surprisingly, your management team shares Cavanaugh's view of your panicky behavior. Few of them believe MedTech can recapture its old momentum. For the good of the company, you decide to negotiate a 12-month severance package with Mitch Cavanaugh and set out for greener pastures.

After you leave, MedTech reports a sales increase of 16 percent, to $365 million, and a profit decline of 16 percent, to $80 million, as shown in the accompanying table.

Ordinarily, you would be sprucing up your résumé, but since this is only a game, you can try your luck again.

Selected Financial Information
(Dollars in Millions)

	Year ended September 30	
	This year	Last year
Operations		
Net sales	$365.5	$315.2
Cost of sales	131.9	88.0
R&D	36.0	32.1
Marketing	66.1	69.5
G&A	51.2	31.0
Operating profit	80.4	94.6
Financial position		
Current assets	124.4	100.8
Current liabilities	64.7	52.4
Working capital	59.7	48.4
Other assets	37.3	30.2
Property and equipment	86.0	82.6
Total assets	247.7	213.6
Other data		
Capital expenditures	17.3	14.9
Depreciation and amortization	11.8	11.6
Return on sales	22.0%	30.0%
Return on assets	32.5%	44.3%
Number of employees	1429	1337

> *If you decide to go back to your last strategic decision, return to Chapter 31.*
>
> *If you would prefer going back to an earlier strategic decision, return to Chapter 19 or Chapter 11.*
>
> *If you're still feeling the sting of defeat and believe you could have made your last strategic choice work in real life, you may be right. After all, this is just a game. However, if you return to your last strategic decision (the first option above) and select the other alternative, you will learn why the author considers it a better choice.*

44

Pursuing a Differentiation Advantage

Wanting to exploit MedTech's strong value-creating activities in component design, assembly-line layout, product testing, computer networks, manufacturing operations, marketing and sales, and service, you choose differentiation as the best track for MedTech's divisions. In less than a week you and your senior team identify 16 different activities that produce unique and highly differentiated value for customers. Anxious to move forward quickly, you ask Mary Updike to help management in both divisions perfect a streamlined process for examining anew the real buyers, the impact of a differentiation strategy on those buyers' value chains, customers' purchasing criteria, potential sources of uniqueness in MedTech's own value chain, the costs of existing differentiation, potential sources and costs of new differentiation, alternative configurations of value activities to create maximum differentiation relative to cost, differentiation sustainability, and cost-reduction possibilities in areas where MedTech's divisions choose not to differentiate. You ask Mary to complete all this within three months, at which time you hope MedTech can launch its differentiation strategy in both divisions and across all niches in order to reap sales and profit rewards by year-end.

At the end of the three months, you unveil the new differentiation strategy to everyone within the MedTech organization, identifying the three major areas where 12 selected value activities will receive special emphasis during the coming months: four in product design, five in manufacturing, and three in marketing and sales. To propel the drive, you make a series of policy changes aimed at standardizing the differentiation strategy across all niches with respect to product features and performance, the rate of advertising spending, the technology employed in configuring MedTech's blood analyzers, and the skill and experience levels of personnel working in the 12 key value activities. As you hoped, the sharp focus of the new differentiation strategy allows everyone within both MedTech divisions to understand more clearly their direct, indirect, or quality-assurance roles in producing unique, value-targeted products.

In the months that follow, MedTech's 42 market-niche managers shift their emphasis from pure micromarketing to maximizing MedTech's positive impact on customers' value chains, which in most niches means finding ways to provide faster, better, and more differentiated blood analysis, collection, and monitoring. By the end of the third quarter, MedTech introduces two customizeable lines of blood analyzers, one in each division, designed to deliver more sophisticated blood testing at the same cost and uniquely tailored for different segments. Customers in many niches quickly perceive the new line of blood analyzers as better than existing models and purchase enough units to push MedTech beyond Benton Pharmaceuticals' growth expectations for the year. At year-end MedTech proves the worth of value-chain analysis by recording sales of $390 million, an increase of 23 percent, and profits of $101 million, also an increase of 23 percent, as shown in the accompanying table.

Selected Financial Information
(Dollars in Millions)

	Year ended September 30	
	This year	Last year
Operations		
Net sales	$389.8	$316.8
Cost of sales	123.6	107.1
R&D	40.1	30.6
Marketing	82.6	63.4
G&A	42.0	34.7
Operating profit	101.4	82.0
Financial position		
Current assets	127.5	104.7
Current liabilities	66.3	54.4
Working capital	61.2	50.2
Other assets	38.2	31.4
Property and equipment	92.7	81.2
Total assets	258.4	217.2
Other data		
Capital expenditures	17.2	14.1
Depreciation and amortization	13.0	11.5
Return on sales	26.0%	25.9%
Return on assets	39.2%	37.8%
Number of employees	1500	1340

Mitch Cavanaugh, your group president, congratulates you on the way you put value-chain analysis to work, confessing that at one time he worried that the undertaking was consuming too much of your time. Now, however, he expects your approach to pay off even more handsomely in the coming year.

As you look back over the year, you realize that the new national health-care act, which guarantees minimum health-care coverage for all Americans, brought with it great pressure to reduce costs and strengthened the appeal of your new customizeable line of blood analyzers. Now your competitors are working day and night to imitate and improve upon the new line. As you ponder the market conditions, you actually relish the challenge of your next strategic decision. To exploit MedTech's micromarketing capability and its value-chain knowledge and to gain real long-term competitive advantage, should the company further differentiate itself by increasing the sources of such differentiation? Or should MedTech zero in on a single differentiating factor, such as technology-driven product design, to offset the competitive attacks that are being fueled by MedTech's success and the new national health-care legislation? Further differentiation would increase long-term sustainability because over time multiple sources of differentiation would provide more opportunities for growth than would more limited sources of differentiation. However, zeroing in on a single differentiating factor, such as technology-driven product design, which currently represents a major part of MedTech's perceived uniqueness in the marketplace, would allow MedTech to advance even further and faster, making it nearly impossible for competitors to overtake MedTech in that single area.

With customers continuing to rave about the design and features of your new line of blood analyzers, you see a clear opportunity for MedTech to reap great benefits from focusing on product design. Better-and-better blood analyzers would surely produce better-and-better bottom-line results. On the other hand, MedTech's ability to introduce a new line of blood analyzers so quickly into the marketplace at a reduced price depended upon value activities in three areas, not in just product design, and you suspect that stressing other value activities could further enhance the perceived uniqueness of MedTech's products.

As you grapple with this decision, you try to peer many years into the future. Five or ten years downstream, which approach will best serve the company, multiple sources of differentiation or a perfected single source? Both approaches would exploit MedTech's strong micromarketing, value-chain analysis, and differentiation capabilities, but would one capitalize on such capabilities more than the other? You invite input from Mary Updike and members of your senior team, but you continue to find convincing pros and cons on both sides. Finally, you must take decisive action.

If you choose to develop multiple sources of product and service differentiation, turn to Chapter 58.

If you believe in perfecting a single source of product and service differentiation, turn to Chapter 59.

45
Developing a Cost Advantage

Reacting to the current recession and rumors that a new national health-care act will soon pass Congress and bring even greater pressure on reducing health-care costs, you believe that MedTech's divisions will benefit most from achieving cost advantages in the years to come. At this point you can see 18 different value activities where MedTech currently enjoys some cost advantage in the areas of human resource management, technology development, procurement, inbound logistics, and outbound logistics. However, when you communicate your decision to Mary Updike, she cautions you that pursuing a cost advantage will require a thorough examination of the cost structure and behavior of each individual value activity and that such cost analyses take time and resources. That may be true, you counter, but you feel it would be a big mistake to retreat after having come this far with cost advantages.

With Updike's help, you launch a companywide strategic cost analysis, telling the management teams in each division that you want them to do whatever it takes to get this analysis right because becoming the low-cost producer in every targeted market niche depends on it. The clarity of your vision heartens your senior management and even convinces Mary Updike to set aside her disagreement and commit to helping you obtain an accurate analysis.

Over the next several months, you do your best to further exploit past successes by maintaining or increasing sales in all market niches. With luck, cost breakthroughs can occur before the end of the year and be applied to an increasing number of targeted niches. With the clock ticking ominously, Mary Updike takes the management teams of both divisions, all 42 market-niche managers, and over 200 first-line supervisors through an exhaustive evaluation process. They analyze the cost drivers in each of MedTech's value activities, identify the relative costs of competitors' value activities, evaluate alternative ways to control cost drivers or ways to reconfigure the value chain, including upstream and downstream values to reduce costs, and test cost-reduction possibilities to make sure they don't compromise product quality and can be sustained over time. In addition, MedTech people analyze a host of cost-influencing factors, including real growth in the industry, the economic scale of competitors, the learning rates of different value activities, technological change, inflation rates, and aging of the work force. In the end, the choices boil down to two ways of gaining cost advantage: MedTech can either control existing cost drivers, particularly in those value activities that represent a significant proportion of total costs, or it can reconfigure the entire value chain in order to more efficiently design, produce, market, and distribute, its products and services.

As the analysis drags on, it becomes clear that reconfiguring the value chains in both MedTech divisions by changing the way the company designs, produces, markets, and distributes products and services will optimize the company's cost effectiveness and guarantee its cost leadership in years to come. Doing so may put MedTech on the verge of solidifying its cost leadership, but time is working against you because it now appears that sales this year will not hit Benton Pharmaceuticals' required growth rates. You make a strong case to Benton executives for reconfiguring MedTech's value chain, but group president Mitch Cavanaugh, in front of Bob Koontz, chairman and CEO of Benton Pharmaceuticals, shoots you down by labeling your plan "strategic tinkering." He accuses you of having become so enamored with the possibilities of future improvements that you are ignoring immediate business opportunities and requirements. He openly chides you for not taking greater advantage of MedTech's micromarketing capabilities. You react calmly by outlining in detail MedTech's cost position vis-à-vis its competitors and relative to each customer segment. And, you do it with such precision, completeness, and strategic vision that you win over Bob Koontz, who recognizes the long-term competitive value of this kind of analytical thinking for MedTech and other Benton divisions. Overruling Cavanaugh, he gives you the green light to reconfigure the value chains of MedTech's two divisions.

You stay clear of Mitch Cavanaugh for the next two months, until the year closes and MedTech reports revenues of $314 million, a decrease of 1 percent, and profits of $74 million, a decrease of 10 percent, as shown in the accompanying table.

Furious over MedTech's poor performance for the year and out-

Selected Financial Information
(Dollars in Millions)

	Year ended September 30	
	This year	Last year
Operations		
Net sales	$314.2	$316.8
Cost of sales	97.9	107.1
R&D	32.1	30.6
Marketing	69.5	63.4
G&A	40.6	34.7
Operating profit	74.1	82.0
Financial position		
Current assets	100.8	104.7
Current liabilities	52.4	54.4
Working capital	48.4	50.2
Other assets	30.2	31.4
Property and equipment	79.8	81.2
Total assets	210.9	217.2
Other data		
Capital expenditures	12.8	14.1
Depreciation and amortization	11.5	11.5
Return on sales	23.6%	25.9%
Return on assets	35.1%	37.8%
Number of employees	1351	1340

raged at your preoccupation with value-chain analysis and reconfiguration, Mitch Cavanaugh demands your resignation. You appeal to Bob Koontz, but he informs you that Cavanaugh has already threatened to leave the company if you remain president of MedTech, a ploy Koontz personally abhors, but, frankly, he cannot afford to lose Mitch Cavanaugh. To resolve the dilemma, he offers to let you pursue your agenda for value-chain and strategic cost analysis as senior vice president of strategic planning for all of Benton Pharmaceuticals, with a 25 percent salary increase. Yes, you will gain a corporate staff position, but no, you will not be making any more strategic decisions for MedTech. "Perhaps," he says with a grin, "you can eventually bring some enlightenment to executives like Cavanaugh."

Upset and dejected by your forced ouster from MedTech, you reluctantly accept the staff executive position, even though you will never be happy until you regain line responsibility. That may happen soon, but until it does, you can revisit your past strategic decisions at MedTech and make new ones, if you'd like.

If you would like to reconsider your last strategic decision, turn to Chapter 32.

If you want to revisit an earlier decision, return to Chapter 21 or Chapter 13.

If you're still feeling the sting of defeat and believe you could have made your last strategic choice work in real life, you may be right. After all, this is just a game. However, if you return to your last strategic decision (the first option above) and select the other alternative, you will learn why the author considers it a better choice.

46
Creating New Approaches to Doing Business

Deciding that MedTech can best gain long-term competitive advantage with fundamentally new approaches to doing business, you ask your senior management team and the more than 40 market-niche managers to incorporate such thinking into the current cycle of business planning. You then ask everyone within both MedTech divisions to take micromarketing and head-on competition avoidance one step further by finding fundamentally new and different ways to meet customer needs in various niches, stressing, perhaps to convince even yourself, that searching for overlooked and underserved niches alone will not win for the company the kind of long-term advantage it needs.

To make your mandate more tangible, you advise MedTech's market-niche managers to identify the *strategic degrees of freedom*, to borrow a term coined by Kenichi Ohmae in his book, *The Mind of the Strategist*, in each of the company's market niches by precisely determining the amount of freedom or number of possibilities for creating brand-new approaches to doing business in those niches. Then together with Amos Gill, Kate DaVaeno, Cam Cardon, and Ken Matsumori, you identify the niches which seem to offer the greatest strategic degrees of freedom or possibilities for fundamental change, targeting them as "special niches." Of the more than 120 market niches served by MedTech, only 23 become special niches, demanding aggressive action in terms of creating new approaches to doing business. For all other niches, you challenge all MedTech's market-niche managers to hold onto the company's current position while you and your senior executives and selected market-niche managers examine customers' true objectives and the basic nature of the product or service offered by MedTech in the 23 special niches. As the team concentrates on the special niches, it finds numerous opportunities for change and redirection, giving you and your senior executives much hope that MedTech really can develop new approaches to doing business that will propel the company far ahead of its competition.

Keeping in mind the likely reaction of competitors to each of your anticipated thrusts in the special niches, you complete comprehensive strategic plans for each special niche by midyear. At that time, the U.S. Congress passes a new health-care act guaranteeing a minimum level of health care to every American citizen. This event strengthens your confidence in your strategy because your industry, undergoing fundamental change, requires nothing short of dramatic new ways of conducting business.

However, you find that having moved the other approximately 100 market niches into a maintenance mode has dampened the motivation and energy of many of MedTech's market-niche managers as well as other sales, production, and R&D people in both divisions working to serve the nonspecial niches. In many cases, competitors easily overtake MedTech's positions, causing sales to decline and placing even greater pressure on the 23 special niches to perform.

By the fourth quarter, you begin to panic as sales continue to shrink in the nonspecial niches and the promise of dividends from any new approaches to doing business in the 23 special niches fades into the horizon. Opting for drastic measures, you restrict the allocation of MedTech's resources to just five special niches where the opportunity for gaining advantage seems greatest and quickest. The five new areas include: (1) introducing blood testing into grocery stores; (2) establishing MedTech research labs to provide sophisticated blood analysis and testing for local and regional hospitals and medical centers at 50 different locations throughout the United States; (3) developing a self-administered blood test kit that screens for as many as 15 different conditions from a single administration; (4) placing and operating blood analysis instruments in California doctors' offices in response to a recently passed California law prohibiting physicians from owning such equipment; and (5) introducing a new blood substitute that augments real blood by a factor of 10 during transfusion. You bet your future and the future of MedTech on these five new game strategies. Your anxiety mounts as the end of the year draws near and you still find yourself months away from launching even one new approach to doing business. At year-end MedTech reports sales of $359 million, an increase of only 4 percent for the year, and profits of $79 million, a decrease of 9 percent, as shown in the accompanying table.

Selected Financial Information
(Dollars in Millions)

	Year ended September 30	
	This year	Last year
Operations		
Net sales	$358.9	$345.1
Cost of sales	125.6	110.4
R&D	28.7	27.6
Marketing	82.8	82.9
G&A	42.9	37.9
Operating profit	78.9	86.3
Financial position		
Current assets	121.1	113.9
Current liabilities	63.0	59.2
Working capital	58.1	54.7
Other assets	36.3	34.2
Property and equipment	108.1	99.9
Total assets	265.5	247.9
Other data		
Capital expenditures	25.0	24.0
Depreciation and amortization	14.3	13.0
Return on sales	22.0%	25.0%
Return on assets	29.7%	34.8%
Number of employees	1377	1351

During a tense session with Mitch Cavanaugh, your group president and Bob Koontz, chairman and CEO of Benton Pharmaceuticals, you receive harsh criticism for pursuing too much novelty and taking unnecessary risks at a time when MedTech's micromarketing and avoiding head-on competition initiatives were producing strong results. They chastise you for failing to solicit their input or listen to their points of view and accuse you of making decisions too rashly, without enough facts or regard for other opinions. To your amazement, they tell you that both Amos Gill and Kate DaVaeno have confided their distress to Benton executives over not having been properly included in your recent strategic decision making.

Having never experienced such a situation before, you feel your pulse racing and your stomach clenching as you wait for the ax to fall. When it doesn't, you offer to resign. To your astonishment, Bob Koontz accepts your resignation without hesitation. Telling Mitch Cavanaugh to work out an agreeable severance package with you, he

unceremoniously ushers you out of his office. Speechless, you acqui-
esce to a severance package that gives you the equivalent of three
years' salary and a lot of time to think about your past mistakes.

Fortunately, in this book you can retrace your steps by going back
to recent or earlier decisions.

---

*If you would like to revisit your most recent strategic
decision, return to Chapter 33.*

*If you prefer reexamining an earlier strategic decision,
return to Chapter 21 or Chapter 13.*

*If you're still feeling the sting of defeat and believe you
could have made your last strategic choice work in real life,
you may be right. After all, this is just a game. However, if
you return to your last strategic decision (the first option
above) and select the other alternative, you will learn why the
author considers it a better choice.*

47
Exploiting MedTech's Relative Superiority

Aware of your tendency to make quick decisions, sometimes without fully examining the situation or listening closely enough to the perspectives of other people, you take great care to include Amos Gill, Kate DaVaeno, Cam Cardon, and Ken Matsumori in the task of assessing MedTech's relative superiority against competitors' weaknesses. At the outset the team argues unanimously that MedTech's micromarketing program far surpasses all competitors in the blood analysis, collection, and monitoring arena and that the company should, therefore, build on that superiority. In light of MedTech's clear superiority in micromarketing and head-on competition avoidance, attempting to create fundamentally new approaches to doing business in selected niches would constitute a grave strategic mistake.

With a strong consensus among your most senior and trusted executives, you take the discussion to lower levels in both divisions. It doesn't take long for MedTech's market-niche managers and other middle managers to lend their full support to the proposed strategic direction, and they promise to assist in the detailed strategic analysis and planning necessary to keep MedTech one step ahead of competitors in micromarketing and avoiding head-on competition. While MedTech can, you believe, maintain its dominant position in some niches without much fear of competitive attack, you know that in many areas, where micromarketing represents the most logical alternative for competitors, your company must work hard not to get "out-niched." To keep you, your senior management team, the market-niche managers, and other MedTech employees focused on exploiting MedTech's relative superiority, you adopt four rules from two respected marketing professors, Robert Linneman and John Stanton, as summarized in their book *Making Niche Marketing Work:*

1. Attack yourself.
2. Make the game too tough to play.
3. Always block competitive moves.
4. Try to minimize "quarteritis."

The more successful MedTech becomes, the more aggressively will competitors try to nip off smaller and smaller market segments for themselves. Incorporating the four rules into MedTech's strategic business and marketing planning system will help prevent this from happening. You encourage market-niche managers to attack themselves, in effect outniching themselves, make the game too tough to play by fully engaging their continually improving marketing databases, make it impossible for competitors to identify an opportunity first, and block competitive moves by aggressively responding even when a very small and minor portion of a niche comes under competitive fire. To ensure that your market-niche managers succeed, you guarantee sufficient funding for the defensive actions necessary to maintain MedTech's relative superiority. You also campaign arduously to relieve undue pressure from Benton for maximizing short-term profits. Over the next few months MedTech's two division presidents, Amos Gill and Kate DaVaeno, lead the charge throughout their organizations so well that the micromarketing and competition avoidance game becomes a virtual art at MedTech.

At midyear, the U.S. Congress passes legislation mandating a new health-care policy that promises all American citizens minimum health-care coverage. The law opens a number of new opportunities for micromarketing in the area of preventative health care, opportunities that MedTech market-niche managers quickly exploit by making blood analysis, collection, and monitoring more accessible to patients. In a short three months MedTech's self-administered blood analysis devices proliferate into dozens of varieties, applications, and niches. As the year continues, MedTech's strength in utilizing its marketing databases to track the smallest discrepancies between customer needs and existing products or services continues to expand, making it very difficult for competitors to hinder or duplicate MedTech's rise in the marketplace. At year-end, MedTech reports sales of $580 million, an increase of 68 percent, and profits of $157 million, an increase of 81 percent, as shown in the accompanying table.

Selected Financial Information
(Dollars in Millions)

	Year ended September 30	
	This year	Last year
Operations		
Net sales	$579.8	$345.1
Cost of sales	179.7	110.4
R&D	40.6	27.6
Marketing	153.6	82.9
G&A	49.3	37.9
Operating profit	156.6	86.3
Financial position		
Current assets	189.9	113.9
Current liabilities	98.7	59.2
Working capital	91.1	54.7
Other assets	57.0	34.2
Property and equipment	123.5	99.9
Total assets	370.3	247.9
Other data		
Capital expenditures	40.4	24.0
Depreciation and amortization	14.3	13.0
Return on sales	27.0%	25.0%
Return on assets	42.3%	34.8%
Number of employees	1624	1351

MedTech continues to attract coverage in the business and health-care press for its marketing prowess and its unmatched responsiveness to the needs of an increasingly complex health-care environment worldwide. But even in light of promises of promotion within Benton Pharmaceuticals and bonus compensation in the form of $1 million in stock options, you grow more and more concerned as your primary competitor, BBX, maintains a fierce tenacity for duplicating MedTech's niche-marketing capabilities, all the while claiming superior technology. You know you must soon deal specifically with BBX's threat.

In an effort to determine how best to counter the BBX threat, you return to Sun-Tsu's *The Art of War,* as well as a number of other ancient Chinese texts, including Lao-Zi's *The Way of Power* and *The Book of Changes.* One book, *Lure the Tiger Out of the Mountains: The 36 Stratagems of Ancient China* by Gao-Yuan, provides a compelling summary of time-honored Eastern stratagems applied by military leaders, tacticians, politicians, merchants, philosophers, and others, which you use to formulate two possible responses to BBX: act from a position of superiority or act for the purpose of attack. Attacking generally proves difficult in both business and warfare, but according to ancient Chinese wisdom, certain attack stratagems can minimize your exposure by drawing the opponent out into the open before you launch your attack. Given the tenacity and strength of BBX, an attack stratagem could work. On the other hand, stratagems relying on superiority to divert a rival's thrust would offer more safety, even though they might backfire on you. No matter how hard you try to divert your opponent's attention in another direction, a strong opponent like BBX may not succumb to such manipulation.

During several penetrating discussions with Amos Gill, Kate DaVaeno, Cam Cardon, Ken Matsumori, and Pamela West, the consultant you used a couple of years ago to help you hammer out the theme for MedTech's direction, you weigh all the pros and cons of both the attack and superiority stratagems. Should MedTech lure BBX out into the open, making it vulnerable to MedTech's strength, or should it use its superiority to fool BBX into assuming MedTech is pursuing one course of action when it is, in fact, pursuing another, causing BBX to follow the wrong course?

You find it hard to believe that you are placing your future and the future of MedTech in the hands of ancient Chinese strategists, but their thinking remains so compelling and so strategically appropriate for your current situation that you and your management team feel confident one of these choices will work.

If you choose the attack stratagem, designed to lure BBX into the open and make it vulnerable, turn to Chapter 60.

If you prefer the superiority stratagem, designed to fool or divert BBX's attention in one direction while you pursue another, turn to Chapter 61.

48
Fine-Tuning Infrastructure and Design

Convinced that you must first engineer the organizational structure and management process that can support the focus on core services and customer monitoring, you ask Bob Shay, whom you promoted to senior vice president at the beginning of this fiscal year, to continue his role as architect, making sure that MedTech designs the right structure, work processes, and systems that will continuously identify unmet customer needs and find unique product solutions to those needs. In a planning meeting with Bob Shay, you suggest he consider several factors, including the role of intermediaries between MedTech and its customers, high-contact and low-contact relationships, individual and institutional customers, delivery time, information about work in progress, capacity constraints, customer repurchase frequency, service complexity levels, and tolerance for service failure. You challenge him to remove all of the failure points that could jeopardize MedTech's objective.

Next, you ask him to scrutinize MedTech's relationships with people, companies, governments, research entities, and universities around the world as well as the company's own physical facilities and offices. No structural or system designs will work if they do not account for the complete infrastructure. You ask him to read two books: Davidow and Malone's *The Virtual Corporation*, which "provides an integrated picture of the customer-driven company of the future," and Regis McKenna's *Relationship Marketing*, which "focuses on building crucial relationships that help a company dominate and own the market in the age of the customer."

Finally, you charge him with three overarching goals: (1) take a long-term view; (2) match the infrastructure to the needs of MedTech customers; and (3) make sure the infrastructure does not overload MedTech's system or overpromise service to MedTech's customers.

As usual, Shay responds beautifully to the challenge and within a matter of months implements a redesigned work system and a network of relationships that strikes you as nothing less than brilliant. Under Shay's direction the selection and preparation of salespeople reaches new heights as a screening and training program comparable to paramedical training and certification makes MedTech's salespeople experts in the field of blood analysis, collection, and monitoring. After initial training, new salespeople spend six months to a year in the field learning how to listen closely to customers.

Another group in Shay's framework, supplier specialists, receive special training to help them discover suppliers capable of injecting new products and services into the MedTech system. In addition, an aggressive continuing education program for salespeople, supplier specialists, and all other employees keeps everyone abreast of new developments in medical research and of changing customer needs and potential product solutions.

Redesigned performance appraisals and reward systems focus not only on sales and profits but also on the application of medical knowledge and innovative business thinking on the customer's behalf. The most coveted rewards and recognition go to people who identify hidden or obscure customer expectations and needs or find new and different product solutions inside or outside the MedTech system.

By the end of the year, MedTech enters into relationships with 10 new suppliers through licensing and other joint arrangements that bring aboard a host of new products and services, ranging from medical equipment rentals during customer peak load times to a throwaway, yet comprehensive, blood testing kit for emergency use in nonsterile environments. Customers express such enthusiasm and manifest such loyalty over MedTech's service, you can't wait for the year-end results that will finally put Benton's and Mitch Cavanaugh's doubts to rest.

When Congress passes new health insurance legislation requiring a minimum level of basic care for all American citizens, MedTech seizes the opportunity, responding to customers' increased emphasis on blood analysis and testing as a means of eliminating other more costly procedures excluded from the minimum-care coverage. With its new design and infrastructure, MedTech quickly introduces a new combined package of virus identification tests and two other inexpensive blood test kits to an eager market.

Selected Financial Information
(Dollars in Millions)

	Year ended September 30	
	This year	Last year
Operations		
Net sales	$351.3	$221.4
Cost of sales	115.8	75.2
R&D	32.2	17.7
Marketing	79.9	52.4
G&A	35.0	23.0
Operating profit	88.4	53.1
Financial position		
Current asets	116.8	74.2
Current liabilities	60.7	38.6
Working capital	56.1	35.6
Other assets	35.0	22.2
Property and equipment	79.4	75.5
Total assets	231.3	171.9
Other data		
Capital expenditures	16.6	10.5
Depreciation and amortization	10.8	11.2
Return on sales	25.2%	24.0%
Return on assets	38.2%	30.9%
Number of employees	1352	1141

At the end of the fiscal year, MedTech reports sales of $351 million, a 59 percent rise, and profits of $88 million, an increase of 35 percent over the previous year, as shown in the accompanying table.

When you receive congratulations from across the Benton organization and Mitch Cavanaugh informs you that the top brass is considering your advancement, you feel vindicated. However, you promise Benton executives that the best still lies ahead, and you state that you would rather remain as MedTech's CEO through the coming year. Benton CEO Bob Koontz allows you another year, but tells you to prepare a successor to take over after that.

You are heartened when people and organizations outside the company begin taking note of MedTech's accomplishments. As one of three experts in a special hourlong discussion on the *MacNeil/Lehrer Newshour*, you specifically describe to a nationwide audience how the new health-care legislation has revolutionized the health-care industry in the United States. As a result of this exposure you become a darling of the news media and a popular commentator on how U.S. health-care product companies, providers, and insurers can create a model for the whole world.

In the early weeks after the close of the fiscal year, you recognize that it will take one more major strategic decision to complete your vision for MedTech. Do you develop a comprehensive measurement system to make sure that the company can continuously improve its core services philosophy, system design, and work infrastructure over time, or do you foster an organizationwide renewal attitude to guarantee continuous improvement? Again the strategic decision boils down to a choice between means and methods for continuing a strategic course you set a few years ago.

The advantage of pursuing the measurement track derives from the fact that concrete and specific techniques can document the company's development for future MedTech management generations. On the other hand, given your recent focus on infrastructure and design, the renewal track emphasizes people and leadership as the avenue to the true progress that springs from attitudes and beliefs deeply implanted in the hearts and minds of people. One alternative represents a quantitative approach, while the other reflects a qualitative approach. As you prepare to turn over MedTech's reins to Bob Shay, you view this as a critical choice because it will so greatly influence the organization after you're gone. Which alternative best fulfills the legacy you want to leave behind?

If you choose the option of qualitative renewal, turn to Chapter 62.

If you prefer the option of quantitative measurement, turn to Chapter 63.

49
Emphasizing People and Leadership

Because you've invested so much time and attention over the past couple of years in the structure and system side of the business, you decide to turn attention now toward people and leadership as the most important elements in delivering superior core services. Once again, your management team trusts you so much that they quickly endorse your decision and align themselves behind it.

Looking ahead to your departure from MedTech, you invite Bob Shay, your new senior vice president and chief operating officer, to create an agenda for focusing on people and leadership in the coming year. Since Shay admits some doubt about his own expertise in this arena, he commits to strengthening his own people and leadership skills. You review with Shay the possible paths he might take, including hiring consultants, holding a management retreat, sending a task force to a series of seminars or just putting himself on an aggressive reading program augmented by discussion with you and other members of the management team.

For starters, Bob bones up on his reading, working through all of the current leadership material; then he attends a couple of seminars. Burt Nanus' book, *Visionary Leadership*, helps him conceptualize the role of visionary leadership in securing the future. The work of William Davidow and Bro Uttal, authors of *Total Customer Service*, greatly influences Shay because it addresses people and leadership in the context of total customer service. Armed with his new knowledge, he hires a couple of local consultants to help him set the direction for MedTech's leadership and people program. When he informs you of his activities, you say you would like to spend one long session with him during which you'll share your own thoughts about what needs to happen at MedTech.

As you begin your meeting with Shay, you remind him that you don't want to tell him what to do, you simply want to provide some input. "Every member of the senior management team," you say, "must actively communicate his or her beliefs about identifying unmet customer needs and finding unique product solutions based on monitoring customer service expectations. Then everyone should back up those beliefs with actions, even dramatic actions, when necessary. War stories about extraordinary actions people have taken to uncover hidden customer needs or find brilliantly simple product solutions will greatly influence MedTech for years to come. The walk and talk of the senior management team will remain a key factor in maintaining and strengthening MedTech's core services strategy and culture." You also encourage Shay to find ways to slice through any red tape and bureaucracy that may prevent people from getting customers what they want.

Knowing that Bob Shay has been strongly influenced by the work of Davidow and Uttal, you conclude your session by reinforcing the leadership and people principles those authors identify: making customer service everybody's business; declaring war on bureaucracy; working ceaselessly to hire the right people; training, training, and retraining; and motivating lavishly.

Your protégé appreciates the session and expresses his gratitude to you for enabling him to assist in guiding MedTech into the future. You feel confident that you've picked the right replacement. He'll face challenges every bit as tough as the ones you've faced, but you think he'll rise to every challenge.

Within 90 days, Bob presents his people and leadership recommendations, addressing all of your concerns and convincing you that he's on the right track. You give him the green light to proceed, and as the year unfolds, you delight in the new vitality that Bob's program instills in everyone at MedTech. People throughout the organization feel more empowered to monitor customer expectations, identify unmet needs, and find unique solutions. You take particular pleasure in watching how cross-functional work teams and task forces develop common purpose, even if only for a month or two, to deliver customers what they thought they would never get.

As the year draws to an end, you count six new product lines acquired through licensing arrangements and three new product areas developed internally, all in response to newly discovered and understood customer needs. The new products include a portable blood analyzer developed internally, complete with its own "power book" computer capable of providing sophisticated analysis of blood samples at emergency sites in the field, in a doctor's office, or in a patient's home. Also, in an unusual move, MedTech enters into a 25-year licensing arrangement with a small firm in Germany to market a new blood substitute that resolves all the major concerns that had prevented mass distribution of blood substitutes.

By the end of year, revenues increase by more than 50 percent to $334 million, and profits grow to $82 million, as shown in the accompanying table.

In the wake of MedTech's successful leadership and people agenda, you realize you've paid too little attention to the recently passed national health insurance legislation, which provides minimum healthcare coverage to all American citizens. Since most of your customers have not yet figured out the ramifications of the new legislation, you know MedTech must move to the forefront, anticipating or even creating new customer service expectations that will inevitably arise from the new legislation.

As you spend time reflecting on this matter during a weeklong vacation with your family, you identify the next, and possibly final,

Selected Financial Information
(Dollars in Millions)

	Year ended September 30	
	This year	Last year
Operations		
Net sales	$333.9	$221.4
Cost of sales	110.4	75.2
R&D	26.7	17.7
Marketing	78.3	52.4
G&A	36.7	23.0
Operating profit	81.8	53.1
Financial position		
Current assets	111.1	74.2
Current liabilities	57.8	38.6
Working capital	53.3	35.6
Other assets	33.3	22.2
Property and equipment	78.6	75.5
Total assets	223.0	171.9
Other data		
Capital expenditures	15.8	10.5
Depreciation and amortization	10.8	11.2
Return on sales	24.5%	24.0%
Return on assets	36.7%	30.9%
Number of employees	1334	1141

strategic decision you will need to make at MedTech. Should you continue with a people-oriented agenda to ensure that a renewal attitude maintains MedTech's continued success, or should you turn your attention back to a more structured and systemized approach by implementing a measurement system that can ensure a continued focus on core services and monitoring customer expectations? Once again, you face a qualitative versus quantitative choice. You ask yourself whether a soft renewal approach or a hard measurement approach will better position MedTech to respond to the major changes that will be brought on by the new national health-care legislation. Which alternative will leave the best legacy for Bob Shay and his people? The measurement approach places more emphasis on infrastructure and design, a decision you opted against a year ago but realize could now benefit MedTech, while the renewal approach furthers and deepens the progress you've made by focusing on people and leadership. Philosophically, you struggle with the question of whether an executive should balance his or her strategy implementation decisions over time, which would argue for the measurement approach, or whether an executive should adhere steadfastly to a single-strategy implementation philosophy, which would support the renewal approach. Before long you tire of too much philosophizing and make your choice.

If you wish to adhere to the renewal approach, turn to Chapter 62.

If you choose to pursue the measurement approach, turn to Chapter 63.

50
Forming Innovative Strategic Alliances

The work of Kenichi Ohmae, Director of McKinsey & Company in Japan and author of *The Borderless World*, convinces you to pursue innovative alliances rather than traditional acquisitions or mergers. Convinced by Ohmae that too many American corporations myopically strive to maintain 51 percent equity in their acquisition deals, you decide to pursue a different path toward globalization. Consequently, you and your four senior vice presidents, Amos Gill, Ken Matsumori, Meg Daniels, and Jack Suhler, formulate a plan for a network of alliances around the world.

Over the next nine months, driven by a vision of finding innovative ways to share both fixed costs and market benefits with business enterprises around the world, you and your four senior vice presidents engineer a total of 36 strategic alliances. MedTech's equity position in these 36 companies ranges from 95 percent to 5 percent, and the alliances include licensing blood analysis, collection, and monitoring products in foreign countries, sharing marketing costs with foreign manufacturers, and codeveloping inexpensive blood analyzers for the Third World.

You hire a new senior vice president of administration, Karen Wilcox, to join your core team and help you develop an organizational approach that emphasizes the sort of high trust and candid communication that fosters healthy strategic alliances. Karen, who was born in Britain and raised in Russia, Indonesia, and France, works closely with you to create a flexible organizational atmosphere that facilitates quick handling of issues, minimizes operating policies, and stresses constant communication through video conferencing, E-mail, and immediate on-line access to financial performance companywide. You earnestly strive to communicate to every part of the growing MedTech network your long-term commitment to establishing a global network unlike anything in the industry, and you find people throughout the organization deeply affected and motivated by your enthusiasm and vision. As news of your success spreads worldwide, more and more doors open up for strategic alliances which enable MedTech to win distinction as one of the most forward-looking companies in the global health-care medical products industry.

In the last three months of the end of the year MedTech initiates 10 more alliances, all outside the United States, but your involvement in this strategy causes you to ignore the passage of new national health-care legislation by the U.S. Congress. Although the new national policy will significantly affect many Benton divisions, you expect little impact on MedTech because most of its global markets already function under some sort of national health-care policy.

At the close of the fiscal year, MedTech reports an 86 percent growth in sales, to $950 million, with a 79 percent growth in profits, to $223 million, as shown in the accompanying table.

Selected Financial Information
(Dollars in Millions)

	Year ended September 30	
	This year	Last year
Operations		
Net sales	$949.9	$510.7
Cost of sales	313.2	172.1
R&D	95.0	56.0
Marketing	190.0	97.0
G&A	129.2	61.3
Operating profit	222.5	124.3
Financial position		
Current assets	315.8	170.7
Current liabilities	164.2	88.8
Working capital	151.6	81.9
Other assets	94.7	51.2
Property and equipment	107.0	97.4
Total assets	517.6	319.3
Other data		
Capital expenditures	26.0	20.8
Depreciation and amortization	13.9	13.2
Return on sales	23.4%	24.3%
Return on assets	43.0%	38.9%
Number of employees	1876	1523

After the end of the fiscal year, you receive word from Bob Koontz, Benton CEO, that the corporation has decided to separate MedTech from the Medical Products and Systems Group and set it up as its own group, MedTech International. He informs you that you will no longer report to group president Mitch Cavanaugh but directly to him as Benton's newest group president. With a wry smile, he asks if you like the idea. Of course you do. You're thrilled. To top it off, you receive stock options worth over $5 million and the promise of increased resources and a free hand in determining the growth and development of MedTech International.

As MedTech winds down after the celebration, you realize that you may have underestimated the long-term ripple effect throughout the world of the new U.S. health-care policy. The pressure to revamp America's health-care delivery system fuels a major restructuring of the whole industry. You also know that the MedTech International Group must undertake a major reorganization in the coming year as you prepare to operate as a group rather than a division.

You and your core team begin carefully weighing the probable impact of these imminent changes on MedTech and the industry. You soon identify two basic organizational options for addressing the changes. One alternative involves organizing the MedTech International Group along product-country lines, not unlike other global organizations, as a means of focusing on product groupings and improving responsiveness to geographical markets. This alternative would further facilitate the necessary decentralization that has made MedTech's alliance strategy such a stellar success. While this alternative represents a safer and more traditional approach, it may also work best.

The other alternative involves organizing the MedTech International Group along customer lines as a means of improving response to the customer needs of different market segments such as medical centers, clinics, doctors' offices, and emergency facilities. This route would help the MedTech International Group standardize the costs and quality of all its products. The former alternative emphasizes specialization and differentiation, while the latter stresses standardization and commonalities. You and your core team see pros and cons for both alternatives, but now you must decide which alternative will best serve the MedTech International Group in the future.

If you choose to organize the MedTech International Group along product-country lines, turn to Chapter 64.

If you decide to organize the MedTech International Group along customer-product lines, turn to Chapter 65.

51
Structuring Traditional Mergers and Acquisitions

While you acknowledge that traditional acquisitions and mergers take much longer to consummate than strategic alliances, you conclude that gaining at least 50 percent control of a venture outweighs that downside. After all, you tell yourself, control and equity remain the key instruments of capitalism, and everyone, including corporate headquarters, stockholders, and industry analysts, expects MedTech to maintain control over its increasingly far-flung global operations. For MedTech maintaining full control means acquiring 100 percent of a new company or at least 50 percent of a merger. With this goal in mind, you charge your core team to obtain 51 percent or more ownership and to enter into 50-50 joint ventures only as a last resort and only when the strategic rewards justify it. You discuss this aim with Amos Gill, Ken Matsumori, Meg Daniels, and Jack Suhler, and the team concludes that only strategic leaders, subsidiaries which provide substantial strategic advantages to the company, warrant a 50-50 merger or joint-venture arrangement. All other acquisitions must be controlled more tightly.

As the year unfolds, a major industry change occurs when Congress adopts a new national health-care policy that will guarantee every American citizen a minimum level of health-care coverage. In response to the new national policy, a frenzy of change and innovation runs rampant throughout the industry, further accelerating the globalization of medical markets. Companies expand internationally, stimulating a wide range of strategic relationships among health-care and medical products industry companies. MedTech works hard to speed up its global expansion but can only complete four new acquisitions and one joint venture before the end of the fiscal year. As a result, sales increase 43 percent to $730 million, but profits, eaten up by enormous administrative and legal costs associated with completing the acquisitions of the previous year and initiating those of the current year, increase only 4 percent, to $129 million, as shown in the accompanying table.

Selected Financial Information
(Dollars in Millions)

	Year ended September 30	
	This year	Last year
Operations		
Net sales	$730.3	$510.7
Cost of sales	248.3	172.1
R&D	65.6	56.0
Marketing	148.3	97.0
G&A	138.8	61.3
Operating profit	129.3	124.3
Financial position		
Current assets	244.7	170.7
Current liabilities	127.2	88.8
Working capital	117.4	81.9
Other assets	73.4	51.2
Property and equipment	107.0	97.4
Total assets	425.1	319.3
Other data		
Capital expenditures	26.0	20.8
Depreciation and amortization	13.9	13.2
Return on sales	17.7%	24.3%
Return on assets	30.4%	38.9%
Number of employees	1752	1523

MedTech fails to keep pace as its competitors BBX Systems and Glaxol Corporation establish extensive networks of strategic alliances and steal the spotlight as the new leaders in forming medical alliances. Alarmingly, Glaxol woos an acquisition candidate away from MedTech during the final stages of negotiation by persuasively arguing that MedTech's approach to mergers and acquisitions represents the old school while Glaxol's approach represents the new. To make matters worse, one of MedTech's recently acquired companies, a German manufacturer of blood analyzers, becomes disgruntled with the protracted negotiation and due diligence process and files suit against MedTech for damages resulting from lost business and extraordinary expenses linked to the acquisition process. The suit causes a great deal of concern at corporate headquarters, leading some senior Benton executives to conclude, particularly in light of MedTech's poor profits, that you have lost control of MedTech's growth initiatives. Mitch Cavanaugh, your group president, suggests freezing MedTech acquisition activities until you sort out all your current problems. He also recommends adding another player to your core team from headquarters. You accept the recommendation even though the new executive's assignment will include keeping a close watch on you with an eye toward stepping into your shoes if you make further missteps.

Over the next few months your job becomes increasingly unpleasant as you find yourself constrained from pursuing further external growth, all the while being watched closely by Benton's planted executive. When Glaxol offers you an opportunity to run one of its divisions, you jump at the chance.

Sadly, your strategic decision making at MedTech comes to an end, but you look forward to a fresh start at Glaxol. Looking back on it, would you alter your past decisions in order to create a different future for MedTech and yourself?

If you would like to change your last strategic decision, return to Chapter 36.

If you would like to remake an earlier strategic decision, return to Chapter 24 or Chapter 16.

If you're still feeling the sting of defeat and believe you could have made your last strategic choice work in real life, you may be right. After all, this is just a game. However, if you return to your last strategic decision (the first option above) and select the other alternative, you will learn why the author considers it a better choice.

52
Researching Cell Transplants and Genetic Mapping

Your decision to focus your R&D efforts on cell transplants and genetic mapping receives enormous support from Jack Suhler and his management team. To launch the new research drive you hold a retreat on breakthrough thinking for senior and middle management of both MedTech divisions. You hire a consulting team from Harvard and MIT to facilitate the program, and you invite a few key individuals from other parts of the Benton organization to sit in on the three-day experience. By the end of the three days, the hired experts have convinced most of the participants that breakthrough thinking begins with a "childlike" attitude of curiosity and wonder toward all facets of life. In a sense, they say, breakthrough thinking results from freeing your mind of all constraints and letting your imagination roam freely in search of new ideas or new ways of thinking about old ideas. Breakthrough thinkers always possess a childlike enthusiasm for discovery which allows them to see things from new perspectives. Everyone leaves the retreat with a lot of enthusiasm, genuinely delighted that they can improve their breakthrough thinking immediately. All it takes is the right frame of mind.

Six weeks later, Jack Suhler conducts a weeklong R&D retreat with 30 group and team leaders to bring everyone up to date on FutureMedTech's intense cell and genetic research program. Various teams have been trying to answer such basic questions as: Why do cells die? Can errors in the genetic code be corrected? What makes cells change and differentiate from one another? Now Suhler wants all the scientists, engineers, medical researchers, and computer experts to share the progress they've made on their various projects and seek input from colleagues. On the final day of the retreat Suhler delivers a stirring speech that elicits an unusual standing ovation from the group.

"Our work on blood and cell analysis has," he concludes, "thrust us into a history-making role in our industry. Our new focus could enable us to introduce the first cures for cancer, AIDS, and other life-threatening diseases. Why do we do it? Not for money, not just for the joy of discovery. We do it for the good of humankind."

After the applause dies down, you speak briefly to the group, saying that the key to innovation and breakthrough lies in acquiring the most talented people and letting them do their work with sufficient resources, minimum restrictions, and maximum encouragement. You reassure your people that Benton Pharmaceuticals stands squarely behind FutureMedTech's R&D priorities, even in light of the fact that a breakthrough in genetic mapping or cell transplanting could eliminate the need for many drugs the company now markets, thereby substantially reducing sales for some of Benton's pharmaceutical and biotechnology businesses. In conclusion, you pledge your own all-out commitment to the cause.

The two retreats tremendously boost the morale of everyone in the MedTech organization as participants enthusiastically spread the word. Even Kate DaVaeno, who argued strongly for improving blood analysis technology, appears strongly committed to the new vision. However, a short two months later, DaVaeno bowls you over with her announcement that she has received an offer she can't refuse to become president of BBX Systems. BBX has offered Kate the very opportunity she had craved at MedTech. With a sick feeling in the pit of your stomach, you realize you should have seen it coming. Your mind racing, you try to counter the BBX offer, but Kate just laughs and says, "I've already accepted the job. I've given my word. And I'm giving you 30 days." When nothing you say dissuades her, you finally accept the situation. Calmly, you reflect on the strategic implications of DaVaeno's departure. She's good. She may well oversee creation of a blood analyzer that will eclipse MedTech's own product. Nevertheless, you remain confident in the long-term value of your own decision to emphasize genetic mapping and cell transplants.

In the months following Kate DaVaeno's departure, you focus almost exclusively on rebuilding the MedTech Operations division from the ground up, reinforcing new operating principles, resetting marketing priorities and selecting the right person to replace DaVaeno. Then, at midyear, just when you feel you've gotten control of the MedTech Operations division, Congress enacts national health-care legislation that mandates a minimum level of health care for all American citizens. Knowing full well that this development will initiate an enormous push for cost control in the health-care industry, you at first feel anxious because MedTech has not well-positioned itself for this kind of industry change. But as you and Jack Suhler and vice presidents from both divisions carefully consider the implications of the new national policy, you perceive, now more than ever, the need for genetic mapping and cell transplant breakthroughs as the best long-range way to reduce total health-care expenditures.

Throughout the rest of the year, you use the combination of the new national health-care policy and the new war on escalating health-care costs to stimulate people at MedTech to throw themselves body and soul into the company's breakthrough program. At the end of the fiscal year, the retrovirology group, assisted by a team of Harvard and MIT researchers, achieves a major breakthrough: a genetically altered cell that, when transplanted in a variety of cancerous animals, permanently halts further cell malformations. It all came together over a few short months with the help of MedTech's blood analyzing technology for examining the minutest detail of cell composition. The scientists, working as a group, discovered a cancer-causing gene that sets off the chain reaction of cell malformations in 95 percent of all cancers. They located the gene's position on the DNA ladder and developed a genetically altered cell that stops that gene's influence on cell malformations. Now the long process of FDA approval, endless tests, and the first human transplants lie ahead. You wish such a momentous breakthrough could cut all the red tape, but the reverse seems to be the case. As news of the discovery hits the media, an equal amount of praise and criticism fills the airwaves and headlines, reflecting both the hope and doubt aroused by the possibility of a cure for cancer.

On the financial side, MedTech posts a 26 percent increase in revenues to $886 million, though profits plummet by 40 percent to $135 million, as shown in the accompanying table.

To improve on this year's results, FutureMedTech's cancer cure must survive the endless premarket approval process and officially enter the marketplace before the end of the year. Otherwise, MedTech's performance will suffer even more.

Worried about this possibility, Bob Koontz, chairman and CEO of Benton, inquires about other projects under way that could lead to new product introductions during the laborious FDA approval process. When your vague answer fails to satisfy him, he asks you to submit a plan to Mitch Cavanaugh, your group president, detailing how

Selected Financial Information
(Dollars in Millions)

	Year ended September 30	
	This year	Last year
Operations		
Net sales	$886.3	$702.8
Cost of sales	283.6	217.9
R&D	180.7	112.4
Marketing	150.0	77.1
G&A	136.8	70.2
Operating profit	135.2	225.2
Financial position		
Current assets	292.5	230.2
Current liabilities	152.1	119.7
Working capital	140.4	110.5
Other assets	87.7	69.1
Property and equipment	117.6	102.0
Total assets	497.8	401.2
Other data		
Capital expenditures	32.7	24.2
Depreciation and amortization	14.6	13.3
Return on sales	15.3%	32.0%
Return on assets	27.2%	56.1%
Number of employees	1812	1642

MedTech will maintain sales levels and increase profits during the FDA and premarket approval process. Koontz obviously recognizes that MedTech has placed all its eggs in one basket and now wants you to start thinking about diversifying the company's activities. Once again, you face a major strategic decision. Should you redirect some of your efforts toward other R&D projects in order to solve the short-term problem, or should you forge ahead, devoting every ounce of resources and effort into the long-term solution the cell transplants seem to offer?

Skeptics inside and outside the company urge less focus on the cancer cure, allowing the premarket approval process to unfold in an orderly fashion and transferring some emphasis to other projects. Optimists argue that every human, financial, and organizational resource should be brought to bear on getting the cancer cure to the market as soon as possible. To make the decision tougher, word reaches you that Kate DaVaeno's BBX will introduce a new high-end blood analyzer later this year that could cut MedTech's market share in half.

Aware of the rumor, some Benton executives expect you to retaliate by immediately shoring up FutureMedTech's blood analysis R&D efforts.

In a hastily convened conference with Mitch Cavanaugh, your group president remarks, "We're not questioning the long-term value of FutureMedTech's amazing breakthrough, but we do expect you to take into account the arduous approval process and the need to offset that delay with viable short-term products." Afterwards, you retreat to your office, realizing only you can decide MedTech's future.

If you wish to redirect some of MedTech's R&D and marketing efforts, turn to Chapter 66.

If you want to forge ahead with a singular focus on getting a cell transplant product to market, turn to Chapter 67.

53
Improving
Blood Analysis
Technology

As soon as you announce your decision to focus on improving blood analysis technology, Jack Suhler tenders his resignation, explaining that he sees no reason to continue working for a company incapable of recognizing its larger responsibilities. Insisting that he absolutely will not reconsider, he leaves MedTech within a week to start a new company with the several million dollars he accumulated through the sale of FutureMed.

It seems you underestimated Suhler's convictions. Now you must solve two big problems: replacing Suhler, which won't be easy, and preventing other key people from defecting to Suhler's new company. However, on the bright side, Kate DaVaeno predicts that a second-generation laser-graphics blood analyzer will double current sales to the research laboratory market during the next two years, with state-of-the-art labs ordering the new instrument and less sophisticated labs ordering discounted first-generation instruments. With Benton experiencing sluggish growth in most of its divisions, a stellar growth year could give MedTech the leeway it needs to pursue a broader R&D agenda at FutureMedTech, albeit without Suhler's genius to guide it.

At midyear, Congress passes national health-care legislation mandating a minimum level of health care for every American citizen and demanding major reductions in health-care costs. Funding for many research labs quickly declines as the entire health-care industry shifts focus from R&D to cost containment. This dramatic turn of events devastates MedTech as a severely depressed research lab market greets its second-generation blood analyzer. You scramble to refocus R&D efforts on low-end economical blood analyzers, but MedTech enjoys so little advantage at the low end of the market, you must resign yourself to slow progress. Turning to the operations and marketing side of the business you attempt to motivate Kate DaVaeno, but she seems so distant, you wonder whether she's looking for another job. As you and she discuss offering deeper discounts on MedTech products to stimulate sales, DaVaeno provides little input, but since you don't want to waste time worrying about personality issues, you take the initiative and set a deep-discounting program in motion yourself.

By year-end MedTech manages to post a 29 percent increase in revenues to $906 million, though profits plummet by 39 percent to $138 million, as shown in the accompanying table.

The coming year will look even worse on paper, unless MedTech can develop and bring to market a variety of low-end blood analyzing tests, devices, and instruments that can offset the decline at the higher end. During the first three months of the new year MedTech shows lit-

Selected Financial Information
(Dollars in Millions)

	Year ended September 30	
	This year	Last year
Operations		
Net sales	$905.9	$702.8
Cost of sales	280.8	217.9
R&D	165.9	112.4
Marketing	200.5	77.1
G&A	121.0	70.2
Operating profit	137.7	225.2
Financial position		
Current assets	296.7	230.2
Current liabilities	154.3	119.7
Working capital	142.4	110.5
Other assets	89.0	69.1
Property and equipment	117.6	102.0
Total assets	503.3	401.2
Other data		
Capital expenditures	32.7	24.2
Depreciation and amortization	14.6	13.3
Return on sales	15.2%	32.0%
Return on assets	27.4%	56.1%
Number of employees	1826	1642

tle progress, but you remain hopeful. Unfortunately, Mitch Cavanaugh, your group president, doesn't share your hope. In fact, he decides it's time to avoid another bad year at MedTech by replacing you with Kate DaVaeno. As Cavanaugh explains, "After Jack Suhler's departure and a disastrous year-end with little evidence of substantial improvement, we just lost confidence in your ability to manage MedTech's future." Later, you discover Cavanaugh had been talking to DaVaeno about this eventuality for months. You should have seen it coming. In accordance with your employment agreement, you receive two years of salary severance. You wonder, should you take a few months off to rethink your decisions at MedTech? Or should you jump right into a new challenge?

If you would like to revisit your last strategic decision, return to Chapter 38.

If you would like to change your mind about an earlier strategic decision, return to Chapter 25 or Chapter 16.

If you're still feeling the sting of defeat and believe you could have made your last strategic choice work in real life, you may be right. After all, this is just a game. However, if you return to your last strategic decision (the first option above) and select the other alternative, you will learn why the author considers it a better choice.

54
Increasing Individual Accountability

As sales of the new generation of low-end blood analyzers increase and solidify the strength of the MedTech organization, confidence in your decision to focus on individual accountability also grows. Together, you and Ed Yates conclude that MedTech's Deming-based total quality management system has already removed the majority of impediments to individual empowerment and productivity, many of the barriers to communication and functional cooperation, and most other inhibitors of real continuous improvement. Now it makes eminent sense to focus even more on individuals, helping them further increase their accountability.

Ed seeks the help of two management consultants, Roger Connors and Tom Smith, coauthors of the book *The Oz Principle*, who have helped a number of organizations recognize the value of full accountability. In a series of meetings and interventions Connors and Smith guide MedTech employees through the differences between what they call *below-the-line victim behavior* and *above-the-line accountable behavior*. According to Connors and Smith, people operating "below the line" make excuses, blame others, and fall prey to confusion and feelings of helplessness when results fail to materialize, whereas those operating "above the line" maintain a sense of ownership over results. People in organizations find themselves thinking and behaving below the line whenever they consciously or unconsciously avoid accountability for individual or collective results. Languishing below the line in what Connors and Smith call *the victim cycle*, they begin to lose their spirit until they eventually feel powerless. Only by moving above the line, onto the accountability ladder, where they "see it, own it, solve it, do it," can people become powerful again.

Armed with this final vital dimension of total quality management and continuous improvement, MedTech continues to develop new work processes and introduce improved products and services at lower costs. These include a new single-supplier relationship with a high-tech computer graphics firm whose equipment greatly improves the usefulness of MedTech's blood analyzers and a series of low-cost blood test kits designed for doctors' offices and emergency units. As levels of accountability within the organization rise to unprecedented heights, improvement becomes a daily ritual at MedTech. No one can function "below the line" in any stage of the victim cycle for very long without an associate bringing that fact to his or her attention.

In the final months of the year, you spend more time at the group level than at MedTech as Ed Yates assumes the bulk of responsibility for running the organization. As the fiscal year ends, MedTech once again reports record revenues and profits. Net sales are $1.1 billion, a 95 percent increase over the previous year, and profits are $337 million, a 125 percent increase, as shown in the accompanying table.

Selected Financial Information
(Dollars in Millions)

	Year ended September 30	
	This year	Last year
Operations		
Net sales	$1,124.4	$578.3
Cost of sales	337.2	190.8
R&D	113.0	63.9
Marketing	247.3	121.4
G&A	89.9	52.0
Operating profits	337.0	150.2
Financial position		
Current assets	365.4	192.3
Current liabilities	190.0	100.0
Working capital	175.4	92.3
Other assets	109.6	57.7
Property and equipment	89.4	83.1
Total assets	564.4	333.1
Other data		
Capital expenditures	20.3	16.2
Depreciation and amortization	11.9	11.5
Return on sales	30.0%	26.0%
Return on assets	59.7%	45.1%
Number of employees	2035	1637

You receive a $1 million cash bonus and $5 million in stock options, but more importantly, the opportunity to influence the operations of other divisions as president of the Medical Products and Systems Group. You immediately begin helping each division president strengthen his or her total quality and continuous-improvement efforts. Even the business press picks up on your record at MedTech and promotes the rumor that you will someday rise to the top of Benton Pharmaceuticals. In *Time* magazine a reporter profiles you as an example of the new breed of corporate executive capable of nurturing total quality and continuous improvement in organizations, personal accountability in people, and real advancement for society.

Over the last five years you have taken MedTech's sales from $147 million to $1.1 billion, an eightfold increase, and you have increased profits tenfold from $32 million to $337 million. You began by choosing an R&D focus for the company, making existing product improvements, lowering costs, and creating a total quality management organization with a flair for jazz improvisation. Ultimately, with the help of Dr. Deming's philosophies and your own commitment to increasing individual accountability, the power of continuous improvement gradually transformed MedTech into an industry leader.

Congratulations! Your strategic decision making has paid off handsomely for you and for every stakeholder in your sphere of influence. You have come to the end of a decision-making track and should be ready for a brand new set of challenges. Choose one or more of the alternatives below.

If you want to compare how the results of your last five years of strategic decision making stack up against the other positive outcomes in The Strategy Game, turn to Chapter 68.

If you want to discover how the alternate decision to improve managerial leadership would have turned out, turn to Chapter 55.

If you wish to review the results that could have occurred had you made different strategic choices on this decision-making track, turn to Chapter 40, Chapter 28, Chapter 19, or Chapter 10.

If you would like to test your strategic thinking ability on an entirely different decision-making track, turn to Chapter 7. (Quickly review Chapter 3 before reading Chapter 7.)

55
Improving Managerial Leadership

Despite some lingering second-guessing from some managers over this decision, you move forward with a program of leadership enhancement. Born out of your gut feeling and Deming's philosophy that employees will not perform well as individual jazz musicians unless the system and environment empowers them to do so, your program aims at developing advanced leadership skills in both the senior management team and the next level of middle managers. For his part, Ed Yates stresses to the senior management team that they must make personal investments of time and effort to improve leadership attributes and management systems that foster total quality and continuous improvement at all levels.

To test current levels of leadership you conduct a Zenger-Miller survey to identify four categories of skills most important in ensuring that an organization's management system accommodates total quality and continuous improvement: individual leadership, work process, team leadership, and customer partnership. Together with Ed Yates, you select Susan Carter as the person to succeed Ed Yates as vice president of continuous improvement, asking her to forge a partnership between the human resources and continuous-improvement departments to teach leadership, work processing, team development, and customer partnership at all levels within the organization. You also circulate profiles of executives at several well-known organizations who have pioneered the quality revolution in America, including Jamie Houghton of Corning, John Hudiburg of Florida Power & Light, David Kearns of Xerox, Bob Galvin of Motorola, Don Peterson of Ford, John Young of Hewlett-Packard, and Roger Milliken of Milliken

& Company. These role models can, you believe, help MedTech vice presidents and directors not only appreciate but emulate the leadership attributes necessary to perpetually foster continuous improvement. When the leadership training of MedTech executives and managers reaches new heights, you feel confident the program will reap great rewards in the years to come.

As the current year unfolds, sales of the new generation of low-end blood analyzers continue to grow, and improvements in products, services, systems, and processes occur throughout the organization.

At year-end MedTech reports revenues of $803 million, an increase of 39 percent, and profits of $209 million, also an increase of 39 percent, as shown in the accompanying table.

While you had hoped to reach or surpass last year's record levels of growth, you take great satisfaction from the fact that MedTech successfully concludes the year with a strengthened management system and leadership awareness for the future. You also appreciate the $500,000 in stock options you receive at Benton's annual conference.

Selected Financial Information
(Dollars in Millions)

	Year ended September 30	
	This year	Last year
Operations		
Net sales	$803.0	$578.3
Cost of sales	265.0	190.8
R&D	79.7	63.9
Marketing	168.6	121.4
G&A	80.9	52.0
Operating profit	208.8	150.2
Financial position		
Current assets	267.0	192.3
Current liabilities	138.8	100.0
Working capital	128.2	92.3
Other assets	80.1	57.7
Property and equipment	89.4	83.1
Total assets	436.5	333.1
Other data		
Capital expenditures	20.3	16.2
Depreciation and amortization	11.9	11.5
Return on sales	26.0%	26.0%
Return on assets	47.8%	45.1%
Number of employees	1866	1637

As you turn over your responsibilities to Ed Yates, you feel a nagging concern that MedTech may yet need a focus on individual accountability to complete its transformation. Some of the company's projected improvements in products and services did not materialize during the past year, and you wonder what might have happened had you chosen to emphasize individual accountability rather than managerial leadership. You find yourself wishing that MedTech's performance had been more spectacular this year, because that would have made it easier for you as group president to sell the other divisions on a MedTech-style strategy of total quality and continuous improvement. Perhaps you can help Ed Yates achieve those results next year.

Regardless, you can take pride in having orchestrated a fivefold increase in sales over the last five years from $147 million to $803 million and a sevenfold increase in profits from $32 million to $209 million. By focusing on R&D, improvements in existing products, and lower costs you were able to implement a total quality management system that truly transformed the organization from a symphony orchestra to a jazz band. Of course, Dr. Deming and better all-around leadership also played a big role.

You have successfully concluded one major strategic decision-making track, but you can continue testing and developing your strategic thinking by selecting one or more of the following options.

If you want to compare how the results of your last five years of strategic decision making stack up against the other positive outcomes in The Strategy Game, turn to Chapter 68.

If you choose to consider how the alternate decision to increase individual accountability would have played itself out, turn to Chapter 54.

If you want to explore how some of the earlier options on this decision-making track might have turned out, read Chapter 40, Chapter 28, Chapter 19, or Chapter 10.

If you want to test your strategic decision-making ability on a new track, turn to Chapter 7. (Quickly review Chapter 3 before reading Chapter 7.)

56
Nurturing the Right Attitude

Having chosen attitude nurturing as the theme of your final year at MedTech, you take three people from your personal staff on a three-day retreat at which you'll prepare the presentation of your career. To get your management team completely on board, you'll need to inspire and motivate them as much as they'll need to inspire and motivate their own people. You begin your preparation by identifying the old mind-set you want the new one to completely eliminate, namely, the belief that performance improves by applying more pressure or resources. Rather, you must persuade your management team that performance depends on continuously restructuring business work methods to achieve ultimate time-based competitiveness.

With this clear distinction in place, you draw on the work of consultant Philip Thomas, author of *Competitiveness Through Total Cycle Time*, to identify three basic elements of a permanent time-based competition attitude: responsiveness, results acceleration, and resource minimization. *Responsiveness* means meeting the customers' needs promptly by reducing long cycle times, the root cause of nonresponsiveness. *Results acceleration* means constantly looking for new ways to compress time, and *resource minimization* means reworking business methods to improve responsiveness and obtain accelerated results without consuming additional resources.

Your presentation the following week garners rave reviews from your management team, who heartily agree with your case for nurturing the right attitude in the coming year. The meeting has accomplished all that you'd hoped for, and more, solidifying the attitudes of your senior management team, so you decide to take your presentation on the road to every MedTech location and employee. Over the next four months you affect the attitudes of every person in the company, further strengthening the company's time-based culture.

You rely heavily on Susan Carter to develop hiring practices and development programs supporting the new attitude. She performs so beautifully, you begin to think that she may well be the perfect person to replace you when you move up. MedTech's reorganization emerges and institutionalizes a constant state of dynamism based on the new mind-set devoted to the three R's of time-based competition. With the MedTech attitude fueling a new stream of cycle-time improvements, product innovations, reduced costs, increased product varieties, and loyal customers, you prepare to accept your new responsibilities as president of the Medical Products and Systems Group.

To conclude your tenure at MedTech, you log a sales increase of 76 percent to $1.2 billion and a record level of profits to $420 million, a 93 percent increase, as shown in the accompanying table.

In a surprise move, the board of directors rescinds your promotion

Selected Financial Information
(Dollars in Millions)

	Year ended September 30	
	This year	Last year
Operations		
Net sales	$1,214.0	$682.3
Cost of sales	315.6	184.2
R&D	145.3	75.8
Marketing	242.8	143.0
G&A	89.9	61.2
Operating profit	420.4	218.1
Financial position		
Current assets	382.4	216.6
Current liabilities	198.8	112.6
Working capital	183.6	104.0
Other assets	114.7	65.0
Property and equipment	141.3	100.9
Total assets	638.4	382.5
Other data		
Capital expenditures	57.3	32.2
Depreciation and amortization	14.4	11.8
Return on sales	34.6%	32.0%
Return on assets	65.8%	57.0%
Number of employees	2068	1697

to group president and asks you to become Benton Pharmaceuticals' president and chief operating officer in preparation for succeeding Bob Koontz as chairman and CEO within three years. In addition to your enhanced promotion, you receive a $2 million cash bonus, $5 million in stock options, and a charge to turn every Benton division into a top-notch, time-based competitor. You give a presentation to the board of directors that includes a thorough explanation of your approach, using MedTech's recent history as a case example. You then listen as CEO Bob Koontz praises you to the board as the most visionary executive within Benton Pharmaceuticals.

For five years now you have been setting a record of performance unparalleled within Benton Pharmaceuticals. Sales increased eightfold from $147 million to $1.2 billion, and profits rose thirteenfold from $32 million to $420 million. Your early decisions to focus on R&D, improving existing products, and lowering costs led to your refashioning MedTech into a time-based competitor with structurally different work methods implemented through a reorganization that emerged from within, and a fundamental focus on time-based competition attitudes.

Congratulations! Your strategic decisions have paid off wonderfully, for you and for Benton Pharmaceuticals. You have reached the end of a decision-making track, but you can keep playing the strategy game by selecting one or more of the following options.

If you want to compare how the results of your last five years of strategic decision making stack up against the other positive outcomes in The Strategy Game, turn to Chapter 68.

If you would like to review the alternate strategy of relying on technique, turn to Chapter 57.

If you want to peruse the outcomes of earlier choices on this track, turn to Chapter 43, Chapter 30, Chapter 18, or Chapter 10.

If you would rather embark on a completely different strategic decision-making track, turn to Chapter 7. (Quickly review Chapter 3 before reading Chapter 7.)

57
Relying on Technique

When you announce your decision to rely on technique for the coming year, your management team reacts with enthusiasm. You suspect they've come to respect you so much that they would have offered equal support had you opted to nurture the right attitude rather than bring technique to bear on the need to further solidify time-based competition at MedTech.

To implement the new thrust, you draw upon the strengths of Ed Yates, who has long supported institutionalizing the management processes necessary to perpetuate time-based competition within MedTech. Gratifyingly, Yates seems to have tempered his view somewhat and he even tells you he's come to oppose *over*organizing before the appropriate experimentation, pilot programming, and breakthrough teaming has occurred. You feel Yates' broadened perspective may well make him a perfect successor. It certainly makes him an ideal candidate to engineer MedTech's technique focus.

Over the next several months, under Yates' direction, your management team identifies and implements several basic processes and techniques that capture the very essence of MedTech's time-based competition strategy, including quick prototyping, competitor benchmarking, early experimentation, program piloting, breakthrough teaming, customer satisfaction measures, innovation championing, sudden product launches, revised performance evaluations, and a host of time-based measures. As these basic techniques take hold, feedback from every part of the MedTech system, from customers to janitors, indicates that the techniques are not robbing the organization of its spirit but are actually stimulating it to new heights as everyone focuses on problems that cause delays or prevent further reductions in cycle time.

Slowly but surely the necessary time-based techniques and processes become securely installed at MedTech, bringing a steady increase in sales. At year-end the company records a 35 percent increase in sales, to $918 million, and a 40 percent increase in profits, to $289 million, as shown in the accompanying table.

Selected Financial Information
(Dollars in Millions)

	Year ended September 30	
	This year	Last year
Operations		
Net sales	$918.2	$682.3
Cost of sales	266.1	184.2
R&D	92.8	75.8
Marketing	171.8	143.0
G&A	98.5	61.2
Operating profit	289.0	218.1
Financial position		
Current assets	296.1	216.6
Current liabilities	154.0	112.6
Working capital	142.1	104.0
Other assets	88.8	65.0
Property and equipment	127.3	100.9
Total assets	512.2	382.5
Other data		
Capital expenditures	43.4	32.2
Depreciation and amortization	14.4	11.8
Return on sales	31.5%	32.0%
Return on assets	56.4%	57.0%
Number of employees	1915	1697

While this year's results don't beat the previous years', they do keep MedTech ahead of other Benton divisions, proving the superiority of time-based competition. You feel confident that MedTech will provide a pattern for other divisions of Benton Pharmaceuticals in the years ahead.

After the end of the year you once again receive an offer to take over the Medical Products and Systems Group as president. Finally, you accept. Ed Yates takes the reins at MedTech, and you move into your new responsibilities after pocketing $1 million in stock options.

In your new responsibilities as group president, you commit yourself to watching over MedTech to make sure that the changes you initiated continue to bring about time-based improvements. After all, in five years you did take MedTech from sales of $147 million to $918 million, a sixfold increase, and from profits of $32 million to $289 million, a ninefold increase. Thanks to your early decisions to focus on R&D, existing-product improvements, and lower costs, MedTech really does provide a model for other divisions in your group. The organization's commitment to time-based competition has created new work methods, an organizational evolution, and better managerial techniques that can benefit all your companies.

Even though you have successfully concluded a strategic decision-making track at MedTech, you can continue your strategic thinking by choosing one or more of the following alternatives.

If you want to compare how the results of your last five years of strategic decision making stack up against the other positive outcomes in The Strategy Game, turn to Chapter 68.

If you wish to review the outcome of the alternate option of nurturing the right attitude, turn to Chapter 56.

If you would like to discover what would have happened had you selected other options on this track, turn to Chapter 43, Chapter 30, Chapter 18, or Chapter 10.

If you want to apply your strategic thinking to a brand-new decision-making track, turn to Chapter 7. (Quickly review Chapter 3 before reading Chapter 7.)

58

Developing Further Sources of Product Differentiation

Agreeing with Michael Porter that the overall success of a differentiation strategy depends on how many sources of uniqueness a firm enjoys, you conclude that sustainability of advantage over time will stem more from multiple, not single, sources. DaVaeno, Gill, Matsumori, Cordon, and Updike agree. The most promising product differentiation will come from coordinating actions in many value activities because doing so will make differentiation more durable and more difficult for competitors to imitate.

Without compromising the strength of the 12 value activities in the areas of design, manufacturing, and marketing and sales, you form a task force under Mary Updike's direction to identify value activities in the areas of procurement (raw materials, purchasing, and materials handling) and outbound logistics (order processing, shipping, and customer follow-up), both of which can provide additional differentiation and create more value. A focus on procurement should enhance the component elements and raw materials involved in the development of MedTech products, thus establishing a greater quality image in the marketplace. A focus on outbound logistics should enable the company to respond faster to customer orders, thus outperforming competitors notorious for backordering blood analysis, collection, and monitoring instruments.

With Mary Updike and her task force researching procurement and outbound logistics, you ask your senior management team to scrutinize all of the other value activities in an effort to find new ways of enhancing buyer value and proliferating the sources of differentiation in value chains of both MedTech divisions. To help MedTech employees understand the importance of finding multiple sources of differentiation that can create real value for MedTech's customers, you cite examples of companies like Caterpillar Tractor, which combines uniqueness in product durability, parts availability, and a strong dealer network. It doesn't take long for a new strategic phrase, *multiple sources of differentiation,* to spread throughout MedTech, and even to customers, who begin expecting more uniqueness from MedTech than from competitors. MedTech seems well on its way toward establishing its reputation as the premier manufacturer and marketer of blood analyzers in the world.

During the first half of the fiscal year, your competitors introduce competing lines of blood analyzers, but MedTech prevents any erosion of its market-niche positions by quickly delivering its own revamped and customized value-added models with no backordering. While some of MedTech's perceived product uniqueness does slip as competitors introduce new products, a new uniqueness emerges as MedTech delivers its own products more quickly than competitors, who still suffer from backordering. As this occurs, people at MedTech watch with delight as one customer after another cancels orders from competitors and switches to the more readily available MedTech models.

MedTech's strategic maneuvering, combined with the usual brilliant micromarketing, becomes the topic of many lunchroom discussions throughout the industry as customers' switching creates a snowball effect in the market, driving MedTech's sales and profits to unimagined levels. By year-end, MedTech reports $1 billion in revenues, an increase of 163 percent over the previous year, and an amazing $371 million in profit, an increase of 266 percent, as shown in the accompanying table.

The avalanche of customer movement in the market drives one competitor into bankruptcy and leaves another with marginal prospects for the future, while MedTech's position in every segment it serves gets stronger making it the clear market leader in blood analysis, collection, and monitoring. Just when you're celebrating with your senior management team, you receive a call from Bob Koontz, chairman and CEO of Benton Pharmaceuticals, who wants you to board an airplane and be in his office the next morning. You tell your management team that Koontz probably wants to hear firsthand the secret of MedTech's success, but you secretly wonder about the unusual urgency in Koontz's voice.

When you walk into Bob Koontz's office the next morning, he

Selected Financial Information
(Dollars in Millions)

	Year ended September 30	
	This year	Last year
Operations		
Net sales	$1,023.1	$389.8
Cost of sales	289.7	123.6
R&D	76.3	40.1
Marketing	203.8	82.6
G&A	82.0	42.0
Operating profit	371.3	101.4
Financial position		
Current assets	338.4	127.5
Current liabilities	176.0	66.3
Working capital	162.4	61.2
Other assets	101.5	38.2
Property and equipment	145.8	92.7
Total assets	585.7	258.4
Other data		
Capital expenditures	52.4	17.4
Depreciation and amortization	16.0	13.0
Return on sales	36.3%	26.0%
Return on assets	63.4%	39.2%
Number of employees	2738	1500

informs you that the board of directors has voted to name you president and chief operating officer of Benton Pharmaceuticals. Shocked by this news, you tell Koontz you never thought things could happen so precipitously at this level, but he quickly puts your mind at ease by telling you that the board has been watching the performance of MedTech closely over the past three years, and he decided not to inform you of your shot at the presidency until MedTech's year-end results came in. He tells you that he personally can't wait to see your experience in creating value for customers drive every Benton division in the future. Then, with a mixture of pleasure and sadness, Koontz confides, "This move may constitute the last significant strategic decision I make at Benton Pharmaceuticals."

Touched by the depth of Koontz's feelings and his unwavering confidence in you, you enthusiastically accept the job and spend the rest of the day discussing timing and transition issues. As you fly home that night, with $6 million in stock options in your name, you can't help but review the crucial decision points you encountered during your tenure at MedTech, and you wonder what might have happened if you had pursued another track.

Fortunately, your strategic choices to focus on marketing and sales, extensive customer segmentation, and separating MedTech's strategic thrusts worked beautifully. And the micromarketing program, with its emphasis on creating value, brought competitive advantages from multiple sources. In five years you increased MedTech's sales seven-fold from $147 million to $1 billion and profits twelvefold from $32 million to $371 million.

Congratulations! Your strategic decision making has won success for you, MedTech, and Benton Pharmaceuticals. You have now come to the end of a decision-making track; however, you can continue playing the game by applying what you've learned to a new set of challenges.

If you want to compare how the results of your last five years of strategic decision making stack up against the other positive outcomes in The Strategy Game, turn to Chapter 68.

If you would like to see what would have occurred had you chosen the option of perfecting a single source of differentiation, turn to Chapter 59.

If you would like to find out what would have happened had you pursued one of the other choices on this decision-making track, turn to Chapter 45, Chapter 33, Chapter 20, or Chapter 12.

If you want to apply your strategic thinking prowess to a different decision-making track, turn to Chapter 4. (Quickly review Chapter 2 before reading Chapter 4.)

59

Perfecting a Single Source of Differentiation

Given the overwhelming response of customers to the technological improvements in MedTech's customizeable blood analyzer, not only in its speed of processing, cost efficiency and diagnostic thoroughness but in its enormous capacity for customization, you decide to stake MedTech's future on getting even better at technologically improved product design. When your senior management team expresses concern that this course of action may dangerously place all of MedTech's eggs in one basket, you rebut their arguments by reviewing what happened in the marketplace last year as customers flocked to MedTech's technology-driven improvements. Hours of discussion ensue, during which you constantly champion a single source of differentiation. Ultimately your tenacity wears down all the opposition, and your senior management team agrees, albeit reluctantly, to focus on technology-driven product design combined with micromarketing as MedTech's single major source of product differentiation and value creation in the marketplace.

Over the next few months, R&D, manufacturing, marketing, and sales in both divisions work closely together on a new technologically advanced line of blood analyzers the company can market before the end of the year. And, even though competitors begin introducing their own new models at midyear to compete with the ones MedTech introduced last year, you remain confident that your next wave of differentiated products will eclipse your competitors' short-term gains by year-end.

All efforts throughout MedTech center on preparing for the next technologically improved line of blood analyzers, with market-niche managers and salespeople hammering customer segments with heavy presales hype just prior to introduction of the line early in the fourth quarter. As the new line of technologically advanced and readily customized blood analyzers hits the market, your hopes for another strong customer response get dashed when customers react to the line with only luke-warm enthusiasm. During the last few weeks of the year, you ask every employee at MedTech to work overtime in an effort to uncover just what happened in the marketplace and why customers responded the way they did. Ironically, MedTech employees quickly discover that the technologically advanced diagnostic capabilities of the new blood ana-lyzers provide too much differentiation, giving customers more diag-nostic capabilities and more speed than they need or want. Customers remain quite happy with the less capable and speedy line introduced last year. This fact leads you to acknowledge that your emphasis on a single source of differentiation did not adequately assess customers' own value chains and how technology-driven product improvements would affect those chains. You mistakenly assumed customers would continue paying for MedTech's increasing differentiation, when, in fact, it added nothing to your customers' value chains.

At year-end MedTech reports a 22 percent increase in revenues, to

Selected Financial Information
(Dollars in Millions)

	Year ended September 30	
	This year	Last year
Operations		
Net sales	$477.4	$389.8
Cost of sales	130.3	123.6
R&D	62.1	40.1
Marketing	107.8	82.6
G&A	51.2	42.0
Operating profit	126.0	101.4
Financial position		
Current assets	176.0	127.5
Current liabilities	91.5	66.3
Working capital	84.5	61.2
Other assets	52.8	38.2
Property and equipment	121.8	92.7
Total assets	350.6	258.4
Other data		
Capital expenditures	36.6	17.2
Depreciation and amortization	14.6	13.0
Return on sales	26.4%	26.0%
Return on assets	35.9%	39.2%
Number of employees	1487	1340

$477 million, and a 24 percent increase in profits, to $126 million, as shown in the accompanying table.

You receive praise from Benton executives, but you know they share your disappointment over the reception of MedTech's advanced line of blood analyzers. Mitch Cavanaugh, your group president, expresses hope that you can make the necessary adjustments in the coming year to capitalize on MedTech's strength in the marketplace.

For your own part, you criticize yourself for relying too much on the logic that customers always prefer technological superiority and for ignoring the real feelings and concerns of customers that ultimately determine value. While this experience lingers as a difficult lesson, you begin making the necessary adjustments to place less emphasis on a single source of differentiation and more attention on value creation at MedTech, remaining confident that the coming year will prove better.

You do gain solace, however, from the fact that in five years you increased MedTech's sales threefold from $147 million to $477 million and profits fourfold from $32 million to $126 million. Your decision to focus on marketing and sales, extensive customer segmentation, and separating MedTech's strategic thrusts allowed you to bring micro-marketing, value creation, and a differentiation advantage to your organization.

Now that you have just concluded a strategic decision-making track at MedTech, you may want to continue applying your strategic thinking skills to one or more of the following alternatives.

If you want to compare how the results of your last five years of strategic decision making stack up against the other positive outcomes in The Strategy Game, turn to Chapter 68.

If you want to review the outcome of the alternate choice of developing multiple sources of differentiation, turn to Chapter 58.

If you wish to learn what would have happened had you made other choices on this track, turn to Chapter 45, Chapter 33, Chapter 20, or Chapter 12.

If you want to test your strategic thinking on a completely different decision-making track, turn to Chapter 4. (Quickly review Chapter 2 before reading Chapter 4.)

60
Pursuing the Attack Stratagem

After a good deal of consultation with your four key executives and consultant Pamela West, you decide to lure BBX out into the open, then attack it with all your might. It makes sense that, rather than plunge into unfamiliar and dangerous ground to reach your opponent, you should try instead to make the opponent come to your turf, where the terrain is more familiar and your opponent will be more vulnerable to attack. You code name the operation, "Lure the Tiger Out of the Mountain." Like generals planning a major military campaign, you, Gill, DaVaeno, Cardon, and Matsumori devise a detailed plan to lure BBX out into a vulnerable position by allowing BBX to "outniche" you in at least two niches, giving your rival a false sense of accomplishment and causing it to intensify even more its focus on micromarketing at the expense of its superior technological strength. Meanwhile, MedTech will prepare for the attack by intensifying its efforts to develop a new low-end blood analyzer that will eclipse the technological superiority of BBX. Then, at the appropriate moment, MedTech will introduce the new blood analyzer with numerous variations aimed at a variety of low-end market niches, thus delivering a knockout blow to BBX that will clearly establish your superiority as both a niche marketer and a technology leader.

Tremendous excitement builds within you and your top lieutenants as you "telegraph" your fake plan to BBX. You make sure that your true intentions never leak out to your enemy who has greatly increased its competitive intelligence in recent months. After identifying two MedTech market-niche managers you can trust implicitly, you prepare them to allow BBX to gain two meaningful wins in their niches over the next few months.

Before long, BBX offers a new blood test directed specifically at diabetics, which MedTech does nothing to counter. Naturally, the new test comes to dominate a niche MedTech had previously controlled.

Only weeks later, BBX introduces a special blood-clotting monitor for patients who have undergone knee or hip replacement surgery and require extraordinary monitoring. Again, MedTech makes no attempt to block the move or to fight BBX over its newly gained niche. Just as expected, BBX executives and personnel exult over the two market-niche wins and begin pouring more and more resources toward micromarketing, exactly what you wanted them to do.

Meanwhile, MedTech's R&D staff, production personnel, and market-niche managers from both divisions work furiously to introduce a new low-end blood analyzer technology that will eclipse BBX's currently superior system. In addition to the R&D emphasis, you instruct a group of 20 market-niche managers to prepare to introduce product variations and service packages that will appeal to carefully targeted niches. Finally, with BBX totally unprepared for MedTech's move, you wheel the new low-end blood analyzer into the market at the beginning of the fourth quarter, causing BBX sales of their own low-end blood analyzer to plummet by 50 percent within 30 days. In addition, the marketing prowess with which MedTech introduces the new low-end analyzer makes BBX's little market-niche wins look like child's play. BBX sales decrease 15 percent, and profits drop 22 percent.

MedTech's sales at the end of the year soar to $852 million, a rise of 47 percent, and profits climb to $247 million, an increase of 58 percent, as shown in the accompanying table.

You and your people receive accolades as the premier micromarketers in the industry, though some Benton executives criticize your stratagem as brinkmanship and argue that MedTech sales could have increased even more in the last year had you not spent so much time playing dangerous competitive games with BBX. While you defend your stratagem by pointing to MedTech's superior results, you can't help but wonder whether your attraction to Eastern philosophy has turned you into too much of a gamesman. Rumors of an imminent promotion for you within the Benton system continue to sweep through the organization, but to date you have received no formal offers. However, you do receive another $1 million in stock options at the end of the year.

You take pride in MedTech's sixfold increase in sales from $147 million to $852 million over the last five years and its eightfold increase in profits from $32 million to $247 million. Your early focus on marketing and sales led you to stress extensive customer segmentation, a separation of strategic thrusts, and micromarketing, while avoiding head-on competition, exploiting MedTech's superiority, and developing an attack stratagem.

Now that you have successfully completed a strategic decision-making track at MedTech, you may want to continue playing the game by selecting one or more of the options below.

Selected Financial Information
(Dollars in Millions)

	Year ended September 30	
	This year	Last year
Operations		
Net sales	$852.3	$579.8
Cost of sales	272.7	179.7
R&D	76.7	40.6
Marketing	183.2	153.6
G&A	72.5	49.3
Operating profit	247.2	156.6
Financial position		
Current assets	281.3	189.9
Current liabilities	146.3	98.7
Working capital	135.0	91.1
Other assets	84.4	57.0
Property and equipment	162.1	123.5
Total assets	527.7	370.3
Other data		
Capital expenditures	59.3	40.4
Depreciation and amortization	17.6	14.3
Return on sales	29.0%	27.0%
Return on assets	46.8%	42.3%
Number of employees	1884	1624

If you want to compare how the results of your last five years of strategic decision making stack up against the other positive outcomes in The Strategy Game, turn to Chapter 68.

If you want to review the outcome of the alternative of executing a stratagem when commanding superiority, turn to Chapter 61.

If you would like to find out what would have happened had you made one of the other choices on this track, turn to Chapter 46, Chapter 32, Chapter 20, or Chapter 12.

If you want to apply your strategic thinking to a new decision-making track, turn to Chapter 4. (Quickly review Chapter 2 before reading Chapter 4.)

61
Launching a Stratagem from Superiority

Leery of pushing your fondness for ancient Chinese strategy too far, you counsel further with Amos Gill, Kate DaVaeno, Cam Cardon, and Ken Matsumori. You design a stratagem that will both advance MedTech's current micromarketing and competition avoidance strategies and sting BBX, a dangerous competitor that has become quite adept at ferreting out MedTech's plans with raids on key personnel and questionable intelligence gathering tactics. You will use BBX's preoccupation with competitor intelligence gathering against them by fooling BBX executives into believing that MedTech plans to introduce a new, technologically superior low-end blood analyzer within the year. You and your senior executives agree that BBX's spies will convince the company's executives that MedTech aims to eclipse BBX's strong technology position, when in reality MedTech will be developing a master plan for establishing minilabs throughout the country that provide a full continuum of blood analysis, collection, and monitoring services with emphasis on lower-end services doctors and small health-care facilities can use instead of higher-priced existing labs.

You and your management team remain convinced that the recent California legislation preventing doctors from owning medical equipment and operating it for profit will spread throughout the country, making it possible for service-oriented minilabs to sweep the nation. If this happens, new market niches will expand to meet new customer needs, creating an environment not unlike those exploited in the past by McDonald's in the fast-food industry and Kinko's in the printing industry. MedTech's minilabs will offer a continuum of blood analysis, collection, and monitoring services designed to appeal to local and regional needs, with efficiency-producing standardization across all labs but also with customization that conforms to MedTech's micro-marketing philosophy.

With a few misleading signals, your people convince BBX that MedTech is secretly laboring around the clock on a technological break-through in the low-end blood analyzer market which masks the real intent of MedTech's effort to introduce 1000 minilabs throughout the country within the next two years. Consequently, BBX works hard throughout the year on its own technological breakthrough in the low-end blood analyzer market, never suspecting MedTech's hidden agenda.

After months of discrete preparation, planning, contract negotia-tion, hiring, and organizing, MedTech announces the opening of 400 minilabs across the country, each of which will come into full opera-tion within 30 days. The news blows BBX so far out of the water BBX's CEO is forced to resign in disgrace. An article in *The Wall Street Journal* alleges that the ouster came about largely because of BBX's overzeal-ousness in industrial spying. Ironically, BBX introduces a new low-end blood analyzer before the end of the year, which MedTech itself immediately employs as an inexpensive testing alternative in many of its 400 minilabs across the country. Fortunately, your strategic assess-ment of changes in the marketplace prove correct as 20 additional states adopt the California legislation, preventing doctors from own-ing and operating medical equipment, further fueling the growth of MedTech's minilabs. With an enormous boost in the fourth quarter of the year, MedTech reports sales of $1 billion, an 81 percent increase, and profits of $325 million, an increase of 108 percent, as shown in the accompanying table.

In a lengthy *Fortune* magazine feature article a reporter recounts the MedTech stratagem blow by blow. You find the piece so well-written, you entertain the reporter's request that you collaborate on a major new business strategy book for McGraw-Hill. You also receive wide-spread praise from health-care industry experts for anticipating the legislation change that created a brand-new market niche in which MedTech has made blood test labs more efficient and, as a result, has helped contain health-care costs for every American. As you assign Amos Gill to roll out the minilab concept internationally, Bob Koontz, Chairman and CEO of Benton Pharmaceuticals, asks you to take over as group president of the Alternative Site and Services Group within six months. As a reward for your past performance, he doubles your salary and gives you $5 million in stock options.

In preparation for your new job, you divide MedTech into two new

Selected Financial Information
(Dollars in Millions)

| | Year ended September 30 | |
	This year	Last year
Operations		
Net sales	$1049.4	$579.8
Cost of sales	304.3	179.7
R&D	73.5	40.6
Marketing	262.4	153.6
G&A	83.9	49.3
Operating profit	325.3	156.6
Financial position		
Current assets	338.4	189.9
Current liabilities	176.0	98.7
Working capital	162.4	91.1
Other assets	101.5	57.0
Property and equipment	175.8	123.5
Total assets	615.8	370.3
Other data		
Capital expenditures	73.1	40.4
Depreciation and amortization	17.6	14.3
Return on sales	31.0%	27.0%
Return on assets	52.8%	42.3%
Number of employees	1988	1624

companies, appointing Amos Gill head of MedTech International and Kate DaVaeno head of MedTech USA. You ask Cam Cardon and Ken Matsumori to join you as new division presidents in the Alternative Site and Services Group, and you persuade Koontz to shift both MedTech companies to your new group.

You look back over the past few years with a good deal of personal pride and gratitude toward all the people who helped carry out your solid, strategic decisions. In five years you have increased MedTech's sales sevenfold from $147 million to $1 billion and profits tenfold from $32 million to $325 million. Your early focus on marketing and sales, extensive customer segmentation, and a separating of MedTech's strategic thrusts gave you the momentum to establish micromarketing as the company's life blood while avoiding head-on competition. Your strategy fully exploited MedTech's strengths as it operated from a position of superiority.

Congratulations! Your strategic decisions have produced solid results for MedTech and new opportunities for you. Now that you have come to the end of a decision-making track, you're ready to apply your strategic thinking ability to new circumstances by selecting one or more of the following options.

If you want to compare how the results of your last five years of strategic decision making stack up against the other positive outcomes in The Strategy Game, turn to Chapter 68.

If you want to find out what would have happened with the option of implementing a stratagem for attack, turn to Chapter 60.

If you wish to review the outcomes of the choices you did not select on this track, turn to Chapter 46, Chapter 32, Chapter 20, or Chapter 12.

If you would like to travel along a different decision-making track, turn to Chapter 4. (Quickly review Chapter 2 before reading Chapter 4.)

62
Creating a Pattern of Renewal

With Bob Shay now ready to take over MedTech, you delegate a good deal of authority for day-to-day activities to him and devote the bulk of your own time to moving MedTech into a steady state of renewal. In the evenings, you mull over an offer from Benton executives to take over one of the company's larger divisions and raise the customer service awareness of that $1.5 billion division to the level you've achieved at MedTech.

While you have not yet given your final acceptance, you can think of nothing that would keep you from taking the new assignment, scheduled to begin at the end of this fiscal year. Your fond memories of struggle, triumph, and success at MedTech will make it difficult to let go, just as a parent finds it hard to let a child grow up. Also like a parent, who wants to see a child mature into a happy adult with as much preparation as possible, you vow to launch MedTech into a mature mode of continual renewal that will make it productive and profitable for years to come.

Building on the people and leadership agenda that Bob Shay so effectively continues to nurture, you begin stressing candid and open communications throughout the organization. Every employee should, you proclaim, remain open, honest, and straightforward in all communications regarding plans, programs, agendas, directions, customer needs, solution opportunities, and everything else that occurs within the MedTech organization.

To help effect this sort of candid communication, you borrow a practice from General Electric, called *work-out sessions*. These sessions are described in Tichy and Sherman's book, *Control Your Destiny or Someone Else Will: How Jack Welch Is Making General Electric the World's Most Competitive Company*. During work-out sessions a team, department, or other work group comes together to address a particular problem or set of problems with no constraints or limitations on discussion or consideration of possible solutions. Just as people do at General Electric, you require the leader of the group to remain silent during the initial discussion in order to maximize the free flow of ideas and criticism necessary to keep communications completely candid and open. The work-out sessions quickly become an ingrained habit for MedTech's culture, making it easier for people to blast through bureaucracy, empower themselves, and solve problems.

By the end of the fiscal year you feel satisfied that your candid communications program has helped set a pattern of constant renewal that will serve MedTech for years to come. To close the year, MedTech reports revenues of $600 million and profits of $155 million, as shown in the table below.

You feel good about the legacy you'll leave behind when you pass the reins to Bob Shay. As a final gesture before your departure, MedTech employees honor you with a lavish company party where your senior team gives you a granite cobblestone bearing a brass plate

Selected Financial Information
(Dollars in Millions)

	Year ended September 30	
	This year	Last year
Operations		
Net sales	$600.2	*See "This year" numbers*
Cost of sales	192.1	*in Chapter 48 or 49,*
R&D	48.1	*depending on which*
Marketing	138.7	*chapter you chose to*
G&A	66.5	*get here.*
Operating profit	154.8	
Financial position		
Current assets	198.1	
Current liabilities	103.0	
Working capital	95.1	
Other assets	59.4	
Property and equipment	94.4	
Total assets	351.9	
Other data		
Capital expenditures	28.3	
Depreciation and amortization	11.3	
Return on sales	25.8%	
Return on assets	44.0%	
Number of employees	1633	

that says simply "The Rock." In the closing moments of the event, you, in turn, award all employees a 10 percent bonus for the championship performance they turned in last year. When the applause dies down, you ask Bob Shay to join you on the platform and present him with a glass-encased metal replica of the MedTech company logo, a symbol of the transfer of authority. Finally, in a brief three-minute salute to the people of MedTech, you express your appreciation for their commitment, trust, and, most of all, undying devotion to MedTech's core services. You promise them that MedTech's best years lie ahead.

That night you take home a check for $250,000, presented to you by Bob Koontz, chairman and CEO of Benton Pharmaceuticals, who predicts a bright future for you with the corporation. On your way home you reflect on how your early choices to focus on marketing and sales and customer service prepared MedTech to narrow its scope of cores and implement careful monitoring of customer expectations. These earlier strategic choices were sufficiently strong to allow either infrastructure and design or people and leadership to establish a pattern of renewal for the company. As a result, sales have increased fourfold in five years from $147 million to $600 million and profits have increased fivefold from $32 million to $155 million.

Though you have reached the conclusion of a strategic decision-making track, you can continue testing and developing your strategic thinking by selecting one or more of the options below.

If you want to compare how the results of your last five years of strategic decision making stack up against the other positive outcomes in The Strategy Game, turn to Chapter 68.

If you choose to review the other alternative of instituting a measurement system, turn to Chapter 63.

If you want to review the other alternatives you could have selected on this track, turn to Chapter 48 or 49 (depending on which chapter you read the first time through), Chapter 35, Chapter 23, or Chapter 14.

If you want to tackle a new decision-making track, turn to Chapter 6.

63
Instituting a Measurement System

You decide it's time to institute a quantitative measurement system. After all, how can you really know whether or not MedTech is delivering "best in world" core services if you lack a yardstick to measure it? With all of the elements of a core services strategy in place at MedTech, the company must now find a way of constantly gauging the impact of its services. However, you know that finding the right yardsticks could prove difficult since it involves measuring some rather qualitative variables, such as the experiences of customers who interact with the company, not just quantitative operational or product factors. Whatever measurement system you use to monitor customer satisfaction, it must be flexible enough to allow Bob Shay and your management team the ability to refine it and even replace it if the need arises.

Although you wish to personally author the new measurement system, you, as always, involve Bob Shay and your senior management team in the process. Together, you develop a system based upon four principles: (1) let customers determine what's measured; (2) never stop adding new measures or refining old ones; (3) make measurement a central part of management; and (4) focus measures on monitoring customer expectations, uncovering unmet needs, and discovering unique solutions.

After conducting numerous customer focus groups to determine what should be measured, new measurements are developed. They include "benchmarking" of competitors' services and "best in world" practices from premier organizations around the globe. As the year comes to a close, sales at MedTech continue to accelerate, allowing you to make good on your promise that MedTech's best years were yet to

Selected Financial Information
(Dollars in Millions)

	Year ended September 30	
	This year	Last year
Operations		
Net sales	$878.1	See "This year" numbers
Cost of sales	272.2	in Chapter 48 or 49,
R&D	70.4	depending on which
Marketing	210.5	chapter you chose
G&A	88.0	to get here.
Operating profit	237.0	
Financial position		
Current assets	287.6	
Current liabilities	149.5	
Working capital	138.0	
Other assets	86.3	
Property and equipment	107.6	
Total assets	481.4	
Other data		
Capital expenditures	41.5	
Depreciation and amortization	11.3	
Return on sales	27.0%	
Return on assets	49.2%	
Number of employees	1758	

come. MedTech records revenues of $878 million and profits of $237 million for the year, as shown in the accompanying table.

The numbers prompt Benton CEO Bob Koontz to award you $1 million in stock options and a 100 percent increase in your salary as you move to your new job as president of the InterMed Division of the company. Looking back, the new measurement system provided a concrete vehicle for moving MedTech aggressively forward. With the new benchmarking, best-practices, and other measurement programs in place, MedTech's management team can confidently carry on, maintaining and growing its devotion to its core services. Bob Shay tells you that this past year has been the most demanding of his career, yet he believes that the measurement system represents the best management tool created by any company in any industry.

Eager for your new assignment, you review your years at MedTech, knowing that both the tough times and the rewarding times will serve you well into the future. You remain convinced that long-term competitive advantage will go to service leaders, not service followers, and you take no small pride in the fact that you've left behind a legacy of service leadership that will keep MedTech ahead of its most earnest competitors. Five years ago you focused on marketing and sales and customer service; then, as the years unfolded, you stressed a narrow scope of core services and instituted a policy of careful monitoring of customer expectations. Because of the strength of these earlier strategic decisions, either the choice of infrastructure and design or people and leadership eventually led to installation of a successful measurement system at MedTech. All your effort resulted in a sixfold sales increase in five years from $147 million to $878 million and a sevenfold profit increase from $32 million to $237 million.

You have successfully completed a strategic decision-making track at MedTech, but you can keep playing the game by choosing one or more of the options below.

If you want to compare how the results of your last five years of strategic decision making stack up against the other positive outcomes in The Strategy Game, *turn to Chapter 68.*

If you wish to find out what would have happened had you chosen the alternative of maintaining a pattern of renewal, turn to Chapter 62.

If you want to discover the outcomes of other choices on this track, turn to Chapter 48 or 49 (depending on which chapter you read the first time through), Chapter 35, Chapter 23, or Chapter 14.

If you would like to pursue another decision-making track, turn to Chapter 6.

64
Organizing along Product-Country Groups

To address the major changes occurring in the industry you conclude that a modified matrix-style structure will best serve MedTech International Group. Therefore, you divide the newly formed group into four major product categories: high-end blood analysis, collection, and monitoring instruments; low-end blood analysis, collection, and monitoring instruments; blood analysis supplies and devices; and diagnostic products. For each product category you establish a product executive. In addition, you establish a country executive for each foreign country where MedTech operates facilities, joint ventures, acquisitions, or alliances. To ensure that product and country managers smoothly coordinate, plan, budget, and implement every aspect of their work, you insist that all 65 business units within the MedTech International Group, regardless of the percentage of ownership, report through both country and product executives.

Your core team backs this approach to the hilt, with the sole exception of Jack Suhler, who considers the organizational structure too complicated. He points to the matrix structures of an earlier decade that worked fine for a few organizations but failed for most. Although he argues persuasively for a customer-based approach that emphasizes flexibility and innovation, he fails to convince you to alter your latest strategic decision. In frustration, Suhler opts for early retirement, agreeing to give MedTech International, over the next 12 months, consulting time of a fourth to a third of his previous full-time work schedule. Although you feel distressed by this first evidence in two years of a lack of consensus among your core team, you continue moving forward with the reorganization.

During the following months, the modified matrix-style organization with its cross-functional components does indeed prove too complex and difficult to implement, chewing up inordinate amounts of your core team's time, as well as that of the product and country executives and business unit presidents. Eventually, the pressures prompt the resignation of group marketing vice president Kate DaVaeno, who complains in her exit interview that the new structure limited her influence and put a stranglehold on marketing. "I feel like I've been hit by a steamroller," she says. "And the product and country executives are also getting flattened by their responsibilities." She also points out that business unit presidents feel increasingly frustrated with all the complicated reports they must submit as part of their responsibilities.

As the year closes, sales for MedTech International increase a mere 12 percent, profits 16 percent, to $1.1 billion and $258 million, respectively, as shown in the accompanying table.

The results reflect MedTech's first setback in five years, and you feel

Selected Financial Information
(Dollars in Millions)

	Year ended September 30	
	This year	Last year
Operations		
Net sales	$1063.9	$949.9
Cost of sales	340.6	313.2
R&D	95.8	95.0
Marketing	223.4	190.0
G&A	145.8	129.2
Operating profit	258.3	222.5
Financial position		
Current assets	351.1	315.8
Current liabilities	182.6	164.2
Working capital	168.5	151.6
Other assets	105.3	94.7
Property and equipment	121.5	170.0
Total assets	578.0	517.6
Other data		
Capital expenditures	32.5	26.0
Depreciation and amortization	15.3	13.9
Return on sales	24.3%	23.4%
Return on assets	44.7%	43.0%
Number of employees	1976	1876

deeply disappointed over the loss of momentum and the defection of two key executives. However, you feel so confident that the MedTech International Group can quickly recover from the setback that you begin immediately preparing your core team for the task of streamlining the matrix-style organization. You receive $1 million in stock options and a promise of more in years to come.

You do find consolation in the fact that you have increased sales sevenfold in the last five years from $147 million to $1.1 billion and profits eightfold from $32 million to $258 million. Your decisions to focus on R&D, to emphasize breakthrough products, to acquire FutureMed, and to create a new R&D division set the stage for your later focus on acquisitions, global expansion, strategic alliances, and a product-country structure.

Although you have arrived at the end of a decision-making track, you can continue to play the game by choosing one or more of the following alternatives.

If you want to compare how the results of your last five years of strategic decision making stack up against the other positive outcomes in The Strategy Game, turn to Chapter 68.

If you would like to see what would have happened had you chosen to organize along customer lines, turn to Chapter 65.

If you wish to review other choices on this track, turn to Chapter 51, Chapter 37, Chapter 25, Chapter 17, or Chapter 9.

If you want to explore a new decision-making track, turn to Chapter 5.

65

Organizing along Customer Lines

The advice of Lester Thurow, author of *Head to Head*, and Ted Levitt, former editor of the *Harvard Business Review*, finally convinces you to organize along customer lines. Levitt offers two simple premises about customer behavior in globalizing markets: (1) homogenization of the world's wants and (2) people's willingness to sacrifice specific preferences in product features, functions, design, and the like for lower prices at high quality. In your own mind, the new U.S. national health-care policy and accelerated changes in the industry worldwide support the premises of Thurow and Levitt and make the customer-product organizational approach the most logical alternative because it will facilitate development, production, and marketing of more standardized products for more homogeneous customer needs.

As you implement the reorganization, you invite input from all areas and levels of the MedTech International Group before finalizing a highly dynamic structure that cuts across countries, existing facilities and locations, product and service groupings, to create seven customer centers or focus areas: medical centers and large hospitals, stand-alone research laboratories, clinics, doctors' offices, emergency and out-patient facilities, long-term care facilities, and home care. You assign each of the 65 business units within the MedTech International Group to one of the seven centers based on which customer group accounts for the bulk of a business unit's current and anticipated sales. Then, you establish seven customer focus area executives at the group level. As part of the reorganization you encourage each new customer focus executive to negotiate innovative and future-looking relationships with customers, which leads to a flurry of new strategic alliances with medical centers, HMOs, preferred-provider organizations, clinics and physician groups, as well as with other manufacturers, R&D facilities, and marketing organizations. As the worldwide health-care industry continues to evolve, the MedTech International Group's aggressive building of relationships and its vast network of strategic alliances prove revolutionary.

With Amos Gill, Ken Matsumori, and Karen Wilcox overseeing the seven customer focus executives which include Ed Yates, Kate DaVaeno, Susan Carter, Bob Shay, Vic Gomez, and two others from outside the MedTech International Group, you, together with Meg Daniels and Jack Suhler, turn your attention to the further growth of MedTech International's network, with the express aim of creating new and more diverse product thrusts that will include joint implants, medical video cameras, surgical power tools, angioplasty catheters, laparoscopic products, and diagnostic test kits.

By the end of the year, the MedTech International Group enters into another 56 strategic alliances, substantially broadening the scope and depth of MedTech International's product and service base. Total sales at MedTech International jump to $1.4 billion, an increase of 51 percent, and profits climb 38 percent to $307 million, as shown in the accompanying table.

Selected Financial Information
(Dollars in Millions)

	Year ended September 30	
	This year	Last year
Operations		
Net sales	$1434.4	$949.9
Cost of sales	487.7	313.2
R&D	143.4	95.0
Marketing	281.0	190.0
G&A	215.2	129.2
Operating profit	307.1	222.5
Financial position		
Current assets	480.5	315.8
Current liabilities	249.9	164.2
Working capital	230.7	151.6
Other assets	144.2	94.7
Property and equipment	121.5	107.0
Total assets	746.2	517.6
Other data		
Capital expenditures	32.5	26.0
Depreciation and amortization	15.3	13.9
Return on sales	21.4%	23.4%
Return on assets	41.2%	43.0%
Number of employees	2192	1876

You receive Executive of the Year awards from the American Medical Association, the American College of Hospital Administrators, the University of Southern California School of Management, and MIT's Sloan School of Business Administration. In November, the week before Thanksgiving, *Fortune* magazine publishes a cover story praising you and the MedTech International Group. In terms of economic rewards, you receive a $500,000 cash bonus and $5 million in stock options. You find yourself extremely grateful this particular Thanksgiving.

In five years you increased MedTech's sales and profits tenfold, $147 million to $1.4 billion and $32 million to $307 million, respectively. Thanks to an early focus on R&D, breakthrough products, the acquisition of FutureMed, a new R&D division, and further acquisitions you were able to turn MedTech into a global player through innovative strategic alliances and a responsive customer-focused structure.

Congratulations! The last five years of strategic decision making have brought you to the successful conclusion of a decision-making track. However, you can continue applying your strategic thinking skills by choosing one or more of the alternatives below.

If you want to compare how the results of your last five years of strategic decision making stack up against the other positive outcomes in The Strategy Game, turn to Chapter 68.

If you want to review the outcome of the alternative of organizing along product-country groups, turn to Chapter 64.

If you would like to review the outcomes of the other choices you could have made on this track, turn to Chapter 51, Chapter 37, Chapter 25, Chapter 17, or Chapter 9.

If you want to play on a whole new track, turn to Chapter 5.

66
Redirecting R&D and Marketing Efforts

Recognizing the prudence in shifting some emphasis away from cell transplants, you immediately begin identifying those R&D projects that can materialize into actual products within three to nine months. You ask Jack Suhler to reassign some people working in the area of cell transplants, with exception of the core team, to agricultural applications. The FDA, Agriculture Department, and Environmental Protection Agency have recently streamlined regulations that have always slowed down introduction of new agricultural and livestock products, and you feel that MedTech can exploit the situation by quickly introducing new products, such as a milk production hormone, a biopesticide for corn, and a lean pork hormone.

Your new head of the MedTech Operations division, Michael Benoit, rises to the challenge of getting several new products to market with such adeptness that you begin expecting good to superior financial performance for the year.

Two new agricultural products enter the marketplace by midyear with solid advance sales, and three more are in the pipeline for third-quarter introduction. All the while, you have been working hard to maintain a strong push behind getting cell transplant products and services through the premarket approval processes. Although Benton executives congratulate you on meeting a tough challenge, you privately worry that the reduced resources you're investing in cell transplant testing and approval will fail to get the job done.

The months pass, and the FDA approval process drags on while you watch MedTech's chances of a preemptory market introduction slip as several competitors begin their own cell transplant testing programs.

Your conscience scolds you for betraying your intuition and logic; you comfort yourself with the excuse that you really didn't have a choice. External pressures always affect decisions.

At the end of the fiscal year, MedTech turns in a respectable performance, with revenues increasing by 37 percent to $1.2 billion and profits rising by 31 percent to $177 million, as shown in the accompanying table.

Selected Financial Information
(Dollars in Millions)

	Year ended September 30	
	This year	Last year
Operations		
Net sales	$1,214.1	$886.3
Cost of sales	376.4	283.6
R&D	182.1	150.7
Marketing	303.6	150.0
G&A	174.7	166.8
Operating profit	177.3	135.2
Financial position		
Current assets	397.6	292.5
Current liabilities	206.8	152.1
Working capital	190.9	140.4
Other assets	119.3	87.7
Property and equipment	142.0	117.6
Total assets	658.9	497.8
Other data		
Capital expenditures	44.2	32.7
Depreciation and amortization	16.8	14.6
Return on sales	14.6%	15.3%
Return on assets	26.9%	27.2%
Number of employees	2057	1812

While these figures please Benton executives, and while most MedTech personnel seem comfortable with their performance, morale within the cell transplant core team and among some of the scientists who had been reassigned to other projects has tumbled over the past year. Complaints about sticking a spectacular breakthrough on the back burner in order to foster shorter-term gains in the marketplace begin to spread through both divisions of the company, but you quickly attack them as counterproductive to MedTech's ongoing effort to gain premarket approval for its cell transplant breakthrough. Calling for patience and perseverance, you remind employees that MedTech has successfully balanced the need for moving ahead on the breakthrough with the demand for short-term profits, all while recovering from a recession and dealing with a momentous industry change.

Persistent rumors about the cell transplant activities of two competitors make you nervous. Who will introduce the first cure for cancer? Even you begin to worry about MedTech's chances. However, you take some consolation from a $250,000 cash bonus and a promise of greater rewards when overall Benton performance reaches higher levels in coming years. You also remind yourself that MedTech's sales have increased eightfold in five years from $147 million to $1.2 billion, with profits growing sixfold from $32 million to $177 million. Your early focus on R&D, breakthrough products, and the acquisition of FutureMed allowed you to establish a new pioneering R&D division that could revolutionize blood and cell research in the future.

This marks the end of one decision-making track at MedTech, but you can continue applying your strategic thinking to other options.

If you want to compare how the results of your last five years of strategic decision making stack up against the other positive outcomes in The Strategy Game, turn to Chapter 68.

If you choose to review what would have happened had you chosen to forge ahead with a singular focus on introducing a cell transplant product, turn to Chapter 67.

If you want to observe the outcomes of choices you could have made on this track, turn to Chapter 53, Chapter 39, Chapter 24, Chapter 17, or Chapter 9.

If you want to move onto a brand-new track, turn to Chapter 5.

67
Forging Ahead with a Singular Focus

Moving forward with more intensity and vigor than you've ever brought to bear on any project or endeavor in your life, you refuse to divert an iota of attention from accomplishing the biggest breakthrough in medical history. If ever there was a time to marshal all the efforts, talents, and time of a group of human beings, that time is now. In fact, you use those very words addressing a special company-sponsored conference in Washington, D.C., attended by key people from MedTech, Benton, the FDA, the U.S. Congress, the President's Cabinet, and the White House staff. To those outside the Benton family, you express your company's commitment to do whatever it takes to move the approval process forward, conducting the necessary research and testing to ensure beyond any doubt that the cell transplant breakthrough is safe, reliable, and long-lasting. As they commit to removing every obstacle as quickly and prudently as possible, you express your heartfelt gratitude for their support and help.

A reporter from *The Washington Post* dubs the conference the "Cancer Summit" and hails it as the epitome of American business and government cooperation. Despite your wariness of the media, you grant interviews to the business and medical press as a means of publicly appealing for additional help. You urge everyone who has ever had cancer or known someone afflicted with the disease to write their senators and congressional representatives requesting the FDA's priority attention to this approval process. You also ask for assistance from the government, universities, and medical centers throughout the country to help with funding and testing.

Almost overnight MedTech becomes a household word and a daily topic of conversation throughout the country and the industrialized world. Funding for tests becomes available from the U.S. government, as well as from Britain, Japan, France, Germany, and India. Universities and institutions around the world offer research and testing assistance to move the approval process along. Spurred by the national and international attention, the U.S. Patent Office grants MedTech full patent rights on its cell transplant discovery and process. With the patent in place, erstwhile competitors hoping to eventually gain licensing agreements for adapting the cell transplant process to other disease areas and product applications eagerly offer their assistance in testing.

In consultation with Benton executives, you and Jack Suhler carefully identify specific markets and applications where licensing to competitors makes sense, while holding on to areas of application where MedTech can effectively meet anticipated demand. Six months into the year, MedTech develops the first genetically altered cells for injection into a person suffering from lung cancer. In the weeks following that experiment, a flurry of tests, diagnoses, and monitoring take center stage throughout the world. The FDA heralds the process as one of the greatest breakthroughs in medical history. The patient who received the first genetically altered cells goes into remission with no evidence of any new cell malformation. While the patient will continue to undergo monitoring for years to come, the FDA grants final approvals. MedTech begins worldwide delivery of packages of genetically altered cell solutions for injection into patients suffering from cancer. Your commitment, devotion, vision, and belief in the face of criticism, skepticism, and enormous challenge yield the success every leader dreams of. At this point, the financial rewards seem almost inconsequential, but you know they will allow you and many others to continue seeking medical breakthroughs for the benefit of humankind.

At the end of the fiscal year, MedTech's revenues soar to $2.7 billion, a 200 percent increase, and profits jump to $473 million, a 250% increase, as shown in the accompanying table.

When Benton CEO Bob Koontz offers you a $5 million cash bonus, you opt to transfer half of it to MedTech's general bonus fund, placing the other half into a special scholarship fund for graduate students interested in entering the cell transplant field. However, you do accept a $10 million stock option. To the board's offer to become president and chief operating officer of Benton Pharmaceuticals, and then chairman and CEO within three years, you say no because you want

Selected Financial Information
(Dollars in Millions)

	Year ended September 30	
	This year	Last year
Operations		
Net sales	$2,658.4	$886.3
Cost of sales	797.5	283.6
R&D	436.8	150.7
Marketing	425.3	150.0
G&A	526.0	166.8
Operating profit	472.8	135.2
Financial position		
Current assets	864.0	292.5
Current liabilities	449.3	152.1
Working capital	414.7	140.4
Other assets	259.2	87.7
Property and equipment	142.0	117.6
Total assets	1,265.2	497.8
Other data		
Capital expenditures	44.2	32.7
Depreciation and amortization	16.8	14.6
Return on sales	17.8%	15.3%
Return on assets	37.4%	27.2%
Number of employees	2416	1812

to remain at MedTech for at least the next five years to continue guiding the leading edge of the industry.

In review, you have not only increased MedTech's sales eighteen-fold in five years from $147 million to $2.7 billion and profits fifteen-fold from $32 million to $472 million, but you and the people associated with MedTech have also changed history. From the beginning your uncompromising commitment to R&D, breakthrough products, the acquisition of FutureMed, establishment of a new R&D division, and your focus on pioneering innovation made it possible for you to continue your dogged pursuit of blood and cell research, cell transplants, and genetic mapping, which culminated, against all odds, in MedTech's amazing cure for cancer.

Congratulations! Your strategic decision making has paid off for you and for all humankind. Now that you have reached the end of a decision-making track, you can continue playing the game by choosing one or more of the options below.

If you want to compare how the results of your last five years of strategic decision making stack up against the other positive outcomes in The Strategy Game, turn to Chapter 68.

If you wish to consider the option of redirecting R&D and marketing efforts, turn to Chapter 66.

If you would like to review the outcomes of other alternatives you could have selected on this track, turn to Chapter 53, Chapter 39, Chapter 24, Chapter 17, or Chapter 9.

If you want to apply your strategic thinking to a different decision-making track, turn to Chapter 5.

68

A Ranking of the Successful Outcomes

Caution: *Your experience playing The Strategy Game will be enhanced if you read this chapter only after you have come to the end of a decision-making track identified as such at the ends of certain chapters.*

By this point you have traveled down one or more five-year decision-making tracks that should have enhanced your strategic thinking and decision-making ability. My intention in writing this book was to broaden, deepen, and strengthen your strategic awareness and competence. But I also wanted to entertain and inspire you with the challenges, dilemmas, and inevitable choices businesspeople face every day throughout our global economy. At a minimum, I hope playing *The Strategy Game* has given you a stronger appreciation for the importance of accurate and sufficient information upon which to base your strategic perceptions and judgments.

In the entire sequence of games there are a total of 18 negative outcomes, ranging from minor failure to absolute disaster, and 15 positive outcomes, ranging from marginal success to spectacular triumph. You may have already encountered one or more of the 18 negative outcomes. In the accompanying table, the 15 positive outcomes are ranked according to operating profits in the fifth year. Each chapter listed in the table represents the end of a decision-making track.

Chapter	Operating Profit	Net Sales
67	$473 million	$2.7 billion
27	$430 million	$1.7 billion
56	$420 million	$1.2 billion
58	$371 million	$1.0 billion
54	$337 million	$1.1 billion
61	$325 million	$1.0 billion
65	$307 million	$1.4 billion
57	$289 million	$918 million
64	$258 million	$1.1 billion
60	$247 million	$852 million
63	$237 million	$878 million
55	$209 million	$803 million
66	$177 million	$1.2 billion
62	$155 million	$600 million
59	$126 million	$477 million

Now that you know how your initial moves in *The Strategy Game* stack up, put your strategic thinking to the test again by choosing one of the options at the end of the chapter you just finished. When you reach the end of another decision-making track, you can return to this chapter to compare your results. Good luck on your next adventure.